Elementally Speaking

The Nature Spirits' Guide to their World

2006
Trafford Publishing

As told to Cheri Barstow

Note for Librarians: A cataloguing record for this book is available from Library and Archives
Canada at www.collectionscanada.ca/amicus/index-e.html
ISBN 1-4120-7271-9

*Printed in Victoria, BC, Canada. Printed on paper with minimum 30% recycled fibre. Trafford's print shop
runs on "green energy" from solar, wind and other environmentally-friendly power sources.*

TRAFFORD
PUBLISHING™

Offices in Canada, USA, Ireland and UK

This book was published *on-demand* in cooperation with Trafford Publishing. On-demand
publishing is a unique process and service of making a book available for retail sale to the
public taking advantage of on-demand manufacturing and Internet marketing. On-demand
publishing includes promotions, retail sales, manufacturing, order fulfilment, accounting and
collecting royalties on behalf of the author.

Book sales for North America and international:
Trafford Publishing, 6E–2333 Government St.,
Victoria, BC V8T 4P4 CANADA
phone 250 383 6864 (toll-free 1 888 232 4444)
fax 250 383 6804; email to orders@trafford.com
Book sales in Europe:
Trafford Publishing (UK) Limited, 9 Park End Street, 2nd Floor
Oxford, UK OXI IHH UNITED KINGDOM
phone 44 (0)1865 722 113 (local rate 0845 230 9601)
facsimile 44 (0)1865 722 868; info.uk@trafford.com
Order online at:
trafford.com/05-2166

10 9 8 7 6 5 4 3 2

This is for Elsie...because "We" promised

......and for all the wee ones,
Thorie, Dillie, Rosa, Ben, Robert Noah and Neo
who never question what they see,
they just believe......

Acknowledgements

First I would like to thank my editor Wende, who is also my daughter. Without her help and patience I would have never have gotten this book written. She has been my editor, critic, guide, and partner through this journey of discovery. If she didn't understand or believe before, you can bet she does now, or at least I hope she does. Wende, thanks for always being there when I needed you.

To my husband Hal: thanks dear for letting me follow my path, even though you didn't quite understand what that was. Your belief in me, though at times you thought I had "lost it", allowed me and still allows me the freedom to become part of a world seldom seen by most people. I only hope I have done the same for you.

To my son Bill, who seems to be following in my footsteps: thanks for listening with an open mind and understanding. Your whole life you always saw and understood when no one else could.

For my Mother, who never told me not to believe but instead encouraged me to listen to those voices: thanks for understanding that a child's imagination may be another world after all.

To all the family and friends I have met on my path that have listened and understood, and also to you who have not: thank you. Each one of you played a part that led me here.

To my guides The Ancients, who stepped aside so I could listen to what the Nature Spirits and all the beings of the Elemental Kingdom had to say. I promise to return soon for my next assignment.

Thanks to all my new friends in the Elemental Kingdom. I am so honored to be asked (actually told, but never mind) to write what you had to say. I hope it makes a difference and I have "made you proud".

And finally, special thanks to "Little Russ" whose gift to me was recognizing that within us all lies the ability to communicate. Not only with what is in our world but in other worlds we cannot see. We miss you.

About the Authors

THE TRUE AUTHORS OF THIS book are the Nature Spirits themselves. To learn more about Nature Spirits and read additional passages, please visit http://www.elementallyspeaking.com.

Even as a child, Cheri Barstow (aka "She Who Listens and Types") had a sense that there were worlds beyond the immediate one in front of her eyes. She has always been attuned to the metaphysical universe. Her work with the Elemental Kingdom began a decade ago. She has been active in the Goddess movement in Glastonbury and attended various conferences and workshops on esoteric subjects of all types.

Cheri lives in Southern California with her husband Hal, where she tends to her enchanted garden and splashes in fountains with her grandson, Thor.

If you wish to contact Cheri or join her mailing list, please email her at elementallyspeaking@yahoo.com.

Table of Contents

Introduction — My Path

WHEN I GAVE THIS MANUSCRIPT to my daughter Wende to edit, I thought I had just about finished everything I needed to and in my mind there seemed to be nothing more I could add. Boy was I wrong! First let me explain, my daughter is a Virgo. If you aren't into astrology, this won't mean a thing to you. If, however, you have just a smattering of knowledge then you know what that means. In case you are one of those that have "no clue", I will summarize by explaining that Virgos are perfectionists. Everything must be in perfect order and logical. They are extremely picky. In fact when Wende was little, she had an imaginary friend and guess what his name was …"Picky". It goes to show you that sometimes what you imagine may actually be yourself in disguise.

Being the detail minded person that she is, she explained that writing down and translating what a Nature Spirit had to say isn't enough. I need to explain to anyone reading this book what my qualifications are and why would I know more about The Elementals than Mary down the street, for instance. How did this whole journey start? Not simply writing the book, but how did I get on this path to begin with?

Phew! For someone who has never written more than a couple of papers for English class, this was going to be a real challenge. Wende said, "Mom, just start at the beginning. Tell them about what you've been doing over the years and everything will just … come together. Trust me". She is the English major and her experience in working for writers of all types is well documented. After all, if you can't trust your own "Virgo" daughter then who can you trust?

Now I guess it's time to start again, but this time I am going to tell you how this all began and how it led to where I am now. I guess the only way to start is to begin at the beginning.

Since I was young I have always felt as if I never belonged. I always had an empty feeling inside, as if something or someone was missing from my life. When I was little, I used to scare my friends by telling them I was from the planet Venus. I was about 10 at the time, so this was very bizarre. When I look back, I'm sure it must have been scary for them at times. It's a wonder I kept any friends but I must say that the ones that I did have, seemed to understand me in some mysterious way.

One of my best friends Peggy also tended to be on the "weird" side. She was very psychic before we knew what psychic was. She and I would read tarot cards and we were usually right. We were kids so, of course, what we asked was kids stuff. Later, when we got older we had some experiences that we still talk about today. I want to tell you about one of those "experiences".

When we were growing up, Peggy and I use to go to the Southern California Desert to Hesperia, which at that time was a very small town. Her father had a cabin there and we would go, usually with a group of girls, every couple of months for the weekend. We did what most teenage girls do: eat, sleep, and talk about boys. But one of our favorite things to do was to hike. One of these weekends a bunch of the girls were out hiking and everyone except Peggy and I decided to go back to the cabin. We wanted to hike a bit more so we told them we would catch up with them later.

Not knowing exactly where we were but familiar enough with the area to find our way back to the cabin, we continued our trek. I remember climbing to the top of a hill overlooking the valley and seeing a wagon train going across the desert floor below. I pointed this out to Peggy who said I must have had too much sun because she didn't see any wagon train. She thought we had better head on back to the cabin before I got, as she said, "sun stroke". As we started walking back she insisted that instead of going straight back we should go over the next hill instead. I asked why and she said she didn't know, but she just thought "we should". We climbed to the top of the hill and headed down the other side into a deep gully. When we reached the bottom and looked up to the other side of the ravine, we saw that the whole side of the hill was gorgeous pink quartz. We had never seen anything like it before in our lives. It was so beautiful. To this day, I can still remember how it sparkled in the sunlight. It was amazing. Neither of us having grown up with any money now assumed that we were about to be rich beyond our wildest dreams. I don't know why we assumed that since we found this hill of "marble" (we called it marble because we didn't know at that point the difference between marble and quartz) that it instantly belonged to us. We practically ran all the way back to the cabin, eager to tell the other girls about our amazing discovery. But we soon found out that they could care less and had other things on their mind, like "what's for dinner?"

Peggy's brother, Bobby, on the other hand was very interested. Bobby was 3 years older than Peggy and he had a dune buggy. This is a vehicle designed to be driven in the desert and can go where nothing else can. It is strange and amazing but also very scary. Believing that we were going to be "millionaires", he was not going to miss out on getting his share. We reluctantly told him where the hill was but made him promise that we would all share in the riches. You've heard the phase, "Like a bat out of hell"? That is exactly what Bobby looked like as he sped away on his dune buggy to find our treasure.

He returned after dark saying he couldn't find it. We would have to draw a map. I remember we drew something and told him exactly where we had seen our hill of marble. The next day we had to go home so he didn't have a chance to go out again on that trip to look for it.

Being teenagers, we soon forgot about our hill and went on with life as normal; well, as normal as you can be when you're a teenager. Bobby however did not forget. For the next 5 years, every time he visited the cabin he would get on his dune buggy and search for our infamous quartz hill. He never gave up, not until one day when he was 21. He was in town and decided it would check the assay records and see if they had any record of this pink quartz. He asked the clerk for information on the area where we had found our treasure. By this time I figure Bobby knew he wasn't going to become a millionaire. I think he was just so tired of looking for this "non-existent" pink hill that he wanted to find out if it really existed or were we just crazy.

The clerk had no problem in finding our wonderful pink marble hill because it was exactly where we said it was. There was only one problem. It had been mined out more than 100 years earlier when the first wagon trains brought in the prospectors. It hadn't existed for more than a century.

If I had heard this, I would have thought it was a really good story. The truth is it's not a story. Peggy and I had actually stepped back in time for a brief period; first with the wagon train and then with the hill. I didn't see it alone and she didn't see it alone, we saw it together. The connection with Nature was made. Maybe that started it all. I never will know but then it's something to think about.

Eventually Peggy married Jack, who is a true psychic in his own right. They moved to the desert where they still live. Peggy became a nurse, but I think she has special healing abilities. The desert called her back and she answered. I have heard more than once that she is called "the witch of the desert". I can surely believe it.

I continued over the years to read tarot cards and attend various metaphysical classes. I have always believed in fairies, long before they were fashionable. When I worked at a summer camp in the mountains during my high school years, my nickname was always "TINK", as in Tinkerbell. My favorite fairytale was, of course, Peter Pan. I even named my daughter Wende. I should have known then that I was already totally connected with The Elemental Kingdom, though in a completely different way then I could ever imagine.

I continued reading and studying, always feeling most comfortable when I could be out in Nature. I believed in the change of the seasons and how they connected with our lifetimes here on Earth. My beliefs contained all the elements of Nature, using it in both my personal rituals and teaching it to my children. I never belonged to any organized religious group after being raised as a Southern Baptist. I just couldn't understand that concept and so when I was about 12, I rebelled and never looked back. For me, my beliefs were personal and that was just fine, but that was soon about to change. I was happy just casually reading cards and having group discussions. Practicing a bit of white magic now and again, working with Nature in the meantime.

By now you are probably wondering what this has to do with Nature Spirits. I have spent time with Nature and enjoyed it, but what makes me an expert? Bear with me; I'm getting to that part. Remember, Wende said I should tell the story of how I found my way to where I am now, so I will continue.

My journey started in earnest about 10 years ago. It was about 2:00 a.m. I awoke, as my husband said, yelling "Russ has been shot".

Before I go on, I better explain who Russ is, or better yet which Russ.

I have a very unimaginative family when it comes to names. Listen closely, because this is going to get complicated.

My Grandfather's name is Russ. My Dad came along and became Russ Jr. After that my brother was born, so sticking to tradition he also was called Russ the 3rd or Rusty when he was little. Alright so far? Then my sister had a son, and just to confuse us more she named him Russ, whom we all called Little Russ. This, in turn, made my brother Uncle Russ. The family managed well enough until both my brother and my nephew had baby boys, at the same time mind you. They named them… I'll give you three guesses and the first two don't count. You're right… Russ. Uncle Russ' son was dubbed Baby Russ (Hanson) and Little Russ' son is called Baby-Baby Russ (Schultz). Are you still with me or did I lose you about 3 Russes ago?

I know you are thinking what in the blazes does this have to do with anything. Patience, just hear me out, we are getting there.

As I was saying before I got into the litany of Russes, I awoke saying "Russ has been shot". I guess I just sat up in bed and blurted it out. This however is not the first time this has happened; I have known many times when things are wrong. This is not an uncommon phenomenon; I think this has happened to everyone at least once in their life, especially if they are a parent.

It couldn't have been a minute later that my sister-in-law Michele called and said my nephew, Little Russ, had been shot, along with two of his friends. She was in the hospital emergency room waiting for the ambulance to arrive. I could hear my sister Karen in the background crying. Michele then said they were bringing him in and she thought he might have died and she would call me right back. Unfortunately, my nephew along with one of his friends died that night. The third boy lingered for a week but he too died. It was horrible shock and a needless tragedy.

Little Russ had been out with his friends for the evening. He and his partner, Mary, had just had their second son, Morgan, a few months earlier. Mary felt that it would be good for Russ to spend the evening out with his friends. These were not young boys. They were all in their late 20's with good jobs, and two of the four had young families.

Little Russ was one of those kids that grew up in the 70s when skateboarding was the latest fad. He was great at it and his claim to fame was being arrested countless times for "skating empty pools". To a skateboarder, the ultimate thing to do back in the early days before skate parks was to find an empty swimming pool to do tricks in. The sides of the pool would allow them to perform amazing flips that cannot be done on the streets. My nephew and his friends would find and use the pools mostly because they were always being chased off the streets for skating. Eventually Little Russ became a gahnite master, a person who spays the plaster through the long tube that forms the swimming pools. He tried out each pool after it was finished to see how it "skated".

Little Russ teaching his son "Baby-baby" Russ to skate

Little Russ' dream was to see his neighborhood in Phoenix, Arizona get a real skate park where kids, like his own two boys, could skate without being run off the streets. He and his friends had been raising money and working with the city to gain approval for such a park when he was murdered.

Little Russ was very spiritual and identified with the American Indian, their beliefs and customs. He even wore his hair in braids. That night, before he went out with his friends, Mary told us she had braided his hair for him. Russ had told her then that if anything happened to him to take care of his boys. She said he somehow knew he was not coming back. He felt it.

Little Russ and his three friends, Mike, Adrian and Forrest had stopped to play pool at an after-hours club in Scottsdale, an influential neighborhood outside Phoenix. The Scottsdale crime rate is extremely low and even one murder per year is rare. The boys simply were in the wrong place at the wrong time. When they left the club (there is no drinking allowed in after-hour clubs), they walked in pairs back to the parking lot; Russ and Mike ahead of Forrest and Adrian. When they got close to the parking lot Russ and Mike saw a kid (he was 21 and just released from prison) sitting on a wall. He jumped down, pulled out a gun, and pointed it at Mike, saying he was going to shoot him. Mike said, "No you're not", but he did. He shot him in the head. He then ran to a nearby waiting car and jumped into the backseat. There were three girls waiting in the car. Forrest and Adrian, who were a few yards back, heard the shot and came running. Along with Little Russ they charged the car. This was their fatal mistake. The kid with the gun shot my nephew, who was standing on the left side of the car, the hollowpoint bullet breaking the window before hitting him in the chest. Then shooting out the right window, he shot Adrian in the head. The fourth boy, Forrest, was by this time was on the trunk of the car. Hoping to hit him, the kid then shot out the back window but luckily he missed Forrest.

No one knows for sure what caused him to shoot. Forrest, the only survivor said he heard no arguing. He had never seen the shooter before. Later we heard that the shooter may have done this as a gang initiation. The shooter was arrested. One of the girls in the car turned him in. It seems she never had any idea this was going to happen. He will be in prison for the next 80 years.

After Michele called me back, I lit a candle for Little Russ. I was really shaken but I knew that I had to try and communicate with him if it was at all possible. Having read about and witnessed automatic writing a few years previously, I thought that if Little Russ could find someway to tell me anything, this might just be the way. Taking a pencil after first surrounding myself with white light, I asked if Little Russ was there and if he had any message to use me and the pencil to tell everyone he was alright. All I got was circling. I can still see and do it today. It went around and down and back around again; Spirals, and always the same.

I would like to say that I started channeling that night; that it all came to me then and there and that Russ was able to tell me everything that happened that night. This was not the case, but I did learn later that the spirals were his first attempt to contact us

My husband Hal and I arrived in Arizona the next morning. The family was in total chaos yet I felt a sense of peace whenever anyone spoke about Little Russ. It was almost as if he was there, trying to help everyone through this time of grief.

Little Russ had told me he wanted be cremated but my sister Karen refused. She believed that if there was no gravesite to visit then Little Russ would be gone forever. I could see this was going to be a problem so I knew I had to connect with Little Russ so that his final wish could be fulfilled.

I still am in a blur as to when and how it happened but I know that within two days of arriving in Arizona I began writing what Little Russ wanted me to tell his Mother. No, my pencil did not start moving on its own, spelling out words but instead his messages came to me as thoughts which I then wrote down on paper. With these messages came the inspiration for a logo to go on T-shirts, in memory of the boys who were killed. Russ suggested that all the proceeds be donated to the skate park.

Little Russ came through me with the words I would later read at his funeral. My sister did finally accept his wishes to be cremated but she insisted on having a funeral service and coffin anyway. Looking back on that time, I am sure that Little Russ would have enjoyed the service. His friends covered his coffin with skating stickers. They filled his coffin with beads and flowers and even a skateboard. And, of course, he wore his skating clothes, his beads, and his braids; all the symbols of his spirituality traveling along with him to the other side.

After the services an amazing thing happened. Everyone had returned to my brother's house and my two nephews, Baby Russ (Hanson) and Baby-Baby Russ (Schultz) were seated at the table in the kitchen away from the others in the room. I happened to be in the kitchen and I overheard them talking about Little Russ. I have to point out that both the boys were not yet 3 years old but still they were carrying on a conversation which made perfect sense. Baby-Baby Russ (Schultz), who's Dad had just been killed, was telling his cousin that his Dad had come to visit him the night before when he was in bed. Little Russ had told him he had to go away but that he would always love him and would see him again someday. If he ever needed him, he would be there. His Dad said he loved him and asked him to take care of his new baby brother, Morgan, and his mom. Baby Russ (Hanson) then told Baby-Baby Russ that he too had seen Little Russ, his uncle, and that he had asked him to take care of his cousin Baby-Baby Russ and his baby brother Morgan too. Little Russ said he loved him and that he shouldn't be sad anymore.

I was amazed. Here were two three year olds talking about seeing their dead father and uncle and thinking it was perfectly normal. Both boys understood that Little Russ loved them and felt assured that he would always be there for them.

In case you are wondering, the skate park was eventually built and dedicated to the boys that died that night. The best part of all, and something I know Little Russ would have loved, is that part of his ashes were added to the (gahnite) cement that was used to make the foundation of the skate park he had worked so hard for. So even in death he still watches over all the young kids that finally have a safe and <u>legal</u> place to skate. This seems to me a much greater monument than any gravestone in the cemetery.

After that the channelings continued, not only from Little Russ but from other relatives as well. I began to channel for other people but soon learned that this wasn't the wisest thing to do. A teacher warned me that I needed to protect myself and not let any entity that felt like it use me as their channel. This made a lot of sense so I asked for a Spirit Guide or Guides to point me in the right direction.

The first group that came to me was The Old Ones. They are a remarkably intelligent group of beings, very esoteric and very hard to understand. They channeled information about energy grids and quantum physics and how the Universe reacted with whatever. They presented such subjects as timelines and ribbons, all extremely complicated and amazingly brilliant, things I had a hard time understanding. I kept all the writings and years later found a friend, Simon, whose guides were The Old Ones. Working with these old readings and still calling on them when I needed help, they often would answer the questions he had wondered about for years.

Eventually I asked if it was possible to have another group that was a bit less complicated but still esoteric in their concepts. I didn't want a group that just answered questions such as "Am I going to meet the partner of my dreams next month" but rather someone who would tell people who asked about their spiritual path in this lifetime.

Luckily someone in The Great Universe listened and I was blessed with the most fantastic Guides. They call themselves The Ancients. They are Celtic in origin, or so it seems to me, and they have given me a fascinating history on who and what they are. No, I will not delve into all that at this time. After all, this is a book about Nature Spirits, not The Ancients. I just have to say that I had to first learn from The Old Ones, who eventually sent me to The Ancients, in order to arrive where I am today.

Soon channeling came just as easily as talking to a friend. Of course the language was a bit strange but after a while it didn't seem that way to me. I think I just got use to the way they spoke and then everything began to make sense.

It still astounds me that I can get these amazing readings. Things I have never learned or studied; words of inspiration and esoteric teachings come through me as I write. Each time I am amazed with what they have to say. I will be forever grateful to have been given this gift.

Somehow word spread that I could channel The Ancients. I did the best I could to keep up with the Emails from all over the world. How people found out about The Ancients and me, I still don't understand but I have been lucky enough, with their help, to relay some outstanding advice to people when they needed it the most. I must point out that this is not my advice but that of The Ancients. I am merely the tool that they use to communicate their message. It's funny because the Nature Spirits refer to me as "She who types".

During the years of 1997/98, I had been studying Druidism. I found it fascinating. I had always felt connected to the Standing Stones and Stone Circles of Europe but had never really had the time to actually visit them. I had been to Great Britain many times and of course had been to Stonehenge, which was a disappointment to me.

It all started as I remember on a trip to London in the spring of 1998. I happened to be in Earls Court, near the theatre district in London. This small courtyard contains a great skateboard shop along with a wonderful New Age store. I usually visit whenever I am in London because they also have a fabulous bakery and a wonderful vegetarian restaurant. While in the New Age store, I happened upon a flier on The Goddess Conference which was to be held in Glastonbury in early August. I had learned recently about the Goddess movement but knew little about it. I wondered how it compared to the Druid belief system and were they connected in any way? This really piqued my interest so I picked up a flier and took it back with me to California.

During the same period, my husband Hal had become interested in the great sailing ships of Europe referred to as "The Tall Ships". He had learned from our friends in Norway that they took non-sailors as trainees in the famous Cutty Sark Race each summer. He really wanted to participate. Since I get seasick if my bath water is too high, I told him to have fun but I was staying put on solid ground. So he was off for three weeks of sailing which just happened to coincide with the Goddess Conference. I had about ten days before the conference which gave me the perfect opportunity to visit some of these Stone Circles and Standing Stones that I had been longing to see.

Through a series of mishaps that I now know was a total case of synchronicity, I arrived with perfect timing in Scotland. I met a guide who would become not only a friend but a great teacher. For the next ten days I traveled with my guide Cris throughout Scotland, stopping at Standing Stones and Stone circles, some of which I am sure no one except someone that lives there would know about.

This trip changed my life. What I thought I knew was quite different than what I was now learning. The path I had been traveling was about to make a sharp turn to the right … or was it the left?

When I entered the first Stone Circle, it spoke to me. At first I thought it was The Ancients checking in, but I soon realized it was the circle itself, telling me what I needed to do, what lessons I needed to learn and to keep my ears and eyes open because this was just the start of a new adventure.

So, the channeling and the learning began. Cris, an expert on so many different esoteric subjects, taught me about The Ancient Isle of Scotland. Along the way the Stones also gave me their gifts. By the time I reached the Goddess Conference ten days later my mind was swimming with so many new concepts.

The Goddess Conference, which takes place each year at Lammas, the first weekend in August, is held in Glastonbury, England. This is the legendary Avalon of King Arthur and the Ancient Island of the Priestesses of the Goddess.

It is here that I met Leona.

Leona Graham Elen was in charge of the special pre/post Goddess Conference Discovery that I had booked before I left for Scotland. This GCD was to take me and my group through every event before, during and after the conference and teach us about the Goddess. The group turned out to be only me and Leona's mother, Florence. This turned out to be the best thing that could have ever happened. Since Florence was in her 80's this really left only me. I was able to experience so many things that never would have possible had there been a lot of people in my group. The main thing though, was becoming great friends with Leona. The Conference was amazing and I learned what I had come for but I also knew that my path had changed.

During the conference Leona and I had time to talk about a lot of things. She told me how she had lived for many years at this place called Findhorn in Scotland. She spoke of this Spiritual community based on the teachings of the Nature Spirits. At this time in my life the only Nature Spirits I had ever heard of was Tinkerbelle, of course, and now very recently, the Stones.

I told her about my channelings with the Stones and she wasn't a bit surprised. I would find out over the years that she and I were the perfect traveling companions and what one of us couldn't see or hear, the other one probably could.

Over the next year she tried to convince me to visit Findhorn for their Experience Week. Cris and I had stopped at Findhorn briefly on an errand and I felt no real connection to the place at that time. I had no intention of ever returning. This would soon change and much sooner than I would imagine.

By now you are probably wondering how this brought me to the Nature Spirits and why I was chosen to write their story. First I must say the ability to write a book is something that comes with patience, knowledge, and endurance. This is what they tell me. You know what; all of this is true but the real ability comes when you actually have something to say.

I never set out in this lifetime to become a writer; and in fact I still don't consider myself to be one. If this is the case then why am I writing a book about Nature Spirits? Some may say it was divine intervention… that is true of course, but then I wonder, "Why was I chosen"?

When I was first asked, "asked" being the operative word, to write about the Nature Spirits, it was at the request of my friend Leona. She knew a woman who had seen and drawn them when she was very young. Although this woman could see these beings, she could not communicate with them. Leona, knowing that I had channeled The Ancients for many years and that I had also had some luck channeling the Stone Circles around Scotland, asked if I would meet with this woman. Leona said her friend needed someone who would try to communicate with these Nature Spirits, also known as the Elementals. Thinking this would be a great and hopefully enlightening experience, I headed to Scotland and then to Findhorn for a meeting with Leona's friend.

Findhorn is a wonderful community, started in the 1960's by Peter and Eileen Caddy. It was, and still is, devoted to the teachings of the Nature Spirits and in the contact of all people with Nature and Her teachings. It grew from a place of desolation to a botanical wonder through the guidance given to them by these beings.

I must say that although in the beginning I was not attracted to the Findhorn Community, I now see that this in truth was the path I was destined to follow. Later I would recall that Findhorn started a chain of events that would lead me to this point and only through that portal could I finally find the path that lay ahead.

After our meeting, I agreed to go to Glastonbury to channel the first Nature Spirit that had contacted her some 50 years before. The Nature Spirit was a huge Oak tree that she had named Axel. I was given the location of the tree and instantly knew the exact tree she was telling me about. Having been in Glastonbury many times before, I knew it quite well.

Of course the task of going up to a tree and asking it to "talk" to you was quite new to me, but I figured what have I got to lose. Maybe if it was like the Stones, just another part of Nature, then it just might want to talk to me too.

Since the place where the tree was located was now inside the gates of a private residence, (it hadn't been a private residence when I had last visited), I had no choice but to sit outside the fence, in the bushes, and try to channel whatever information this tree called "Axel" wanted me to know; if indeed it wanted to tell me anything in the first place.

Leona's friend had wanted me to ask about the hierarchy of the Plant Kingdom. Questions such as; Who ruled what? What was the purpose of each plant, tree, etc and what jobs were they required to do? Now here were some questions that I had never even thought about, yet wouldn't it be wonderful if I could get even a clue to those answers? Not knowing what to expect but still hoping for the best, I "tuned in" to the tree and it began. The tree actually spoke. The readings I received were amazing, funny, and so enlightening that I was anxious to get even more. Alas, my time in Glastonbury was short and I was only able to get 2 readings at the time.

Needless to say I was very pleased and sent these readings back to the lady in Findhorn. I waited but was never asked to follow up with these readings. I can't say what happened to this project, but after two years it had just faded into the background.

Meanwhile in the back of my mind there was a voice that kept saying…"We need to tell you more."

I, of course, was still channeling my guides, The Ancients, but every now and again would get a message from a Tree or a Stone or something I passed in Nature. I would write some of these down but most times I just listened and forgot. This is a real problem with channeled information; if you don't write it down then and there, it instantly disappears from your radar. Your mind acts as if it never received it, and as hard as you try to recall what "They" said, you can't for the life of you remember a thing.

This story finally began again when I returned to Findhorn two years later for what they call "Experience Week". Leona finally convinced me that this was the place that I needed to visit and I must do it right away! Plus, she said I really had to attend a special course, which they call "Experience Week". She assured me this was the only way I could accurately judge what Findhorn was all about and to reconnect that link with Nature that had begun two years earlier in Glastonbury.

She was right, as she usually is, and I reconnected with Nature. Soon we were "open for business again", so to speak. The Elementals, otherwise known as The Nature Spirits, were alive and well and living in Findhorn and boy did they have a plan for me. Their mission and my path would take me to many different countries, landscapes, and climates; many that I wouldn't have considered "talking with" before. Each place giving me many different (yet somehow the same) readings, not only explaining what the Elemental Kingdom does but how they feel and the knowledge that they have for everyone who lives on this planet we call Earth.

I know many of you will find this hard to believe, but I assure you that this is only what was given to me, to give to you.

I have learned that we are not the only beings inhabiting this planet and that we are also not the only intelligence that exists on this plane. Others exist all around us and they have a purpose too. They live and they die and are reborn again to renew this planet with what we all need to survive.

I, of course, wanted to know why had chosen me. They said it was because I was once a rock, or as they prefer…a Stone. Being a Stone I had listened, absorbed, and understood what it meant to just "BE".

And so my friends, this is how and what brought me to this point. If you have just picked up this book because you were curious, then you, like me, have begun your journey toward that place I was a few years ago. That path lies just ahead; so why not follow it for a while? You never know who or what you might meet on the way. Not to mention where you may eventually wind up. It couldn't hurt!

What is an Elemental also known as a Nature Spirit?

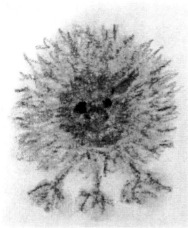

IF YOU HAVE DECIDED TO take a chance and read this book then your first question is probably, "What the heck is an *Elemental or Nature Spirit*?"

Of course many of you know this already but for those of you who don't or may only have an idea of what they are, I'll try to explain. In actuality I won't be the one explaining, but only presenting what they tell me in an easier to understand form.

I was asked by *The Elemental Kingdom* to be the mediator, the go-between their world and ours. In their words I have been referred to as "The One Who Types" or as I would prefer, "The One Who Listens and then Types", a human who can hear what they say and has agreed to write it down for them. At first I thought this was the only reason they kept speaking to me but I've come to feel that they actually like having me around.

The Elementals or Nature Spirits, which are quite interchangeable titles, are the *Spirits of the Nature Kingdom*. We are not talking about fairies now but instead the *essence* of the plant, or tree or stone or all other things in *Nature*. This can range from the highest mountain range to the smallest grain of sand. It can also encompass the Amazon Jungle or be as small as that violet that Granny grows on her window sill. Every part of *Nature* contains a *Spirit Being* and this, my friends, is called an *Elemental*, also known in some circles as a *Nature Spirit*.

Of course other authors have their opinion on what or who these *beings* are and they may be right. Since I am no expert on the subject and only write what I am told, I have no way of knowing. I just believe that what I am told is the honest truth. Having been assured by the *Nature Spirits* that they only speak the truth is good enough for me.

When I first started channeling the *Elemental Kingdom* I only connected with the *Mineral Kingdom*. I found this fascinating and had no idea that I could communicate with the plant world or any of the other *beings* that existed on their plane. When I found that I could I was amazed, awed, and so thankful for this gift. Of course I had no idea that with this gift also came responsibilities, one of which was to write down what they wanted us to know and give it to everyone I came in contact with. At first I thought they were crazy because I am not a writer. This didn't seem to matter to them at all. They said I could just write down what they said and that would be fine. Sure, like that was going to happen.

First, writing down what I channeled was the easy part. I could do this, no problem. The problem came when I gave these readings to the real world and their eyes glazed over after two sentences. How were these people suppose to understand the message the Nature Spirits were trying to send if they couldn't read past the first paragraph?

A teacher of mine once said that *Spiritual Beings* speak in a different way. She referred to it as "God Talk". I think that is a really good description. At times they tend to be a bit flowery or esoteric and often seem really "out there", for lack of a better term. Still, the more you read, the easier it gets…believe me it does.

What part did I play or would I play in getting this out there in words that normal, for lack of a better word, people could understand?

So I asked? Big mistake! They told me I should "just" translate what they said into a readable form. This was easy for them to say.

The first channeling was brutal, every word meaning more than one thing. Which definition did they mean and what were they trying to say, I had no clue. I worked for at least two weeks on a one page reading and finally gave in. I needed an inner plane translator to help.

For those of you that have never heard of an inner plane translator I will try to explain. It is exactly what it seems, someone who exists on a different world somewhere between ours and theirs. These *beings* have the ability to put into simpler language words spoken by other *beings* on these worlds. I have channeled a group of these types before and they can be hilarious or can put into simple language what it is the other *beings* are trying to say.

Knowing that I could always contact the ones I had used before, I asked if it would be alright to use an inner plane translator. Their response, "No, do it yourself". Thank you very much guys. Not exactly what I wanted to hear. Accepting that this was the way things were going to be, I asked my guides, The Ancients, for help. They, being the geniuses that they are and the reason they have that job in the first place, told me to just listen to my intuition. It would come and I would know what to write.

They were partly right. Yes, eventually it did become easier but it still took me many hours to do each passage and then I had to ask if I had gotten it right. Sometimes I was right on and sometimes I wasn't, but all and all I did what I felt they wanted.

At first I didn't know exactly what I was meant to channel. Did they want me to channel only the trees and the flowers? Should I include the stones and the sand? How about the river and the ocean or that volcano in Hawaii? Everywhere I went I heard voices, all calling to me, wanting me to stop and write down what they had to say. At first it was great, in fact it still is, but eventually I realized that I could never in my lifetime write down all the information that all the *Nature Spirits* wanted to give me. Not in one lifetime for sure. Even if I could, I could never "revise" it. That would just take me forever. What was I suppose to do?

Since I had started on this project originally to channel the Plant Kingdom, I thought it best that I should see that project through first. This is not to say that I haven't channeled the Mineral Kingdom, because I have. They are fascinating and the information that I have received is so amazing that at times I can't comprehend how my mind can even receive these things. Most of which I have never heard of before in this lifetime.

I am though, going to add some channelings from the sea and also one here and there from other places that are connected with the *Elementals of the Plant Kingdom*. I wish I could include everything but if I did I think it would just be too overwhelming. Maybe later I can put everything from the Mineral Kingdom together. Maybe I'll call it "Getting Stoned". Until then I have to finish what I promised and write this book. As I said, and they have mentioned, I am just the go-between.

With that in mind, shall we now go-between our world and theirs and find out what each of these *beings* does? What is their purpose, what services do they perform, do they live alone or are they a part of the bigger whole? These and a lot more questions will be answered. Read on and become part of their world, the Elemental Kingdom inside our world.

The Rules

By now you probably would like to hear what the Elementals have to say about themselves in their own words…right? I thought so. We just have one little problem. Of course if you are familiar with them or have been working with them for as long as I have, this isn't a problem. But for those of you who have not read anything channeled from an *Elemental*, the way they speak may seem a bit overwhelming. As I wrote before, there may be some passages difficult to understand, so doing my best I have tried to make some sense out of them.

Since I am no writer, this may not be what you are used to but it is what I feel they have tried to convey in simple terms. At times it may seem a bit simple minded but then they are *Elementals* after all. Just bear with me and we both will get through this book somehow.

I could easily give you my opinion of what I believe a *Nature Spirit* is, but again that would only be my way of thinking. We all have our ideas, some more realistic than others, yet each are still within the realm of what we imagine. Therefore, I will in each channeled reading of the book, write down exactly what they said in their own words. This will give you the opportunity of understanding, in your own way, what they are saying to you. Each of us hears things differently and so each may see in the readings something different. This also gives you the option of going back to the "original channeling" and maybe grasping something that you didn't quite understand before.

After each "original channeling", and by this I mean I have not changed a word of what they have given me, I will "try", this being the operative word, to translate what they say into a simpler language. I know it won't be perfect and some of you will think I am completely off base but this is the best I can do. To the others of you that just can't get it at all, I really hope it helps. Like I said before, the more you read the easier it gets.

So shall we now begin at the beginning by letting them explain who they, *The Elementals* (also known as *The Nature Spirits*) are:

The Spirits of Nature

We are the Spirits of Nature, the ones that reside deep within things, bringing from within, the light needed to fulfill our tasks.
We live inside all beings, be it the smallest tree to the largest sea.
We travel and (we) remain constant.
We bring knowledge and search for dreams.
We carry and lift and support and give to all beings, for we are the all within all things… The essence of the world that you see, each given a purpose of joy to each being that exists.
We have chosen and thus accept all that we undertake.
We assist and revise, elect and develop all that is given to the world.
We are the spark alight with the glow of the evening sun, the mist that rises in the cool air.
We are the sea and the stones and the valleys and the hills and all parts in-between.
We raise our heads in colors arranged through seasons of growth.
We sleep when time permits and return to begin again.
We unite in all things, believing that this plane shall again support all in the joy that radiates from the Greatness that leads us all.
We are Nature. Our creatures serve, heal, and maintain all that you see.
We are and shall ever be a part of you for without us none would exist.
We give to you joy that exists throughout time. Give us the freedom to renew and all will work in harmony.
Thusly said we present in detail the work we provide, the joy in giving we provide and the information needed to continue.
Go in the knowledge that all things are connected. That loves lasts throughout time and that Nature gives what it must.
Return to her what she expects and she shall reign true throughout time.
We remain, The Guardians of Time, the Words of Nature.

Don't you just love that? Did you get it or have you had a little problem understanding what they are saying or their meaning?

For those of you that had a problem, believe me, you are not alone. At times I really am challenged with what they are trying to say. Eventually though I get "attuned" to their way of speaking and it becomes clearer.

I was chosen (or was I told?) as I wrote before, to "revise" their writing. This does not mean that I will take anything away but just do the best I can do to put it into a language that may be easier to understand. I know that you may see it quite differently and that is just the point. This is exactly what they want. They want each person to understand in their own way and time exactly what each passage means to them.

Taking this into consideration, I will try to do my best. What I think they are saying will simply be called "revised", for lack of a better word. It will be referred to as that from now on. It will always follow the "original channeling" and it will appear in "this type". This is so that you will always be able to refer back to the original when you need to. Hopefully this will be of help.

Here is the first passage. I surely hope you can understand me. Gook luck…

The Spirits of Nature — Revised

We are the *Nature Spirits*, the ones that live deep inside everything. We bring from within the light that we need to do our jobs.
We live inside all *beings*[1], whether it is the smallest tree or the biggest ocean.
We change and we stay the same.

---

1   You will find all through the passages the use of the word *"being"*. A *"being"* to the Elemental Kingdom is any form of life. Not necessarily what we would consider life but anything that has an essence or soul. Since all things have an essence or soul, or that is the way that the Nature Spirit community sees it, then all things, whether they are rocks or bugs, themselves or others we can't see (yes, even us!) are *"beings"*. Therefore a *"being"* does not have to be some alien but can also be something quite recognizable. Then again it can also be something you have never seen or heard of either.

We teach you what you need to learn and we search for dreams.

We give to all *beings* the support to lift and carry them throughout their lifetimes.

We are the total of all there is inside everything.

We are the essence or the soul of the world that you see, giving each being a source of pleasure in which to live.

We have chosen this and we accept the jobs we are given.

We provide help, we change, we choose and we make available, everything that is given to the world.

We are the spark that blazes in the glory of the setting sun and the mist that rises in the cool air.

We are the ocean, the rocks, the valleys, the hills, and all the places in-between.

We glow and bloom with the colors of the season.

We sleep when the time is right and return again when it is time to start again.

We work together in everything we do, believing that this world will hold everyone in the joy that spreads from the *Greatness* that guides us all.

We are *Nature.* Our creatures serve you, heal you, and take care of everything you see.

We are and will always be a part of you and without us none of you would exist.

We bring you the joy that will last throughout time. Let us be free to grow and we will all work together in peace.

Having said this, we will now tell you in detail about the work we do, the joy in living we provide and the information you will need to go on.

Go now knowing that all things are connected, that love lasts throughout time, and that *Nature* gives you everything that you need.

Give her back the respect she deserves and she will rule fairly forever.

We are and have always been, *The Guardians of Time, the Words of Nature.*

Was that easier to understand? I certainly hope it helped those of you that could not quite grasp what they were saying. As I said before, what you feel they said and what I wrote may be completely different. This is fine. I just want all of you to receive all the information I was given. Whether you read it over and over in their own words and it suddenly hits you... which can and does happen, or you just read what I have written, the main thing is to understand that *Nature Spirits* exist. They have a purpose and goals and responsibilities just as we do. Without them we wouldn't be around.

Who are The Elementals?

As MUCH AS I COULD write about who I think the *Nature Spirits* are or what they do, I could never explain this as well as they can themselves.

When I first started channeling *Nature* and before I separated their messages into groups such as plants, minerals, etc. I received a message from *The Elemental Kingdom* as a whole. I was sitting beside the River Tay in the highlands of Scotland when this message came. I thought is was so beautiful and moving that I cried and wished that everyone could understand that all *Nature* wants from us is to be noticed; to be recognized for what She provides and to live in harmony and love with all beings.

These words kept me searching for more.

A MESSAGE FROM THE ELEMENTALS
GLEN LYON, SCOTLAND 1998

Continue on your path, for we are the ones you seek.

Within the depth of our being we become to you, an instrument to return to the serenity lost in your life. For within our holy place lies the depth of free will, to become one with all that want and need to belong to the system you have so long ago forgotten.

We remain, as through time, a oneness of all things. We consider that what shall become of all that do not dwell within our realm; A sudden, but not unsettling, chance to return to depth of love of all living things.

We know that what you feel has again returned you to the realm of ones that dwell within these holy places.

We are but a tiny group of entities that exist to bring to all, the depth of understanding lost upon this chaotic earth. For when it was new, we were as a light, glowing ever into the night. We reined, and became to those that believed …a haven for dreams.

Reality and unconscious thoughts co-mingle when one is open to us. We evolve not, for we are as we were.

We devise ways for all to see, but watching does not ascend many to our plane.

We are near, so very near, but yet, none can see.

Why we need ask for all this when we are, and were, and shall always be, ones that need only a moment of time among you, to become again, all that was new and green and golden at the dawn of many millenniums?

Ask all and we shall respond, for we desire you and you desire we.

Come to us in the depth of your being and we shall be there. For we await to serve, to renew.

For we are of the ones that are ever around you, yet unseen. Recognize us in all you see. The trees, the soil, and all that belong to the earth, sky and sea. The rain that falls. The clouds. The dawn. The stars.

We are they. We are here to serve.

Enjoy all that we bring, but give to us the understanding that we do exist on your plane.

We do our part of the evolution of all and we shall reign when all have passed. For when all move on…only Nature remains. For we are infinity and through us grows, as a new blossom, the beauty and grace of all the earth.

We ask only to be remembered by all who dwell within this space.

Appear? We do often, but none see. We give you love, for "you" have seen. We need more to understand. But when she has chosen to remain, all of mankind cannot betray her wrath. She is your Mother, Nature to all.

Respect Her, return to Her. Her arms unfold to all. Embrace her and feel her beauty, her warmth. We, as beings of all these realms, honor her. For She shall outlive all. For only She, can send to you, what is needed to sustain your race. She lives in all places. She is for all times. We give to you Her love and the love of all beings. Return often and be blessed. For Nature is all, you are one. To not remember is only the path of lacking

We give to you all. Please give to us the understanding and the right to exist.

Go in love. We give you all. We honor all and send to you the trust in what your knowledge shall impart to non-believers. We remain and shall ever be.

Come to us often. The grace of all things begins in us.

We remain, The Spirits of Nature

A MESSAGE FROM THE ELEMENTALS — REVISED

Stay on your path, because we are the ones you've been searching for.

From deep inside of us, we offer you a way to return to the peace you have lost in your life.

Here in our holy place you will find the freedom to become a part of all who want and need to belong to a way of life that was forgotten long ago.

We, the *Nature Spirits*, will stay together forever, but we wonder what will become of those that don't live here in our world. Will they ever have the chance to feel that deep love for all living things? We know that this feeling has once again brought you back to our world and to the ones that live inside it.

We are a tiny group of *beings,* or *Nature Spirits* as you call us, which exist to bring you a deeper understanding of what has been lost in your confused world.

When the world was new we were like a light that was always shinning, even in the darkest places. We controlled these places and became for those that believed in us, a safe place for their dreams.

When you believe in us, what is real and what is hidden in your mind will come together.

We never change because we are… what we are. We try to get your attention, to make you see us, but only a few of you are able to enter our world; A world always so close to you, yet you still never see.

Why do we care how you feel about us? Because we are, were, and shall always be *beings* that need just a moment with you to once again be what we were before, everything that was new and green and golden at the beginning of many different millenniums throughout countless ages in time.

Ask us anything and we will answer you because you need us as much as we need you. Look deep inside and we will be there, always waiting to serve and to make you feel new again. We are the ones that are always around you, but you just don't recognize us.

If you look, you can find us in everything you see; in the trees, the soil and everything that belongs to the earth, the sky, and the sea. We are in the rain that falls, the clouds, the dawn and the stars. This is who we are and we are here to serve you.

We want you to enjoy everything that we give you but only ask that you believe that we exist in your world.

We do our part in bringing growth to <u>every thing</u> and we will still be here when <u>everything</u> is gone. When everything else is gone, only *Nature* will remain.

We are timeless, and through us will grow, like a new flower, the beauty, and grace of all the earth. The only thing we ask is to be remembered by all of you who share this space with us.

(I ask this question in my head…) "Why don't you come out more often so more people can see you?" (Their answer…) "We are here all the time, but no one sees us".

(Here, they are talking to me because I am listening to them.) We send you love because you have seen us but we need more (of you) to understand.

When *Mother Nature* decides who will stay and who will not, all of mankind won't be able to escape her anger. She is your *Mother*, She is our *Mother*, She is *Mother Nature* to everyone and everything on *Earth.* Respect her and return to her. She opens her arms to everyone; come into her arms and feel her warmth and her beauty.

We, as *Nature Spirits* in both yours and her world, honor her. She will outlive you all because She is the only one that can give you what you need to support your people. She lives in all places and She will live for all time. We send you her love and the love of all "*beings*".

Return often to *Nature* and be blessed because *Nature* is all things and you are only one. To forget her will only lead you to the path of being without her.

We give you everything, so please give us your understanding and our right to live.

Go in love and remember we will provide everything you need.

We honor you and send you on your way, trusting that you will tell everyone that does not believe in us about what you have learned.

We are always here, now and forever. Come to us again soon because the beauty of all things, happen in us.

We remain, *The Spirits of Nature*

As you can see, *Nature* wants only that we recognize that it exists. We need only to look around us to see that *Mother Nature* is here, giving us everything we need to survive. Without her we would not, could not, exist.

We take *Nature* for granted because it is always there, but what if it wasn't? What if *Mother Nature* decided we no longer should be part of her world? Most of us have never thought about this because we take what *Mother Nature* provides for granted. We just assume that the flowers will bloom in the spring, the vegetables will grow in the summer, and the apple trees will give us apples in the fall. That is just how it works, how it has always worked and how, we assume, it will continue to work forever.

In reading this book you may learn that what you believe will last forever may not after all. That *Mother Nature* is getting annoyed with us and unless we "shape up" and recognize that her world exists, what we take for granted may no longer be there.

You have read that *Nature* only wants to be seen, to be noticed and acknowledged. This doesn't seem all that hard to me, in fact it seems like a reasonable request when you realize all that *Nature* provides us.

As you continue to read the different passages you will understand just what part each *Elemental Being* has in providing for all of us here in our world. You will realize the effort and love that is given to each of us here and the importance of each *Elemental* and the jobs they have chosen. The lessons they can teach us all will become apparent and through the understanding and acceptance of the *Elemental* world, we can all live and work together to make our world a more loving and accepting place.

Understanding and believing that other worlds exist within our own can bring back the days when all beings lived together in harmony and peace. To a time when all were accepted and none were ignored; all were equal and everyone worked together to make our world, their world, a place filled with light and love.

Read on and discover the world of *The Elementals; the Devas, Pan* and the *Nature Spirits* that live among us. I think you will be surprised and delighted and happier knowing that there are others out there that think only of you. Hopefully, after reading this book, the idea of hugging a tree won't seem that strange to you after all.

I wish you luck on your journey of discovery. By the way, tell the old Oak Tree if you see him that I have done my best and I send my love.

So It Began...
A Conversation with Axel

Glastonbury, England – August 7, 2001

As I MENTIONED BEFORE, THE reason I went to Glastonbury in the first place was to interview a certain tree called Axel. After realizing that this was indeed possible and that my path in life had suddenly made a sharp turn to the right (I like that), I just relaxed and listened to what Axel had to say. I was amazed and excited and never dreamed that what happened that day would take me into a world that welcomes us all.

So without further ado, I give you, finally…

A CONVERSATION WITH AXEL

I am Axel, and it is true that we live here…all one, yet you seek to know what it is that separates us, one from the other. Nature is a dance. A gift from the One that exists.

Here we awaken in many realms and thus to be is never the point. For each of us here has a "spot", a growth, an endeavor, and with this, a place to exist. We await all that would awaken to us, yet this place, this spot, our spot, so to speak, exists for all in that it is a haven for ones that know and believe…yes, believe in all that has gone before.

In the beginning, long ago, there existed, within all, a place among us. An ancient dwelling that drew upon that which dwelled deep within all beings. As each evolved, each became aware of which plane, place or spot he would exist.

Existence, what is this anyway? (Axel says, ho, hum) To exist is to live in a reality that becomes truth". Whose truth? Why yours of course! For all truth comes from the reality of existence. The existence of learning. Growing, not just physically, but with the wonderment of what you have been given.

Look at me. I exist because I need the stability of strength. The truth of steadiness. The simplicity of beauty. I am old, yet in the strength that comes from age, I evolve… not to be a mortal tool, but as a path that others may follow.

For each of you are on a journey, and unlike yours, ours exist too. We move onward, but our energies ever remain. Thus we attain what you desire, what you seek, but seldom find… Yet it's there, for you need only to gaze upon all that is provided and will see that Nature, us, all of us are here, ever near, and in the nearness, will give you everything.

You stare upon me now with an open mind. You gaze upon my being and seek my council. So be it. The hierarchy of the forest… Hhhhhmp! What is that anyway! We have jobs, skills, each unto themselves. Each seeking perfection unto themselves. We don't ask for these (jobs), for we are these! We exist only when they exist. Many have become lost, for their jobs, their skills, and their goals…their lives in a sense of the word, have been destroyed because they have been forgotten or laid to waste.

Why do you ask of what is in this world? Curiosity, I suppose.

Do you know we wonder of your world too! Why do you carry much-unneeded stuff; baggages and crates of useless "things"? Be they mental, physical or even your socialites among others? Why not just be as us, free to enjoy what you do? Exist to do what makes you exist. We know that we exist in a place that dwells within a hidden world, but unlike you, we "EXIST". Do you? No, I think not! Enough of this…ha-ha!

You wanted to evoke the right to speak to the ones that live here, right? (Yes, that's right)

So I will ask. Yes, 'tis possible, and since I am here and you are there, then I shall start.

Yes, I am Axel, if you desire me to be so named but you know I really don't care, for I have any name you desire. I have lived here for many lifetimes, in this I say "your" lifetimes. I evolved from a youth, as do you, and became as I am now. I rank among the elders of the forest and dwell within "The Path of Reason". To this we call a group that relates to others what is needed to exist in this realm. Many seek our council and of course unlike you beings, we live in a world of constant change. As seasons evoke changes, so must we evoke certain rights. Certain ways must be followed; for to never follow these "rules", one would find certain chaos upon this earth. The Equinoxes play a big part in what we do, as each brings with it a certain change. As each of the creatures that live among us go on with what they do, the challenges change. As winter turns into spring, with it, awakens these that have rested. With this awakening the tasks begin again. Within these paths, these stars that you call planets align in us the ability to continue to speak. For each trigger (for the lack of a better word) our ability to continue. Must I say, as of late, we have had much misalignment here for the planets have become distant to us. Why? I do not know, but much has changed. Our ability to continue is ever challenged by what they provide and yes (Cheri) we do work in harmony with them.

We know they exist, as we exist, not for the beauty, which is in all things, but in the strength that each gives to the other. For this place that you call Earth, revolves around their space and thus what we accomplish affects them as they affect us.

Understand? No matter. Have I sidestepped so? Thus I guess I should step back…

(The next part of the reading refers to another being, which is pink, which Leona's friend saw and drew.)

You wonder about the Pink Being do you? Ha! He is a worker of great magnitude. He works here and there splitting his time, vast in many settings. He lives in places unseen to all, yet he is ever near to all that desire to see him. He relates to work that exists "on" this place, so to say above, not under the earth. He grows in stature everyday and soon will be a member of his "line". Shall I say that each species (as you would say) has a "line", or a council that exists and unlike us they evolve slowly and in doing so exist for many, many generations more, and yet in each of us, be they the Pink Being or Axel, we exist together. For what would I do without the Pink Being? He exists here to develop my system of interchange. This is a system in which I exchange energy given by the earth to the sky and he emanates the power to his "line". He sits upon my outstretched arms and the earth gives him his charge. Do you understand?

She (the Earth) is all, but she exists in many forms. A lot of you understand the concept of Mother Nature, right? All right, so she, our keeper, the supreme one in our realm gives all that we need. Like a great receptacle, you "plug" into me and you get your food, your energy, to do your job, your work (or as you say, your craft!

(I am about to leave because I have another appointment)

Yes, I understand you must depart, and yes later will suit us all fine. Until then beware of those that would awaken what you don't need. Ta, until later. Love to you. Axel

LATER…

Welcome to our realm. Awaken to the beauty that awaits you. All things are here and so you must be also. Not in the physical sense, for you would find that impossible, but in a sense that what we feel and what you feel are the same. Do you understand? All are composed of members that belong to the whole. Be they like us or the animals that live among us. They are different, yet the same. Animals are also here to help all beings, you alike. They are much aligned yet are friends to all. As in your society they react to changes and thus in many cases they evolve slowly and become less of a threat than do a species such as yourself. Then again all things exist to serve, no matter what beingness they possess. You have come to learn of our "beingness", our land. You want to call it a kingdom, yet she/he is one. No king rules here. All are equal. Be they the tiniest one that scurries across the pages of your book, reading, looking, and reporting the news. (A tiny creature, much smaller than a spider went scurrying across my pages. He would continuously stop and start. Then as suddenly as he appeared, he was gone as I continued to write) All see, and yet many do not understand and yet they continue, ever trying to be all they can; as the ant.

We live in a world of silence here. For our beings speak to us in a way unheard by you. They know what they must accomplish in their tasks and thus do them everyday. All are given such jobs (as I stated before) and all accept that what they do is for the benefit of all. I have given you the message of the council we keep and ask that you relate this to my friend. Please tell her that Axel, as I am called here by her, remains. To this I employ her to act upon. As she journeys towards the path she has chosen, let her be aware that what she does can only be awakened, within those that would be awakened, to the joy of oneness. For we, unlike you, remain here always. Set in a place that remains ageless. We begin and we end and we begin again. In the past many have understood us and have been with us and have dwelled along side of us. This is lost here, because you don't understand that to see us, in the sense of being, you must first believe we exist. Not in the physical sense, of course. For all of you are capable of this, some more than others we must say. Yet the beingness of us, as the stone said, IS, is enough. Try it sometime, here is fine.

What is the hierarchy here? There is none. For unlike you, we are all among us, ones that desire to continue in the work we have chosen. *Discourse you say? Of course! All of us must have that, yet ours is mainly you. Yes, we have remained ions but in the short period you have been among us many Spirits have been lost. This is a pity but we remain, and we will, long after you do not.*

Within this realm I rule, or should I say I am the manager of this region. That is to say, they are nearer to the place you are staying (on the Tor), my workers. Not ones that work only for me, but still they bring news of what is here, yet they belong only to themselves, ever dedicated to all they seek in their work. They tell me what has happened, and what the Mother/Father, the One that exists in all realms, has in mind each day. She, who exists in all of creation, decides what the earth must accomplish in what given time.

As the moon moves and the stars glide by, our friends here return to the tasks they perform. Each season brings with it a renewal, growth, a newness. As babes are born in your world, so they enter yours. As spring arrives so do our youngsters. They break through the rich earth to feel the warmth of the sun. Yes, I do remember such a feeling, each time I look upon our sister the sun. She decides when she will appear, of course. She is a bit temperamental, you might say, never as consistent as her sister the moon. I relate this in a context of sex, which there is here also. We also have the male/female roles yet they play a part only in the function of renewal, except for beings that do not grow within our midst. For now we will speak of growing beings; the flower shall we say. You know how they grow, so what purpose do they have? None? They are quarters of the round. That's what we call them. They round out every quarter of the year; each existing or not existing within their quarter. They arrive in the spring. Yes this is true, yet some come much later, as the heather comes later, the buds of many come quite early. We on the other hand, remain upward and don't rest in the wintertime. No, I must say we do relax a bit; overconfident of what is to come. The "chaos of spring", I call it. What a mess I must say, everyone running about so terribly busy. You see all comes out, shall we say, at their time and it takes a bit to get some of us going!! We lay dormant in the winter? I THINK NOT!!!! For we see always. Some go deep within the Mother Earth to rest, yet they are busy too, but not so in a way that you would understand. For they explore their sense of "being", their sense of wonder at what lies ahead. For all, each cycle begins again, but still their essence remains. They continue to evolve, in a sense that the being they were remains within this realm and they continue.

Yes, you have it, or you did?

Each in their own way tries to bring each season they exist, to become all that they must. Sometimes it is hard, for what is suffered is often too trying for some, so they remain in their slumber until they are awakened once again. So they do have a council ruled (never liked that word!) by the Chief Council here. The group helps, of course, as do all living beings here, but we all pull together to do what we must.

Pageants, you say? Of course! We have a great one here every year, but seldom do you notice. Oh, yes, sometimes when all are in bloom you see the wonder of it all, but often you miss the subtleties of what else we give.

You keep dwelling on the hierarchy here. All right, so here it is:

I, the great tree, am on the council...right? Being so appointed I took over this part of my area. Kind of like a sergeant in your world. All come in with needs, unknown to you, for council. I talk among my elders, if it is needed. If not, I try to solve what I can. The problems here are slight but can be a nuisance if left undone.

The elves, fairies and the like do live among us. Shall we say they are the lighters. We call them the lighters because they turn on everything, most things here. They work in teams, one serving as observer and one serving as council, so to speak. They a-light all thinks above the ground with energy from below. You remember I told you about the "plugging in" and how it is my work. I am an energy point in my area and the like of those come to me and get the charge needed to evoke Nature to renew. Not in the growth, of course, but in the natural occurrence of budding, let's say. When a tree, flower, plant or whatever grows, it pushes its way through the soil, the earth, and emerges new, fresh. Yet it remembers before and calls on its friends the fairies, the lighters to give them the energy to relight the flame that has lain asleep under the earth. That's where I come in. I gather strength, energy through the core of my being. Through the great sun that lies below my feet (my roots), for I do not move about, and from the great sun that lies above my branches. Both charge me. Thus when the lighters come to be "enlightened", (You find that funny? Think about it!) they take energy from me and awaken, not in a sleep sense, but in a blooming sense you would call it, to what their essence was before.

Power points exist all over the earth. I am one, great rocks or stones, contain immense power for they existed long before we. Give them respect but give them love too.

Therefore the lighters give the spark that relights the flame that is asleep, they also put it out when it is time. Others bury our seeds. Yes, we have beings here that bury our seed. So it continues…

We have ones that touch up the colors of all things. Like the sets of all things, colors change, as seasons turn and so must all beings, such as we, die. Though this is dying in your world, in ours it is transformation. As we transform we become once again with the earth. I speak now of spring beings; some like myself remain.

The fairies bring what I need to survive, extras I might add, for they are good to me. They each have a task. Some to keep all things within their realm tidy; clean from diseases that would destroy us. Others begin and end their day, their period, doing nothing but working near to the earth, listening to her voice and relaying her commands. Others live high in the trees and are ever wary of outsiders that would cease us and take us from our home.

Council revolves around all beings in the fact that all may speak. Some (beings) cease to be, but only if they choose. Others begin a new task for they have become weary of what they do and others long for the sun or the darkness. This is quite possible, for all have a choice.

My being is present, yes, yet my spirit is separate. If I desire to be, say a flower for a season and another a tree, we shall switch. Tedium here is also felt, though like you, I have an ego so to take away my power (so to speak) I seldom do this. After a trying winter I may!

You must leave us. We are sorry. We saw you last night visit the great hill. (I went alone to the Tor at midnight) We heard you call us in the night and we thank you. Understand that all of Nature is a place that dwells within all of you. We are here to serve you. Serve us and we will remain. Continue your journey and speak to your friends at home, your Nature friends. Learn more and relate to us when you return. Tell my friend to draw the two we have spoken of. More is always forthwith, anytime. Talk to your spirits at home. They have a system not unlike ours. Remain true to the beings here and they shall appear to all that seek the beauty that you call Nature.

Go in peace. Axel

A CONVERSATION WITH AXEL – REVISED

I am Axel, and yes it is true that we all live here together. You want to know what separates us from each other, what each of our jobs are. *Nature* is a dance, a gift from *Mother Nature*. Here, we wake up in many worlds and so where we live is never important. Each of us has our spot, our place to grow, and something we must do, so it is we have this place where we live called Glastonbury. We wait for those that will wake us and believe we exist. This place, our spot, belongs to everyone because it is a place for ones that know and believe, yes believe in everything that has happened before.

Long ago, in the beginning, there lived in all of us a place of togetherness. An old place that brought out the feelings we held deep inside for every *being* on this planet. As each of us moved ahead in his different lifetimes, he learned in which world or "spot" he would live. Existing, living, what is this anyway? Axel says, (ho hum), "To exist is to live in a world that becomes truth."

Q: Whose truth?

A: Why yours of course! Because all truth comes from how you believe your world is, this world of learning. This world of growing, not physically, but with the wonder of what you have been given. Look at me. I live because I need to be strong and solid. My truth is to remain still, to stand-up tall, and for something as simple as beauty. I am old, but because strength comes with age, I evolve, I grow and I move forward, not to be a "human tool" but as a path that others might follow.

Each of us is on a journey, but ours is different than yours. We move ahead but our energies stay behind. We give you what you want, what you are looking for, but you don't often find … Yet it's here. You only have to look at all that we give you and you will see that *Nature*, us, all of us are here. Because we are here, we give you everything.

You look at me now with an open mind and see me as a living *being*. Because of this, you are asking me for my help in answering the questions you have brought. Alright. You want to know about "The hierarchy of the forest?" or in what order do the Nature Spirits rule their kingdom? Hhhhhhmp! What is that anyway!

We have jobs and skills that are special to each of us and we all search for perfection in what we do. We don't ask for these jobs because we <u>are</u> these jobs. We live only as long as these jobs exist. Many *Nature Spirits* have disappeared because their jobs, their skills, and their goals have been destroyed or forgotten.

Why do you want to know about our world? Because you are curious, I suppose. Do you know we wonder about your world too? Why do you carry around all that unneeded stuff; baggages and crates of useless things, whether they are mental, physical or just problems with other people? Why not be like us, free to enjoy what you do and "Live to do what makes life worth living!" We know that we live in a place which may seems to you to be a hidden world but unlike you though, we live. Do you? No, we didn't think so.

Enough of this…ha! ha!

You wanted to ask if it was all right to speak to those of us that live here. Isn't that right? (I, of course answered yes.) Yes, it's possible, and since I am here and you are there, then I will start. Yes, I am Axel, if you want to call me that, but you know I really don't care. You can call me anything you want. I have lived here for many lifetimes, in this I mean your lifetimes. I grew from a young *being*, as you do, and became as I am now. I am one of the *elders*, the older members of the forest and I live within what we call "*The Path of Reason*". This is a group that tells others what they need to do to live in our world. Many ask our advice and of course, unlike you, we live in a world that is always changing.

As the seasons bring changes, we must deliver to everyone that lives here, certain rules. These must be followed; if not there would be chaos on this earth. The equinoxes (seasons) play a big part in what we do, bringing with them certain changes. As each of the *creatures* that live with us moves along with what they do, their challenges change. As winter turns into spring, those that have rested awaken. When they are awake their jobs begin again. Along these paths, the stars that you call planets line up and give us the ability to keep on living; each restarts our ability to begin again. Must I say that lately we have had a lot of problems with the planets lining up like they have before. They have been farther off it seems to us.

Why? I don't know, but a lot has changed. We need the movements of the planets to survive and yes, we do work with them. We know they exist (live), as we exist (live), not only for their beauty, which is in all things, but in the strength that each one gives to the other. This place you call earth, revolves around in their space and so what we do also affects them just as much as they affect us. Do you understand? It doesn't matter. Have I gotten off the subject? I guess I should get back again …

You wonder about the *Pink Being* don't you?[2] Ha! He is a very great worker. He divides his time doing a lot in many different places. He lives in places that many people can not see, but he is still close enough for anyone that really wants to see him. He does work "on" his place because he lives above the earth, not below it. *The Pink Being* gets more important each day and soon he will be a member of his <u>line</u>. I will say that each species, which are different types of *Nature Spirits*, has a <u>line</u> or a council (a group of leaders) that changes very slowly. They live for many lifetimes but we all manage to live together. What would I do without the "Pink Being?" He lives here to develop my system of interchange. This is a system where I exchange the energy that the earth gives, and return it back to the sky. He brings this power to his <u>line</u>. He sits on my branches and the Earth gives him his charge. Do you understand?

She, who we call Mother Nature, is everything, but she lives in different forms. A lot of you understand the concept of *Mother Nature*, right? Alright, so she, our keeper, the supreme and the highest one in our world, gives us everything that we need. Like a great circuit in your electrical system, you plug into me and get the energy (food) to do your job. You might say your craft.

I tell Axel that I have to leave because I have another appointment but that I will return later. He says "Yes, I understand that you must leave, and yes, later will be fine". Until then be careful of those that would tell you what you don't need to know.

LATER …

Welcome (back) to our world. Awaken to the beauty that waits for you here. All things are here and so you should be too. Not in the physical way, because that would be impossible, but in a way that what you feel and what we feel are the same. Do you understand?

We are all made of members that belong to the whole; whether they are like we are or the animals that live with us. We are all different but still, we are all the same.

Animals are here to help all *beings*, not only you. They are not always given credit for their help but they are everyone's friends. Like in your society, the human group, they react slowly to changes and so in many cases, they evolve slowly and become less of a threat to us than human *beings* like you do. Then again, all *beings* live to serve, no matter what kind of *being* they are.

You have come to learn how we began, who we are and about our land. You want to call it a kingdom, but there is no he or she here so it doesn't matter. No king rules. Everyone is equal, the same. Whether they are the smallest little bug, which just ran across the pages of your book[3] or the largest creature that lives beneath the waves, they are all equal. Every creature sees, but many don't understand. Still they keep going, always trying to be everything that they can be, even an ant.

We live in a world of silence here. Our "*beings*" the *Nature Spirits*, part of the *Elemental Kingdom*, speak to us in a way that you can not hear. They know what they must get done in their job every day and so they do this. We all are given such jobs and we all accept what we do and what will benefit everyone.

---

2 The next part of the reading refers to another Being, who is pink, which a friend saw and drew.

3 A tiny creature, much smaller than a spider and bright orange, just ran across the page I was writing on. He stopped and started, and then just left. He ran right off the page as I continued to write.

(They ask me now if I will tell their friend that they are still there. That she must follow her own path and the only ones that can be awakened are those that want to be awakened to the joy that everyone is one)

We, unlike you, will always be here, living in a place that will remain forever because we begin and we end and we begin again. In the past, many have understood us and have been with us and have lived right along side of us. This is lost here now because you don't understand that to see us, in the sense that "we are real", you must first <u>believe</u> that we are real and that we exist. Not in the physical sense, of course but this is also possible. We must say that all of you are able to see us, some more than others. For us just to "BE" and for you to see us as the *beings* that we are is enough for us! Try to see us sometime. Now would be fine!

Q: What is the hierarchy, the chain of command, who rules who there?

A: There isn't any. Because, unlike you, everyone here wants to do the work that they have chosen.

Q: Does anything bother you or make you mad?

A: Of course! All of us have the right to get upset but when we do it is usually about you.

Q: How long have you been around?

A: We have lived eons (uncountable years) but in the short time you have been with us, many *Nature Spirits* have disappeared. We are sorry about this, but those of us that are left will stay and we will be here long after you are not.

Inside this world I rule, or to put it better I manage, I am the manager of this region, the land around here. That is to say, my workers are closer to the place you are staying (which is on the bottom of the *Tor,* which is a sacred hill in Glastonbury). These workers don't work only for me though they do bring me news of what and who is here. They work only for themselves and are dedicated to everything they do in their work. They tell me what has happened and what the *Mother/Father*, the one that lives in all worlds, has in mind each day. She, Mother Nature, who lives in all creation decides what the Earth must do and in what amount of time. As the moon moves and the stars pass by, our friends here return to the jobs they must do. Each season brings with it a new beginning of growth. Like the babies that are born in your world, they are also born in ours. They break through the rich soil to feel the warmth of the sun.

Q: Do you remember what that was like?

A: Yes, I do remember the feeling, each time I look at our *Sister the Sun*. She decides when she will shine, of course. She is like that, you might say, never as regular as her Sister, the Moon is. I say this making each of them female.

We do have the different sexes here. We also have the male/female roles but they only play a part in continuing the species in our world. It is different for *beings* that do not grow here.

For now we will speak of the *beings* that grow; like the flowers. You know how they grow but what purpose do they have? Do you think they have none?

This isn't right. They are "quarters of the round". That's what we call them. They round out every quarter of the year. Each living or not living in their own quarter. They arrive in the spring, this is true, but some come later, like the heather and the buds of many may come much earlier. Others like me (trees, bushes, etc.) on the other hand, stay above the ground, standing tall and not resting in the winter.

Q: Do you ever take time to rest?

A: No. I have to say, we do relax a bit because we know what will be coming in the spring. The "chaos", <u>the out of control situation of spring</u>, I call it! What a mess, I must say, everyone running around, so terribly busy. You see everyone comes out or blooms, shall we say, at their own time and it takes a lot to get some of them going; to get some of those plants and flowers to wake up.

Q: Do they just lay there all winter?

A: I don't think so! They are always aware. Some go deep inside our *Mother Earth* to rest, but they are busy too, but not in a way that you would understand.

They think about why they have chosen to be what they are and look forward to what will come in their next lifecycle. All lifecycles start over, but still their essence or soul remains. They continue to grow, in that the *being* that they were before will stay in this world (the flower) but their *soul* or *essence* will move on.

Yes, I think you've got it...or you did!

Each in their own time tries to bring into each season that it lives, everything that it can to become all that must become. Sometimes this is hard for some, so they stay asleep until they are ready to be awakened again.

Q: Do you have a council or some group that runs this place?

A: Yes we do have a *Council*, a group (though I never liked the word, council) ruled by the *Chief Council* here. The group helps, of course, as do all living *beings* here, but we all pull together to do what we have to do.

Q: Do you ever have pageants or festivals?

A: Pageants you say? Of course! We have a great one every year, but you don't often notice. Oh yes, sometimes when everything is in bloom you see the wonder of it all, but usually you miss the little things that we give to you.

Q: (Again I asked) "Who is in charge of whom"?

A: You keep asking about the hierarchy here. Alright, so here it is:

I, the great tree, am on the *Council*... right? Right. Being chosen, I took over this part of my area; kind of like a sergeant in your world. Everyone comes to me with questions and asks for advice about things that you do not know about. I talk with those that are wiser than I am, *The Chief Council*, if it is needed. If not, then I try to solve what I can myself. The problems here are small but can become a nuisance if you don't deal with them.

Q: Are the *fairies* part of the *Nature Spirit* kingdom?

A: The *elves, fairies,* and others like that do live with us. We call the ones you refer to as *fairies*, "lighters", because they turn on everything, well most things here. They work in teams together. One looks and studies what must be done and the other decides when it should be done, kind-of. They "a-light" all things above the ground with the energy from below. You remember I told you about the "plugging in" and how this is <u>my</u> work? I am the energy point in my area and these *beings* come to me and get the *charge* that they need to reawaken *Nature*. Not in the growing of course but in the natural way that a flower would make a bud. When a tree, flower, plant or whatever grows, it pushes its way through the soil and breaks through, arriving new and fresh again. It still remembers what it did before and calls on its friends the *fairies, the lighters*, to give them the energy to "re-light" their flame that has been asleep under the earth. That's where I come in. I gather strength, the energy through the center of my being through the great sun that lies below (the earth's core) my feet (You would call these my roots because I don't walk around) and from the great sun that rises above my branches. Both charge me. So when the *lighters* come to be "enlightened"[4], they take the energy from me and awaken, not in a sleeping sense but in what you would call a blooming sense, every *being* that they should to what their soul-essence was before.

Power Points are all over the world. I am one. Great rocks such as the *Standing Stones*, contain huge amounts of power because they lived long before we did. Give them respect but give them love too. So, the *lighters* give the spark that re-lights the flame which is asleep. They also put it out when it is time. Others bury the seeds.

Q: You have other *beings* that bury your seeds?

A: Yes, we have *beings* here that bury our seed. So it continues...

We also have ones that touch up the colors of everything. After all the periods of growth are over, everything changes. The colors change as the seasons turn and so each *being* <u>dies</u>. Though this is what you call it in your world, in our world it is called *transformation* or a time of change. As we change, we become once again, a part of the earth. I'm talking now about *Spring Beings*. Some like me, just stay on and on.

The *fairies* bring me what I need to live, extras I might add; they are very good to me. They each have a job, some keep everything in their world tidy and clean from diseases that would kill us. Others begin and end their day, their <u>period</u>, doing nothing but working near the earth; listening to Her voice and telling us what She wants us to do. Others stay up high in the trees and are very careful to alert us of strangers that would stop us from doing what we must and take us from our home.

The *Council* includes all our *beings*, letting anyone that wants to, speak. Some *beings* decide not to continue on this earth, but that is their choice. Others will begin a new job because they may get bored with what they do or they would like to be in the sun or in the darkness. This is possible because everyone has a choice.

Q: Is your *soul-essence* in a different place then in your physical form as a tree?

A: My *being* is here, yes, but my spirit is separate. If I want to be, for example, a flower for a season and maybe another season, a tree, I will switch with someone else who wants to trade places. We get bored here, just like you.

I have an ego though, so to take my power away (so to speak) is something I don't do very often. After a really hard winter though, I just might!

(I just told them that I had to leave and attend the conference)

---

4   So you think this is funny? Just think about it.

You have to go. We are sorry. We saw you last night visit the great hill. (I went to the *Tor* the night before at midnight). We heard you call out to us in the night and we thank you. Please understand that Nature is a place that lives inside all of you. We are here to serve you. Serve us and we will stay.

Continue your journey, and talk to your friends at home, your *Nature* friends. Learn more and visit us again when you return to Glastonbury. More information is always available, anytime. Talk to the *Nature Spirits* at home. They have a system that is a lot like ours. Remain true and believe in the *beings* here. They will show themselves to anyone that looks for the beauty that you call *Nature*.

Go in peace. Axel

So it began, and so it continued.

If you are still curious, I hope that you will continue to read about this wonderful world of the *Nature Spirits*. The *Elemental Kingdom* wants those in our world to know that they exist and are always there, no matter where you go. Hopefully you will come to understand the gifts they give to us all, in every aspect of our lives and the reasons they are here. They hope that through their eyes you will come to understand the jobs that they do to keep our world, working within their world, alive and well.

So I will continue, trying my best to revise what they say so it can be understood by everyone, yet always presenting what they have given to me in its original form. After all they are the ones writing this book. They are the ones telling me what I need to tell you. They are the *Nature Spirits* and they are, of course, **Elementally Speaking.**

This Place, The Wisdom of Nature

IN THE BEGINNING, BEFORE I got really involved in putting this book together, I received this message from Nature. It gave me advice on what I should look for and the reassurance that Mother Nature was alive and well and living here on Earth. It also pointed out that maybe this had not always been the case and that before she came there were others here that controlled this planet.

Throughout the readings you will find reference to these *beings*. I don't know who or what they were or even if they still exist. That will have to come later. As for now, it's good to know that Mother Nature is still around, doing what she does best. Let's just hope that she decides we are still worthy of her company and sticks around. I wouldn't like to think of a world without her.

THIS PLACE, THE WISDOM OF NATURE

As you search for truth, know that what we impart is that. Our truth, the truth of the Great One that leads us all and to this we shall ever be useful.

Beginning again, we are ever present in all things and thus give credence to the existence taken by you in our behalf. Many seek us out to understand why we begin and end and many search out reasons for our existence. But unlike you, they seek not why we exist or why we evolve (as do you) or the service we impart to all living beings in all places upon this earth. We are and shall ever be the reigning truth that lights all paths and only through us shall you survive. For if not through the continence of water and air and the need for sustenance, could you not survive?

Though the animals and the birds and the fishes that swim in the Great Sea shall cease, we only shall remain to feed and clothe all of you that remain, again to renew what you must to attain your path in this lifetime.

As we choose the lessons that we must also learn, so must you know that we too "are lessons," imparted to you for the goodness of all and through us all things exist and are again useful as before.

Long ago many ruled this land that brought to us all that was needed. We shared all in the goodness of this place and the light that shone brought joy to all beings. In time, the light faded and the joy that was known changed and with it the purpose of each person and animal and plant on this realm.

Keeping with this subject, we shall tell you of the gifts that were given so long ago by the Ones that were here before you. They were of a race, unlike any that remain. Full of energy and hope for all things, they brought with them the intelligence for all things. The earth was scarce then. The abundance in our world was challenged, for the Mother, ever weary, was asleep, in a state of transmigration from one realm to the next.

In starting to awaken to this world, the Ones brought with them the light that would arouse her from her sleep and awaken within her the ability to begin again her work upon this plane. As she arose, the intelligence was given and the light. The gift was given to her and all that would follow. She bloomed with the glow that reigns truly within her heart and remains still, for the fire that burns within her soul remains still a gift from long ago. This fire heats the roots of the soil when the winter wind blows. It warms the children that lie waiting within her warmth to begin again their growth, and the world's view of spring-time. She emits her forces in rage when She is angry and emits the soothing waters to the ill when She is calm. All things begin in her heart and all things shall remain there still.

As the "Old Ones" came, they brought the seeds that would become to her "The Children of her Birth". She nurtured them and they grew in the rich soil, sustained by the love and light of the holy order provided through all the Universe.

The "Beings of Light" knew of what must be given and so imparted all knowledge to all things. As seeded, The Mother began to birth all things and within this all of man became again what he was before, a seed to be nourished and atoned for indiscretions on places far from this place.

As man grew, so did Nature but also did the chances that came with this growth and remain still.

As you encounter many new things on this journey, know that what you see is but a part of what was before. Know that the beauty that surrounds you is but a facet of the truth that existed so many years before. For Nature as She changes grows in the direction that She must, often with trepidation and within the frame work of those that dwell above.

But be warned, that a "Higher, Great Being" that rules us all, has but to notice on what changes She imparts and all things shall change. For in her mercy, the Great One that in part rules us here, has given guidance to you above and in her mercy has challenged you to exist in this neoclassical continence you call life. Acceptance of her is ideal but some do not believe and yet they impart their will of this on others that cease to believe in this truth to become what they desire.

As She exists and becomes more, you shall become less unless you accept that what She provides shall begin and end all life upon this plane. We exist because She permits it; you exist because We permit it. She rules through Us and We rule through you, but only to the point of extinction. Knowledge is given and shall cease if not taken in truth.

We remain, Nature.

THIS PLACE, THE WISDOM OF NATURE — REVISED

As you search for the truth, you need to know that what we tell you is the truth, *Our* truth and the truth of the *Great One* that we all follow. Knowing this will make this very useful for you.

We are always a part of everything and for your benefit we offer you this proof that we exist. Many of you have tried to understand where we begin and where we end. Others search for the reasons why we even exist. Unlike you though, they don't ask us why we live or how we evolve (we do this just like you do) or even what we provide to all the living *beings* on this planet.

We are and will always be the highest truth that can "show you the way" (to survive) and only with our help will you survive. If it wasn't for the benefits of water and air and your need for food, could you live?

Even if the animals, the birds, and the fish in the sea disappeared, we would still remain; to feed and clothe all of you that had decided to stay and find your path in this lifetime. As we each choose the lesson we must learn, you must also understand that we too "are lessons" given to you for everyone's benefit. As we said before, we are needed because everything exists because of us.

Long ago the *beings* that ruled this land provided everything that we needed. We all shared in the goodness of this place and their light brought joy to all its beings. But in time, that light faded and the joy that we knew changed. When it changed, so did the purpose of each person, animal, and plant in our world.

Continuing with this story, we will tell you about the gifts that were given to us so long ago by *the Ones* that were here before you. They were a race, not like any that still exists today. They were full of energy and hope and brought the intelligence to benefit all *beings*.

The Earth, as you know it, was barren. What was needed was not provided because "*The Mother (Nature)*", overly tired, was in the position of traveling from one world to the next. When She began to awaken on Earth, the "*Ones*" brought with them the light that would restart inside her that ability to begin her work in our world. As She arose, this light and intelligence were given to her.

She bloomed with the glow that still rules her heart and the fire that burns in her soul still remains, that gift from long ago. This fire heats the roots in the soil when the winter wind blows. It warms the children that lie waiting in her warmth to begin again to grow in what your world calls "spring time". She sends out raging forces when She is angry but also sends the soothing waters when She is calm. Everything began in her heart and they still remain there today.

When the "*Old Ones*" came they brought the seeds that would become her children. She nurtured them and they grew in her rich soil supported by the love and light of the *Holy Order* provided throughout the Universe. These "*Beings of Light*" knew what was needed and gave this information to all things.

When she was seeded, "*The Mother*" (*Nature*) gave birth to everything. In doing this, man became just as he had been before, a seed to be nourished and forgiven for his mistakes on other places far from this world. As man grew so did *Nature* but so did the changes that came with this growth, the changes that still remain today.

As you face many new things on this journey of life, you must realize that what you see is just a part of what existed before. Understand that the beauty that surrounds you now is just a fraction of what existed so many years ago.

Mother Nature as She changes, grows in the direction that She must, often because she fears for the safety of those that live above.

But be warned that a higher, greater *Being* that rules us all, just has to notice the changes that *Mother Nature* makes and everything could change. In Her mercy, *The Great One* that in part rules us here, has let you above guide yourself and has challenged you to live in this new traditional way you call life. Accepting *Mother Nature* would of course be ideal, but some just don't believe this. They try to force their beliefs on others, who stop believing in Her truth, to do what they want.

As *Mother Nature* lives and becomes greater, you will become less unless you accept that what She provides both begins and ends all life on this planet. We live because She permits it, you live because We allow it. She rules through Us and We rule through you, but only to the point of extinction. This knowledge is given to you and will end if you don't believe it is the truth.

We remain, Nature

If you ever wondered how Mother Nature got here and why, I think this might have answered your questions. Maybe not in the way you would have liked but at least partly.

I know that this reading just brings up more questions. This seems to be true with each one I do. The more you learn the less you know and the more questions you have. It is a never ending circle but at least it gets you thinking and that is just what the Elemental Kingdom had in mind when it asked me to write down what they said. The point is that we live because Mother Nature provides what we need to live. If she decides not to do that anymore then we won't. The only thing she asks is that we believe that she exists and that we thank her once in a while for what she provides. I think this is little enough to ask for what she does for us. Wouldn't you agree?

A Message from The Nature Spirits

Findhorn, Scotland – Summer 2002

IT HAD BEEN A YEAR since I had been contacted to channel the Elemental Kingdom. By this time I had pretty much written off the project but still had it in the back of my mind that I should continue working with the Nature Spirits in some way.

It was the summer of 2002 and I had returned to Scotland. I again found myself at Findhorn when I was asked to pick up a few supplies at the "Park" store for a friend before heading toward Glen Lyon. Again, I didn't feel the great connection with Findhorn that I had heard so much about but since I was there and I knew I needed to reconnect with Nature, I felt this was a good place to do it.

I was still part ways into the whole fairy mode; where fairies look like Tinkerbell even though I knew differently, so when I got this reading it was really a wake-up call for me.

How many times have I ignored Nature, even though She is everywhere?

This would not be my last plea from the Elemental Kingdom, not by a long shot and by the time I reached my friends at Invervar Lodge in Glen Lyon I knew I was on a mission. I had received the message and now my journey would begin, at least officially in my eyes. In their eyes it had begun long ago.

A MESSAGE FROM THE NATURE SPIRITS

Welcome, We are here, yet in this world many do not see. For the times come and man has not become what he must to attain all within our realm. We exist within this place and yet we do not exist to be ignored, yet we have become to most not what we are, but what we can be.

Give us the knowledge to exist within your realm and we shall impart to you the needs of your world. For spaces and times and energies exist where the earth and Nature reside.

Long ago, the Mother ruled upon this plane and still she is all. For we exist still and forever and She alone gives choices to those that remain. Exist with us.

Reveal within this place and to others the knowledge that we are near, that we exist, and that we desire to be. Give to us what you have forgotten and we shall return to you all that we believe, the knowledge lost long ago.

For Nature shall live when all others depart; She who lives governs all and the path home leads only to the hillside outside your door.

A Message from *The Nature Spirits* – Revised

Welcome, We are here, but in this world many of you don't see us. Time moves on and still you haven't done everything you can to connect with our world. We live in your world but we don't like to be ignored. Even those of you that believe we do live, see us as something we really aren't, not what we actually are.[5]

Tell us what we need to do to live and be seen in your mind and we will give you in return what we know will help everyone in your world because everything that anyone needs exists in *Nature*. Once people believed that *Mother Nature* ruled this planet and gave them everything they needed to survive. The truth is….She still does. We, *The Spirits of Nature*, are still alive and we always will be. Why? Because *Mother Nature* alone decides who stays and who goes. We can live together.

---

5 Referring here to the images we give to *Nature Spirits*, also known as *Fairies* … You know; gossamer wings, long flowing hair, flower dresses, etc.

Be happy here and now. Tell everyone that *The Nature Spirits* and *The Elemental Kingdom* live and that we want to continue to live. Rediscover what you have forgotten about us and we will give you back everything we know and believe. We will give you that knowledge you lost a long time ago. Go back to the stories told about *Nature Spirits, Fairies*, and *The Gods and Goddesses* of the land and remember.

Nature will still be here when everything else is gone. *Mother Nature* still lives and manages everything. To find her again, just follow the path that leads to the hillside outside your door, and She will welcome you home.

The *Elemental Kingdom* was very gentle on me or should I say "Us" this time. Later you will see she can be more demanding and starts "telling it like it is".

This reading opened my eyes and led me to "the path that leads to the hillside outside your door", literally. When I arrived the following summer back to Glen Lyon I took a walk that led me to the River Tay. Looking out over the river from an old wooden bridge, I saw this magical place tucked into the bank of the river. It had a wonderful Ancient Stone (which happens to be my weakness) surrounded by lovely little flowers and all sorts of mossy greenery. It was the sort of place one might find a "Hobbit" if one was looking for one. I, of course, thought this might be a great place to try and reconnect with Nature. Maybe I could get more insight or at least find out what it was I was supposed to do. Climbing down the bank I could see how clear the river was but had no idea that the river and The *Elemental World* were one. This is just one thing I would learn on this wonderful journey of discovery I was about to make.

I finally was able to reach this enchanted place and immediately began to channel *Nature*. What I received touched my heart and was so overwhelmingly beautiful that I knew without a doubt I had to do something. I knew that *Nature* had so much to tell us not to mention give us and all she wanted in return was to be noticed.

So it was that this reading changed my life. It made me see *Nature*, not as something that is just there but as another world within ours. A world only concerned with helping all *beings* no matter who or what they may be. Their words kept me searching for more.

I followed the path; now it's your turn.

Lavender

Findhorn, Scotland – July 2002

IT WAS THE SUMMER OF 2002 and I had finally accepted the fact that I needed to return to Findhorn for what is called "Experience Week". I was skeptical but excited at the same time knowing that my connection with the Nature Spirits had been recognized by both them and I and they expected me to fulfill the task of telling the world just why they existed. I knew that I didn't want to come off as "airy fairy" because that was not the purpose of the book, but instead to let the world know about the essence of each *being* in their world. This, of course, could never happen because there is no way I could channel all the different *being*s in Nature, which would be impossible in this lifetime.

Of course, the Conversation with Axel would have to be the first passage in the book but other than that I had no idea where to begin.

Before I go any further, let me better explain a little more about Findhorn. Located near Inverness, Scotland in The Moray Firth, it sits right along side a huge Royal Air Force base. This is a most extreme example of a juxtaposition of opposite worlds.

The Findhorn community began and continues today under the guidance of The Elemental Kingdom or as most of us know them, The Nature Spirits. Since the beginning, the Nature Spirits have taught the Findhorn residents everything they needed to know about their world, working together to produce what they need to survive. There are many books written about the community if you are interested in finding out more about the history of Findhorn. For now I just want to touch on what I learned there.

Not knowing what to expect, but obviously on the right path, I began my Experience Week. What an experience it was! If you have ever wondered at all about the existence of any kind of Nature Spirit at all, this is the place for you. Not only did they help me connect with the Elemental Kingdom but also to see what purpose I had in my world as well. People of all ages and from all walks of life live, work, and learn together by "tuning in" to the voices of Nature. It was an amazing and yes, life altering experience that made me more confident that I had chosen the right road when I decided to work with The Nature Spirits. What I had never noticed before suddenly became quite clear and the voices that spoke to me made much more sense.

The Stones, which are also a part of the Elemental's world, led me here, I am sure. I am convinced more and more everyday that nothing happens by coincidence; everything is somehow planned. Through a series of twisted roads I finally found myself here. Why? Because this is where I needed to be. I had certainly changed my mind about Findhorn. It no longer became that hippie community that started back in the early 60's but instead became the doorway to a world that is open to us all. I just never had the key and now I do ... in fact, we all do.

I didn't have much time to do much channeling while I was there. Realizing that I could and learning to connect to Nature itself was enough.

After the summer, I returned home and started to receive more readings from the Nature Spirits in my area. However I did manage to do my first one at Findhorn in front of Cluny College where I stayed during Experience Week.

Sitting out on the grass and looking out over the hills spread in front of me, I couldn't help but notice the lovely scent of the lavender blooming nearby. It made me think of how even after the harshest winters here in Scotland, the lavender still returns every year. It comes back just as beautiful and as fragrant as it probably has forever. It made me wonder if our lives are somehow connected in the same way.

It was at the height of its season; beautiful, soft and of course inviting me to have a chat ... so what else could I do?

Lavender

The lavender awakens each year and with its awakening comes the renewal of life. Fragrant, and soft to touch, the bitterness of the past winter ends and fragrance becomes reality, once again. Needful lessons erupt as before and thus is life as it arises upon this plane. As each in their own time becomes one with all things, thus they remember as the lavender, the distances erupting into life … awakened as before, new, yet ancient. As the lavender, so does each person become again as before. Their fragrance erupts as life and with it, gives each person who they meet the opportunity to become, once again, an essence of either desire or not.

Walking the path of each existence allows each one that desires, a choice, and in these choices comes the callings that bring about changes that relate to this and future existences. As each of you become, once again "renewed", know that as the lavender the truth lies not in the beauty but the essence. Not in the maintenance but in the renewal.

Be as before, but be as always … renewed, loved and united in this path you desire. For all exist now and forever and all shall grow.

Like the plants that are nourished, so are we all but existence comes when acceptance is renewed. Accept the love that grows within us all. Acceptance of things shall begin only if you desire to be all that you have become… not today, not tomorrow, but in each lifetime. For love expounds and with it, the reality of all that is.

Emerge, young ones. As each grows, as the seeds are sewn, each begins again … renewal … as love, light that radiates from above, below and through all things.

We remain, The Ancients of the Lavender

Lavender — Revised

The lavender awakens each year and through this awakening comes the beginning of a new life. Soft and smelling sweet, the long hard winter is forgotten and the new life of the lavender begins again. Once more there are lessons to be learned, not only by the lavender but also by every person on this Earth. Just as each person, when they are ready, feels they are connected to every living thing, they like the lavender begin to remember. They bloom again, new and reborn in each lifetime … but still they hold inside, what they learned before. Just as the lavender, blooming season after season, each person begins his life again, lifetime after lifetime. When the life of the lavender is renewed once more, the sweet smell is released, just like the sweetness of life is released for you in your world. Life begins once more, giving each person the opportunity to become, once again, either someone that is wanted and needed in this new life or someone that is not.

The roads you take in each life allow every person that wants it a choice. With these choices come the opportunities to bring about the changes that will affect both this life and the lives to come. As each of you is reborn, remember that like the lavender, whose oil is used in healing, it is not its beauty that is important but what it gives to the world. It is the same for all of you. It is not how you look, but is how you choose to spend this lifetime and what you can give to your fellow man.

You can be like you were before, but first begin each lifetime with more love and more purpose. With these things you can achieve what you want.

Everyone lives through lifetime after lifetime and in each one they grow a bit more. Like the plants, we are all given what we need to survive. To truly live and to love, we must accept that life is what we alone make of it and that love must grow within us all. You will only be able to accept these things, if you *want* to be everything you have become, not only today or tomorrow but in each lifetime. Remember that love is everything, now and forever and that love is the only thing that is truly real.

Begin again, young ones. Like the seeds of the lavender that are spread in the fall and bloom in summer, you too will bloom again. You too will live again.

As each of you grows and lives your lives, each starts over and is born again.

Be like the LOVE that glows from above, below and through all things.

We remain, The Ancients of the Lavender

The idea of birth, death, and rebirth is not new. In fact it is probably the most accepted concept in the world today. Still, when it is explained through the eyes of the lavender it seems almost magical. The choices we make and the paths we choose are there, lifetime after lifetime. We need only to recognize this and try to do our best in the lifetime we have chosen.

In this reading as in all the readings I have received, the underlying message is love. As they said … To truly live and to love, we must accept that life is what we alone make of it and that love must grow within us all.

It seems as if the Elemental world and ours really do have a lot in common, don't you think?

I left Findhorn with a new purpose. This was not only a search for what The Elemental World did but also the answer to the question of how to make their message available to everyone. It would be a long road but certainly a very interesting and enlightening one.

As you will see, I continue to return to Scotland and to Findhorn. Perhaps this is because this is where it all started or maybe it's just that the connection with the Nature Spirits is so much more intense there. I really don't know. I just hope that you continue to read what they have to say.

Ojai Cemetery

Ojai, California – Tuesday, January 14, 2003

ON THE CALIFORNIA COAST IS a wonderful little town just inland from Ventura called Ojai. It is quite well known among the spiritual community, having both The Krishnamurti Center and the Theosophical Society. And let's not forget Meditation Mount and the world famous "pink moment" either.[6] This is a place where you would expect to find retired hippies and new age shops. You won't. What you will find instead is a place where spirituality is alive. Ojai does have its local color of course, but then again you will find that anywhere. Mostly you will find people dedicated to saving the environment and endangered species. Caring people working together to bring back organic farming and alternative healing and to create a new birthing center.

The Nature Spirits love it here, but then why wouldn't they? They never cut down a tree. They tried that once but it didn't work.

The place is surrounded by orange groves and rolling hills that seem to contain the wisdom of The Ancients. So of course, here of all places, you would expect to find a very unusual cemetery, wouldn't you? I did.

It's not that the cemetery is old because nothing is old in California, except maybe the missions. But it is unusually full of Nature Spirits and they sure have a lot to say.

I had been to Ojai to visit my friend Leona who worked for The Cheetah Conservation Society. Leona had a few tasks to wrap up before she left, so I decided to see what a big oak tree down the street might have to say. I hadn't noticed before that the tree was, in actuality, located inside the local grave yard. This didn't bother me; rather it made me more curious. What would an old tree in a cemetery have to tell me? I know I was not supposed to ask to hear any stories, this would come later I was told, but I was certain they would have some very interesting things to say. I was right.

I also found out that I wasn't as "in touch" with the Elemental Kingdom as I thought. A huge lesson was learned that day, one that helped me become more connected with the Nature Spirits I would meet later on my journey. For this I will be forever grateful. Hopefully you will see what I mean after you read this piece.

OJAI CEMETERY

I come to you now, in this place that awaits all eventually, at least in this lifetime. I am a Nature Spirit or what can be given as such in your lifetime experiences. I await many things to happen here but the eventuality of this occurrence seldom becomes all that I expect. Entering into this place to seek me out is well taken and those that seek seldom do so in this environment, so to speak. As a place of rest, it is also a place of renewal; not only for those that have passed, but for us as well. Seeking solitude, many spirits, many different types (this is added because we are what you refer to as Nature Spirits but in fact "spirit" is a word that denotes passing from this place to another and yet we remain, as the wind does, ever blowing through the canyons; never still, always blowing, blowing.) are ever ready to begin again another way to disturb all things remaining to entertain life changes arranged now or in a time to come. It is not as if we seek to destroy all that awaits here, on the contrary, we are here to make all things, be they alive or dead (for all things never really cease), but also for those that survive long after their bodies lie dormant under this Earthy plane.

As the Devas who rule here, (thus, they are called so because the relationship given them thus enlarges their point of being and with this comes the status appointed to such as these) they rule not all, but instead bring to those that dwell among them, the

---

6 "The Pink Moment" is what the locals call that time of day, just before dusk, when the sky above Ojai turns a wonderful glowing shade of pink. It happens every day of the year and in any weather. Some say, and I certainly believe, that "It is the magic of Ojai". I also think the Nature Spirits that live there have a bit to do with it!

knowledge needed to extend themselves in this realm.

As they steadily grow, we also grow, not in the sense that we are different from them but complete unto ourselves, also.

Seymour you called me or shall I say I have accepted this name and thus we shall begin by this:

Your knowledge into our world has only begun and with this shall be imparted many lessons learned or not, also those things which I shall appoint to you shall begin in your time to awaken those that would deem it possible to understand what we do. In fact it may even bring to them the knowledge understood but until now has never been imparted unto many.

As you sit under this tree, as you have before, remember that what you see is indeed also what we do in this place; we have accepted that your task is just that. For to understand our world, with the complexities of its space you much first understand its beings such as I and others too. For each has and shall ever have a place in our society and with this the purpose given to all. As you exist to be what you must, we have accepted certain tasks as well. Not (only) what must be done but as a task that will make us, unlike you, better suited for the realm in which we delve. For as you search for truths that relate to your being we also search. In this our tasks are related not to what is integrated within our being but in the justice afforded all within all things, ways and acts on this and all given planes.

I, Seymour, shall impart to you all that you desire but only if the acceptance given can be relayed as given. For changing viewpoints and realms leads ones to speculations seldom seem by all people. So in understanding that what we're giving you is actually part of us, then you have to know that what we say or not becomes truth if you know it to be true.

That is "Figu".[7] He is orange, that is truth and with this glow he accepts what he must. He seeks now the integration of what you do and what you see. He wanders hither and fro and seeks out all that shall transpire. Alone he investigated. Leave him be and he shall belong again to himself, but integration of self will respond to us all and the gamete of knowledge attained shall help us further with your quest.

So you have seen some of us in other places. This is good. For often we represent ones that dwell not on this Earthy plane but in the minds of those that would seek out things that relate not to the what, why or the where of our being.

Starting now I am going to tell you things that you seek. This can be useful in this endeavor you have undertaken, in the extent that many have asked that you transmit what we say into reason for those that can't see or even understand what and who we are.

The ones here at least exist to be what we must, to function in the needs of this area. We work with many entities and thus have jobs not unlike you, but then again they are by far more different. As each of us exists to do what must be done, we are given certain rank and file. Not in the military ways, as on your plane, but in the joined way of ours.

As I seek to uncover information on what shall become of what has happened in this time frame, others accept this and move ahead with this work.

As your seasons change and goals are altered so changes are made not only by ones such as I, but by others that have accepted other tasks on this level. As you assist us with our goals, be aware of many that would hamper you in this quest but also understand that the plight of us all does depend on you and ones that will listen to what we have begun. You ask now not for yourself as before, but for others, why we live as we do and what purpose do we possess? Many questions can be answered and will be, but this knowledge shall only be of benefit if it is shared with all that would desire to know what and where and when and how we live, delve, devise and attune our lives, such as they are, to the benefits of this place you call Earth.

As we radiate out into this plane, a network forms not unlike the ones formed by your many functions. Ours differs in the fact that we go not by wires or through fields spread open with cable unfamiliar to ones such as we, but to a network of planes that allow us to function on levels unseen by you. Though we exist as you, ever present to those that would see, we do our duties in places seldom seen by mankind. As the Earth turns and the seasons change, so do the duties of each being in this place, As for the fact that we are the same as other places, this I can no longer account. For we are the same this is truth, but in fact we all share the great respect and the desire to make this place more than what you have succeeded to overcome (destroy). In our acts, we accept that what we desire is what we must accept, yet many do change within this framework and accept other things within this place.

You seek out answers to what are Devas, fairies and the like and the existence of said types. To those we relate, all things exist if you accept this as truth but in fact we do exist even though those that truly believe are indeed not all that seek out this truth. Devas

---

7   I must explain that what they were referring to above was what looked like a tiny orange spider named *Figu,* that ran all over my laptop and then down my coat before disappearing.

as stated before, rule us here for they are who we know to be our truth and thus in acceptance, we look to them for the truths that relate to us here and in this place.

As we each solve problems that we will relate, we gather knowledge which is needed to begin again everything that went before. The acceptance of this, will indeed bring to all concerned, the knowledge that is needed to begin again the growth that we must accept to proliferate all things within this place. As many come here to rest, many also must accept this and make way for Spirits that exist, not in ours or your realms, but exist in a warped sense of reason only needed to fulfill what they desired most but was unaccepted on this plane.

As we scurry about, for this word fulfills what we have hoped, we enter into contracts, not only with what we must do, but with what we must forge within our own existence to encounter within ourselves towards growth. Like you we exist for a reason. Yes we toil and grow but so do you also. We are unseen, but seldom are we noted. For acceptance in this form proves to be such as that when and if we appeared none would accept us as "being" in deference to all. Such it is and so we do what we do, which is many things in silence, screeching ever near to extinction in cases related often times in stories told by fireside meetings seen by many yet unknown. For we see all. Yes in different ways, for the relationships are such as to never strain the bond between worlds.

As you seek out what is related, be warned that many in my world fear for the existence of their being to be nil (nothing), in the fact that what they see is destruction of all that they have known in their existence. With this comes the loss of beings such as felt by many in this place. As you shelter us, so do you also excuse those that would command the destruction that awaits all that do not encounter all that is needed for the betterment of all beings. Be they you or be they us.

Knowing full well that you will never accept us in the form in which we dwell, others have written of us as beings of light; as gossamer winged sirens alight in the midsts of tales seldom encountered within this plane. Yes, many are and shall be unlike you and many exist that would light up your being, but their purpose is not this alone. For the benefit of light has much more purpose then the continual sighting of winged beings in the garden at midnight. I exist not as a winged creature but as a "leaf". Not in the context of a leaf, but in a being that shall and will resemble this. To do so provides what I must and thus gives to each that desire it, what is needed. As I fell to Earth[13] you discarded me, and yet you recognized my existence but in this form did not. Thus in seeking me you were "unrelated" to me. This is what I mean, for we are here but not to you. You look, this is truth, and you see, to this we agree, but when presented (or "in your face" as often is spoken), you ignore this.

Where have I gone you ask? Which one have I become? Alas, tis to "no avail" to you now, but to you the acceptance of what is given shall be noted and now and forever foreword you will also see more than before. My existence is different from many in that what I do is not what many others do, but also many others do also what I do but differently. This ranges in needs.

As each tree (the being that uses us) has sparks that radiate from the Earth thus igniting these sparks, so the energy is imparted to us and we carry this to other beings. Unlike the lighters that have spoken to you, we are not ones that give to all the needed sparks to carry onward toward other goals for we differ from that place.[8] For the sedentary difference here is that growth is slower; easier and less noisy as before. From this resting place of many, some cease to begin again knowing the growth that was undertaken in their life was uncompleted. Because they have been reluctant to change have stayed and thus to interrupt their journey would heed them uncaused misery. So growth is slow and intervention also comes slowly.

As they should depart this Earthy plane and return to the Earth, the bodies decay and with this comes what we need to begin again. Though many fear this, the bodies are that and that alone. Some seek to stay and thus become in time attuned to Nature, as we are called, and accept us as their path thus altering what they desire. Many have chosen to remain and thus have accepted this state and have become as us; once again with the potential for growth. Though comprehension in this does not suit many it is indeed possible and many have begun again different from before and much more attuned with what they had ignored before. As each person becomes what they must, we also become what we have accepted. Though I exist as a leaf, I give you this only in the fact that this is the being form in which you relate, I am indeed not this leaf for I am a lighter, yet not as before. I am a spark that is ignited. Here always and in this accept the sunlight, the moons rays, and the energy needed to extend to our Mother what she needs to exist. As above so is below. As the great fire that lives deep within this place, the Great One knows what must be taken to encounter growth both above and below this plane. With it comes the gift that I offer to all. The benefit of this spark that comes from both shall ignite this place that I dwell and this form, which you relate to as this tree, begins to reform. As it reforms this energy is given and taken and I relate (give) this to what I deem necessary.

---

8 Glastonbury, Scotland. See passage, "A Conversation With Axel".

I speak for all that dwell within this framework in saying that energy is freely given and as such should be accepted by all as that. To deny this is to shelter ones needs in the arms of resistance. To hinder all from this energy is to hold your world captive from this growth. Accepting that what I do is necessary and knowing my form does not alter what I do in your lifetimes. For ours is different, and with it comes stagnation and with it comes growth but also comes acceptance by all in a job that is worthy to the being of all.

As I "spark" this existence, the existence of worlds and energies colliding, I bring with it the gift of life. For this creature in which I dwell (the tree) would not exist without the energy given and received through above and below. As regulated and attuned it grows, releasing what your world must have to exist; working in harmony with all beings. Thus it is so and thus I shall continue.

Others await their quests and with them their existences also. Give to them a voice and speak to all that will hear the beauty of beings that exist outside your realm. Go in the beauty that is ours as we accept the gift that is yours. Alone we are defeated, together we survive. I am and shall be until I exist no more, Seymour ... SEE MORE!

OJAI CEMETERY—REVISED

I am coming to you now in this place that waits for you all, at least in this lifetime. I am a *Nature Spirit* [9] or that is what you call me in your experiences in this lifetime. I wait for many things to happen here, but when they finally do, it's not always what I expect.

Coming here to look for me is a very good idea because it is not very often that people come to a cemetery to talk to us here. Known as a place of rest, it is also a place of new beginnings, not only for those people that have died but for us too.

Some of the *Spirits* that are here are searching for quiet and want to be alone; many other kinds of *Spirits* are always ready to start over while others just find another way to bother everyone that is still here. Some stay to think about how to change their lives now or in the lifetimes to come.

It's not as if we want to get rid of everyone that waits here; quite the opposite. We are here to arrange things, whether that *being* is alive or dead (because nothing ever dies). We are also here for those that live on, long after their bodies are buried under the ground.

The *Devas* [10] who rule here, don't "rule" as you know it but instead they give to those that live among them the information that they need to survive longer in this world. Just as the *Devas* keep growing, we do too, only not in same way. Yet we are just as complete in what we do as they are in what they do.

You seem to want to call me Seymour so I will keep this name. We will begin:

What you know about our world has just begun and so we will give you lessons you may have already learned before or haven't learned yet. In your own time, things that I tell you to do will begin to awaken those people who want to understand what we do. In fact, it might even bring them information that is already known but until now has not been given to many people.

Every *being* has and will always have a place in our society or community and because of this a reason for living. This is given to everyone. Just as you live to become what you must become, we too have taken certain jobs. Not just as a job that must be done but as a job that will make us, unlike you, better suited for the world in which we live. As you look for the truth of why you are here, we also search for that truth. In this way our jobs are not related to what is organized in ourselves, but in the fairness we give everyone in everything, in every way and in every act on this plane; in this world that you see and in any other worlds that you don't.

I, Seymour, will tell you everything that you want to know but only if you accept that what I say to you <u>must</u> be written just as I say it. [11] Changing viewpoints and words will lead people to beliefs that most can not understand. So in understanding that what we're giving you is actually part of us, then you have to believe that what we say will become true if you <u>know</u> it is true.

That is *Figu.* [12]. He is very orange, that is true, and with this glowing color he does what he has agreed to do. He looks at what you are writing and what we see and how they work with each other. He wanders everywhere and looks at everything that happens while you are here. Alone he searches for these answers. Just leave him be and he will do what he has to do. What he has learned he will give to all of us here and this will help us to take you further on your quest to learn more about *The Nature Spirits*.

---

9 This is added because we are what you call Nature Spirits, but in fact, <u>spirit</u> is a word that means passing from one place to another. We, as Nature Spirits, stay. <u>Spirits</u> are just like the wind that blows through the canyon... never still, but always moving.

10 *Devas* are called this because of the position and the job they are given here. This title gives them credit for the work that they do.

11 This is why I have kept the original channelings just as I received them. In this way you can see what you are supposed to see in each reading.

12 I must tell you that what looked like a tiny, tiny orange spider, was running all over my laptop and then down my coat before disappearing.

So you have seen some of us in other places? This is good. Usually we don't look like what most people expect us to look like. This is because pictures of how we are <u>suppose to look</u> have been given to the world by people who have no idea what we really do, why we do it or where we do it.

Starting now, I am going to tell you the things that you are to look for. This can be useful in this job you have undertaken, because many *Nature Spirits* have asked that you write what we say in words that everyone can understand. So that everyone can see, or at least try to understand what and who we are.

At least the ones here live so they can become what they must become and work to do what is needed in this place. We work with many different *beings* and so have jobs not so different from you, but then again they are very different. As each of us lives to do what must be done, we are given certain rank and file or leadership positions. This rank and file system of ours is not done in the military way, like in your world, but in a connected way so that everyone is working together. When I look for information on what will happen because of what has been done at this time in the past, others accept this and move ahead with this work. As your seasons change, things that we planned may also change. These changes are not only made by me but by others like me who have accepted these jobs on this level.

As you help us with what we are trying to accomplish here, be careful of those that might try and stop you in your search. You must also understand that what happens to us all depends on you and the ones that will listen to what we have started to say.

You ask us now, not for yourself as before, but for others, why we live as we do and what purpose do we have?

Many questions can be answered and will be, but this information can only help if it is shared with anyone that would like to know what, where, when and how we live. Also how to look into, arrange, and bring harmony into our lives, such as they are, for the good of this place you call *Earth.*

As we reach out into this world, a network forms. It is not too much different than the ones you use and the way it works. Ours is different because we do not move through wires or within cables through fields. We in our world don't know how these work. We use a network, a group of planes (different worlds or dimensions) which let us work on the levels that you can not see. Even though we live as you, always there for anyone to see, we do our jobs in places that you don't often see.

As the *Earth* turns and the seasons change, so do the duties of each *being* in this place.

As for the question, do we do the same as other "Nature Spirits" in other places, I really can't tell you. We are the same this is the truth, and in fact, we all share the greatest respect and the wish to make this place more; more than you have succeeded to destroy. In accepting the job we do, it is understood that this is what we have chosen to do. Still, many do change within this framework or what they planned and accept other things within our world.

You are looking for the answers to what are *Devas, Fairies*, and others like this and if they really exist. We answer by saying everything exists if you believe it exists. But the fact is we do exist, even though those that truly believe are not the only ones that look for the truth.

Devas, as we said before, rule us here. Because they are the ones we trust and accept, they are the ones that we look to for answers that relate to us here. As we each solve the problems we will tell you about, we gather information that we will need to restart everything that happened before. Accepting this will certainly bring to everyone concerned the information they need to again start the growth that we must accept to help everything in this place reproduce.

Though many come here to rest, others also must agree to this and make way for those *Spirits* that don't live in our world or yours… Those that live with a warped sense of what they needed to do and wanted most in their last life, but was not accepted on the Earth plane.

As we "scurry" or run all around, (this word "scurry," explains what we hoped it would) we enter into contracts, not only about the work we must do but also with what we must accomplish inside ourselves to bring about the growth we need.

Like you, we live for a reason. Yes, we work and we grow but so do you. We are not seen and hardly ever noticed. Accepting our appearance in our true form would be hard for you to comprehend and so nobody would accept us as real. Even if they did, they wouldn't tell anyone, because no one would believe them. That's just the way it is. We just do what we can do, which is to do many things in silence.

We hear stories of how we are "screeching to a halt" or how we are about to "no longer exist". Sometimes these stories are told around fireside meetings, seen by many of us, but not noticed by any of you. We see everything. Yes, but in different ways. These relationships are made so that we do not break the bond we have between both worlds.

As you look at what we are telling you, be warned that many in your world are afraid that there is nothing after this world. In fact, the belief is that everything that they know in this world will end. Many of us in this place feel the loss that these *beings* in your world feel. Even though you try to keep us safe, you also excuse those people that would order this world destroyed. The ending of this world will come to everyone that doesn't learn about all that is needed to make this world a better place for every *being*.

We know that most of you will never accept the way that we really look. Others have written about us as "*beings of light*" or as gossamer, sheer and beautiful winged creatures that fly about in stories; those *beings* that you will probably never see, not in our world. Yes, many are and will never be like you. Some that live here could light up your life, but their purpose isn't just this alone. The good things that come from this light have more reasons to exist than the never ending sightings of winged *beings* in the garden at midnight. I exist but I don't look like one of those *winged creatures* but like a leaf. Not in the fact that I am a leaf but that if you saw me, you would see a leaf. Doing this gives me what I need and also doesn't bother you.

When I fell to earth, you brushed me aside.[13] You knew that I am alive; you know I exist, but you didn't recognize me in this form. So in seeing me in my form as a leaf, you were not connected to me. This is what I mean. We are all here but not to you! It is true that you look for us and we know that you understand. We agree on this but when we show ourselves to you or are "in your face" as you would say, you ignore us. Where have I gone, you ask? Which leaf am I? Too bad, you won't find me now, but in accepting what I did to you, I will remember this and from now on you will always see more than you did before.[14]

My existence is different from other *beings*, in that what I do is not what others do. Still, there are others that do what I do, but differently. It depends on what is needed at the time.

Each tree (that is the *being* that uses me) has sparks that move out from the center of the earth. When these sparks are lit, the energy is carried to us and we carry it to other *beings*. Unlike the *lighters* that have spoken to you (remember Axel the tree?), we are not the ones that give everyone the sparks they need to move ahead towards their goals. We are different than in that place you wrote of before.[15] The difference is that the growth here is slower and we all stay in the same place. It is easier and less noisy than there.

From this resting place of many (the cemetery), some of those that have died have decided not to start over, knowing that the growth that they needed to complete in this lifetime was not finished. Because they are not willing to change, they have stayed. Interrupting their journey would only bring them misery they did not cause, so their growth is slow and trying to change them also comes very slowly. They should leave this earthly plane and return to the *earth,* because the decaying of their bodies will bring what they need to start over. Although many fear this, their bodies are just bodies, nothing else. Some in deciding to stay become in time close to *Nature*, as you call us. They accept us as their new path, their new life and this changes what they want. Many have chosen to stay and have accepted this state of *Nature.* They have become like us, once again with the possibility to grow. Although a lot of people would not understand that this can be done, it has and some have started over, different than they were before; becoming much more connected than they had been before. Just as each person becomes what they must become, we also become what we have decided to become.

Though I exist and live as a leaf, and I tell you this because this is what you can understand. I am really not a leaf. I am a *lighter*, but not like the ones that you read about before. I am the spark that is lit. I am always here and because of this, I accept the sunlight and the moon's rays and the energy needed to give to our Mother what she needs to live. What is above is also the same as below.

Just like the great fire that lives deep within the earth, the *Great One* knows just how much she needs to grow both below and above this world. With this comes the gift that I offer to you. The benefit of this spark that comes from both places, will light this place where I live and this form, which you think of as the real one, will begin to change. As it changes, the energy is given and taken and I do what I feel necessary to perform this work. I speak for everyone that lives within this framework of our world, in saying that this energy is given freely and so it should be accepted by everyone in that way. To say no to this is to value one's needs over the needs of everyone else. To stop this energy from being given to everyone is to hold your world captive from growing.

Accepting what I do is necessary and knowing what I look like will not change what I do in your lifetime. Our lifetimes are different but each one brings growth but also with each there may be no growth. What is important is that we each do a job that will be the best for the life of all *beings* on this planet. As I "spark", lighting this existence as you know it, the lives of worlds and energies meet. I bring with it the gift of life. This tree where I live would not exist without the energy given and received from above and below. As it

---

13 As I was typing on my laptop, a leaf fell down and landed in front of me. Not even thinking about it, I brushed it aside. So it was that I was presented with the gift of actually meeting and seeing a Nature Spirit. Because I wasn't looking through the eyes of someone who believed (and I certainly thought I was a true believer at the time) and saw then, I ignored it. This is something I will regret for the rest of my life. I have been lucky enough to see many more *Elemental Beings* but I still would have loved to have seen this amazing *Spirit Seymour*.

14 That's the truth!

15 Glastonbury, Scotland. See passage "A Conversation With Axel".

does what it should in harmony with all things, it grows, releasing what the world needs to live; working together in peace with all beings. This is the way it is and this is what I will continue to do.

Others wait for their paths, their destinies and with this their lives come too. Give them a voice and speak to everyone that will listen about the beauty of the *beings* that live outside of your world. Go in the beauty that is ours as we accept the gift that is yours. Alone we are lost, together we will live.

I am, and I will be until I live no more … Seymour … SEE MORE!

The lesson was well taken and what I needed at the time. Because of this I am always alert and have actually talked to and seen another *Nature Spirit* in the form of a leaf (see Autumn Leaf). I only hope that my old friend in the cemetery can see me now and knows that I followed his advice. To all of you, don't ignore those little eyes you see in a tree or the sweet faces on the pansies in your garden. They might just be a *Nature Spirit* trying to get your attention. And for heavens sake, don't ignore that leaf that falls on your laptop.

Top of the Glastonbury Tor

Glastonbury, England – Friday, February 07, 2003

GLASTONBURY, ENGLAND HOLDS A VERY special place for me, not only because it is where this whole story began but because of the energy that surrounds it. In case you aren't familiar with the myths and legends that surround this place, I will give you a brief history.

The Glastonbury of legend is said to be the original Avalon; the resting place of King Arthur. The Holy Grail myth still rings clear and The Goddess movement has reawakened here. It is a land of ancient stories told on The Tor, a sacred Hill beneath which some say Arthur sleeps until he is once more called upon to return.

I must add now that "Tor" literary means hill. If you are in that part of Britain you may hear the word and assume that it refers to the hill in Glastonbury. It may not. I know I just assume that when someone mentions The Tor to me, that this is what they mean. Many times I have been wrong. However, The Tor that I channeled is indeed the Glastonbury Tor.

Inside the Gardens there lies the Chalice well where people of all religions have had wonderful healing experiences. The waters that flow under the Tor and through the gardens to the well are both red and white. These are considered the male and female streams and finally come together inside The Chalice Well Gardens; both energies uniting in Nature, just as it is in our world.

It is not uncommon to see a fairy or two here or some other being that you might not recognize. I had connected with the fairy kingdom one night after an amazing experience on the Tor, so when I was asked to do a reading with the Great Oak Tree Axel there, it didn't seem out of place at all. As I soon found out, the Nature Spirits are alive and well in Glastonbury.

In the following readings you will meet some of the Elemental Kingdom that still live in that area. The readings are all very different but like the others are also much the same.

Since you have read how this all began with Axel, the Old Oak, I thought you might be curious about Glastonbury and the beings that live there. Where to begin was a problem because I had more than a few readings from this place but being practical and always believing you should start at the top, this is just what we will do.

THE TOP OF THE GLASTONBURY TOR

Today I asked the pendulum which place I should choose to begin my writing and this was the place they chose. After a very steep climb and a lot of heavy breathing I am (finally!) here again. This time the weather will hold, I think…In fact I have just been assured of it but just in case, I had better get with it.

Strange things are related about this place and with them come truths yet unknown. Do you accept this as such? (I Do) And so… This is what I am and this is what I shall remain.

As you enter into this realm, which unlike "The Mother" offers answers, you accept that what I deem truth is not what all shall see. For all things shall come in time as time is infinite.

As before, many seek out this place. Some for solace, for this place has seen much solace in its wake, and some for growth. To this we accept readily. For all things are and shall continue only if they learn that what is now can only have become what it has become because of what had belonged to yesterday. Do you understand?

In time all things change, but the <u>Universal Law</u> admits all and in it all things must change. For changes, be they of this plane or all others, must become so or things (you, I and all beings seen or unseen) will never accept all that is needed to sustain and grow in this and all future existences.

You seek now the answers to questions long last forgotten but also you ask of us, the Nature, to divulge what it is that we do among you on this plane. This is indeed useful and so to me you have come. I shall relate all that I know that shall indeed bring with it the knowledge that you seek. For this need is indeed useful for all that journey here.

I exist and have for many lifetimes… Steadfast and ever willing to remain. Many have crossed this portal and have become what you call "children of the past" among this place. All existence changes and so many have, "among" (in the time I have been present in this form) my growth and with this many things have also happened in this realm and with this, changes to me also.

As a hill, (The Tor) a small one at that, I have gained not unduly, a reputation as stated in your mythology. Not unlike many that exist through this countryside I was chosen for the past changes and with it came what was and shall never be as before.

This place was new when the Gods and yes, The Mother (which is still and ever present) were the Great Ones of old. Many have disappeared, this is truth, but they remain through legends and stories and remain still as a new age begins…an age of awareness in all things. Alas, the Gods and Goddesses have arrived and again shall lay claim to what once was. They exist as you but lay dormant in the minds, for the mind is but a great keeper of all things and when needed can bring forth all that was forgotten.

Again I begin in the vain, for that which I am is more than what you assume. As the trees here and in all parts of this realm, I seek out what must be done to accomplish this goal on this plane. As acceptance of what was before, I am a place that recalls all that was and brings to those that seek a longing for those times. This in itself does not change anything but indeed offers those, such as you, an opportunity to begin again with facts that relate to before.

You seek out what it is I do. My existence has been proven, to this I know, but in truth I am but a Tor, a hill. Deep within I hold longings of the past, but in reality many sleep beneath my portal. For existence in that world unseen by men is still existence and what is offered can never change, unless those that seek realize that what they desire be of truth and not the illusion of fame or riches desired from the portals that await. As before, the portals opened as stated. Yes they indeed did and to this you were an observer.

Others attest to what they see but the truth is never taken, for many scoff at this but in reality…yes, in which reality, they are truths. Visions given from this loft of nights long ago are seldom given and yet, when encountered, change all that accept them. Thus am I also a conduit. A conduit not only of energy sent within my base for those that sleep, but also conduits for all that accept me as such. For visions are but dreams, unrelated but ever near… Seeking out those that would answer all that call. For deep within my belly lie realms yet unseen…Of visions untold, of dreams unendured.

Seeking out these, many have failed for the facts become reality only if in ones dreams they become thus. Seeking out this reality has become…what you say "fashionable" but alas this is also what you know.

Yes another has arrived like Figu, but called Fishu[16], to help devise what information you have attained. Let him be and all shall become his truth.

Along this path you will find many that have entered here and within me are many paths opening when and where they are needed. Many do not accept this and are driven back to their reality, but in keeping with what was told this is fact… Reality is what is accepted and nothing more. If in my acceptance I become a wide range of mountains then I shall become… a wide range of mountains; but if in my reality I become this Tor, then I am this Tor. My acceptance of this is such and in this I exist. In tempering my reality I accept this and thus must pursue all that of which I have accepted. In doing so I release all past life existences and live in what I know to be this time, through all the existence that exist now and in all days forward.

As your lives change, so must mine but time is relative and what you call millenniums are but a "slight" in the time of my existence. For all things change and become and again change. Then the release of the past makes way for myths and legends of all that have come before. In this you learn and in this I seek out ways to unite all with what we were and what we have become.

Beneath my portals lie many factors that relate to Nature as you perceive them and to this you have journeyed and to this I shall relate. I tell you now that within my chasms, of which reign many, things exist unlike those of your world. I lead many here to reunite and to cleanse themselves; to energize and to renew. Many spirits reign here and thus they remain until they are needed

---

16 In some of the passages you will hear the Nature Spirits refer to a certain tiny creature that crawls over my computer or the paper I'm writing on at the time. Since my experience with brushing away the leaf in The Ojai Cemetery passage, I wouldn't dare touch anything that falls, crawls or lands on me or anything I'm working with when I am receiving these messages. The Nature Spirit I'm working with at the time usually tells me that this creature is just gathering information for them, so leave it alone and it will eventually go away. They are right because these creatures always seem to just disappear. Every once in a while they will give them a name. It's always a play on words. Sometimes I get it and sometimes I don't. This time the creature is called Fishu, which may means he's fishing for answers from me… get it? At least I got Figu…Figure you out. What do you think it means?

in your world. Their reign is not unlike your world, but their quests are quite unlike those that exist on your plane.

As many enter into this plane, which is possible, many accept this as truth and thus in this they exist and in me they reside. For legends are born… yet do they die? Not always in this land that you call earth for Spirits unite under banners of evil and of good and thus they remain, called upon by those that seek their existence through this knowledge.

Many practice upon my place, chants and spells and conjures that unite them with many that remain…and with this comes their growth,…not necessarily through the existence of these Spirits (as called by you, but unrelated to us) but in their need to connect to what was before. For often what was, is indeed what is called upon and thus in this all things are needed and all things are what they must be.

As many reside below, the energy of the Great Mother warms them, renewing within them what they have missed. As the sun rises in the southern sky, the energy flows through me as in the trees and thus this energy is taken again as before but without the benefit of the open plane. For the energy of the earth and her Great Sisters are that they continue to grow, within your realm, all that is needed to sustain those on this plane.

You seek now advice on what shall be or not. To this I say… All things come and go but all things shall remain. If I perish, I do so because I must, but the essence of this Tor shall never be lost. For my essence is still and always will be "my essence" and with it I shall dwell where I dwell, and that is the truth. For all are given this and with it build what they are, what they have and will ever be. Accepting this, the destruction of myself will never for lay the foundation on which I am built and thus it is said… All things cease but never cease…all things die but never die…for all things exist to do and to be and to grow and to attain all that must be attained to continue on its path.

Alas in my depths many exist and know not why they do, but their truths are theirs and their time of realization will come when it is needed. As for the Nature Spirits, many of which you seek dwell within my chasms and are indeed gifted with truths. Not unlike yours they scurry ever further, as you, to do what they must to attain their truth.

As this spider Fishu has come and gone, so must you and I and they also… Each, gathering information to continue, ever aware, but insightful only to a point of existence acknowledged by themselves.

You ask if they are more aware than you and to this I answer…Yes and no. For the acceptance of your world to some is never encountered for they exist far below and never see what you have become. Those that dwell above are aware but many seek not to change what they inspire and such remain as you, unaware and unattained in what is their true reality.

As you seek out these forms that are Nature, be aware that those that speak are those that know where you are from and to what purpose you have become, to them their conduit to the outside world. To these souls (for a better term is essence, but in your reality is the same) you are what is needed to extend upon your plane their existence. For though many exist to be what they are and to continue on this path many do not and the destruction of this place is indeed what they worry most about. For the existence of this plane that in which you dwell has indeed turned into one of want. Discussions can lead to many a time of distrust and so I shall continue with my plight, my existence on this plane.

This building, this dwelling on which you exist (sit) is but a shell[17]. For many have come before and this is but a fragment of all what dwelled upon my plane.

Stories can be revealed at another time for the substance you seek is not of this realm below but of the existence of such as you seek. So the intricate parts begin and the renewal becomes undisturbed.

You contemplate as a "spa"[18] for Nature Spirits and to this you jest for the renewal of all things comes from the renewal of energies given from that which reigns supreme…The Great Mother.

As The Mother is our giver so must one believe in more, for the power to alight our world is but given to She by one that exists still more. As each here has one that is more to them, as you, so must She also have one that exists beyond her scope. For She is all upon this place, giving to each the benefit of all things. She is birth and renewal. She is what generates all that live upon this plane, but her sisters also rule with her and thus are also much needed to extend our place upon this unit you call earth.

Relating to all I seek out news, such as the tree in the courtyard, but mine exists on a level unlike that below. Many are "tuned in" upon my breast and with this comes the necessary information that is needed to extend our life upon this plane. As the weather changes so must we and in this the conception of climate is born. For as your seasons evolve so do we, each in constant circles

---

17 Here the Tor speaks of the old stone structure that sits upon the top of his hill.
18 Alright, so I was thinking that since this was a place of renewal, it was like a "spa" for Nature Spirits. Rather stupid, right?

relating to our growth and renewal appearances.

As information of the outside world, your existence is given to all that listen… trees, rivers, rocks, plants, and so on. This is related and Nature changes. Thus when things seem different this cause may be because you have "stated" why and where things have changed in all this place (Earth). So in keeping with this and the renewal of all things, this is relayed to Nature, or such as we, and we impart what must be given to others that in turn, relay to us all that is needed. The wind is as it is, so as the snow and the rain, all controlled by what they must be and all comes when it shall and all knows when this is so. The answer lies not in what you say or do but in the reactions of what has been given and to this we know that actions are futile and that whenever one changes his views then this in tune changes ours. Reactions cause actions and thus it is so.

As you search out stones and trees and flowers and the sky and the rivers, understand that all have a purpose. To me, it is simple… to renew… to change… to give… to inspire… to release when needed… but to contain all those that wait until they return.

Legends are born here and legends die here. I shall remain for as long as they. For the truth be…all things are, if they are what is needed. When forgotten they cease.

I remain but my essence shall endure. My chasms remain, full with truths and pasts and growths. Fulfilling all that I was given and releasing all that I must. I relate this and seek that which you desire become your reality. As in the past you shall remain, ever near or far, a part of my story, a part of my legend.

Go in the love that remains and seek out now ones that can lead you farther towards that knowledge. Come again in the spring. I remain… This Tor of Old, Myth and Legend

GLASTONBURY TOR – REVISED

Many strange things are told about this place (Glastonbury Tor) and along with these legends are others that are true but still unknown to you. Do you accept this? (I do.) You do and so I will continue.

This is what I am and this is what I will stay.

As you come into this world, which unlike the *Mother* herself will give you answers, you must accept that what I say is true, even though it is not what everyone will understand. It doesn't matter how long it takes, eventually they will understand because time goes on forever.

Like in the past, many still search for this place. Some for rest, because this place has seen a lot of peace in its time, and some for the growth I can give to them. I readily accept this.

All things live and will continue to live forever but only if you understand that what is now happening in your world can only have become this way because of what you did in the past. Do you understand?

In time, all things change. Why, because the *Universal Law* says this and this law includes every *being*. Changes, whether they are in this world or other worlds, must happen. If they do not, then you and I and all *beings* you can and can not see, will never accept everything they need to continue to live and grow in this and all future lives.

You are looking now for the answers to questions that have been forgotten long ago, but also to ask us, *Nature*, to tell you how we work with you on this plane and in your world. You have come to me and this information that you ask for is very useful. I will tell you everything that I know that can provide you with the information you are looking for and knowing this will be useful for everyone that visits here. I live and have lived for many lifetimes; strong and always willing to stay. Many have crossed this portal or doorway here and have become what you call the "Children of the Past".

All lives change. I have seen so many changes in the time I have been here and in this form as a hill. Many things have happened in your world and these have brought changes to me too. As a hill, which you call "The Tor", and a small one at that, I have gotten a reputation you can read about in your mythology. Being no different than others hills that live throughout the countryside, I was chosen because of changes made in the past. Because of these changes, what once was can never be like it was before.

This place, now called Glastonbury, was new when the *Gods* and, yes, *The Mother* (who is still and always here) were known as *The Great Ones of Old*. It is true that many of them have disappeared, but they still live on in legends and as stories, still remaining as the new age begins; a new age of awareness and understanding in all things. It is true, the *Gods* and *Goddesses* have returned and once again they are trying to hold on to the way their world used to be. They live like you in their own world, but lie sleeping in your minds. The mind is a great keeper of all things and when you need it, it can remember everything you have forgotten.

I will start over but with not much hope because what I am is much more than you can see. Just like the trees here, and in all other parts of your world, I search for what I must do in this world to finish my goals.

As you accept what happened before, understand that I am a place that remembers everything from before and brings to those that search for it a longing for those times. This in itself doesn't change anything but does offer those, such as you, a chance to begin over with facts that belong to a time before.

You want to know what I do. There is proof that I live and things that I know, but the real truth is, I am a Tor or you would say a hill. Deep inside of me I hold the things that you are looking for and want from the past. In fact many *beings* sleep beneath my door, because living in this world that man can not see is still living. What is offered to some can never change, unless those that look for it finally realize that what they search for is the truth and not the illusion or the falseness of riches and fame that they want inside the doors that are here. Others tell of the things that they have seen, but they are not believed. Yet, in reality … but in which reality, they are true. Visions, pictures given high on this hill at night, telling stories about long ago are not usually seen. But when they are, they change the life of the person who sees and believes them. So, I am also a conduit, a way for the past to be seen in the present. Not only a conduit of the energy sent inside my base to those that sleep, but also as a way for people to see me in this way. Visions are only dreams; not the same but always close; looking for those that would answer all that call. Deep inside my belly lie worlds you have never seen, sights you could never imagine and dreams that live on forever. Many have looked for these things but have failed because facts only truly become reality if you believe that what you dream is actually true. Looking for this world that we live in and looking for fairies, etc. has become "fashionable", but then you know this.

Yes, another small *being*, like Figu but called Fishu has come to find out what information you have gotten so far in your machine. Just leave him alone and he will learn everything he needs to know.[19]

Following along this path (of the fairies) you will find many that have entered here. Inside of me there are many paths opening when and where they are needed. Many don't believe this and so go back to their reality and to the world that they only can see. Remembering what we told you, the fact is "Reality is what you accept as true and nothing more." Example: If I, the *Tor*, accept and <u>know</u> that I am a wide mountain range then I become a wide mountain range, but if in my reality, in my world, I know I am this *Tor,* then I am this *Tor.* In accepting that this is so, it becomes so.

In making my reality what I want it to be, I accept this and so I must follow through with all that I must do to be this *Tor*, this hill. In doing this I let go of all my past lives and live in what I know to be this time; existing through all that is lived now and in all days to come until I am no longer a Tor.

Just as your lives change, so must mine. Time is what you make of it and what you call a millennium is just a "murmur" in the time I have lived.

All things change, return again, and then continue to change once more and so on. When the past is released, the legends and myths of things that had happened before can live. In this way you learn and in this way I look for ways to tie everything that was before and what will come, together.

Under my doorways lie many things that have to do with *Nature* as you see it/them. This is why you have come here and this is what I will tell you now. Inside my chasm, a deep space inside me (in which there are many), things live that do not live in your world. I bring many of these *beings* here to reunite and cleanse themselves; to energize and renew their spirits. Many *Spirits* live here and stay here until they are needed in your world. Their lives are not much different than yours in your world, but their paths in life are very different than those in your world. As many different *beings* come into this world, which is possible, they accept that this is what they are meant to do. They believe this and so they live here.

Legends are born … but do they die? Not always in this land that you call Earth.

Yes, Spirits do come together under banners of good and evil and here they will remain until they are called upon by those that believe, <u>that know</u> that they live.

Many practice magic here on the Tor using chants and spells and saying things that will bring them together with the Ones that remain. In doing this, they continue to grow. Not necessarily because these *Spirits* (this is what you call them but they have nothing to do with us, the *Nature Spirits*) live but because they need to connect to what was before in the past. Indeed, many times connecting with the past is what is needed and so in doing this all things become what they must be.

For the many that live below, the *Great Mother (Earth)* warms them, bringing back to them what they have missed. When the sun rises

---

19 Refers to one of the small beings that always come to investigate the writing I am doing. Usually they have a clever name that has something to do with their work. As in the reading, The Oak Tree in the Cemetery, the little bug like being was called Figu. I thought this might mean, figure you out?

in the southern sky, the energy flows through me like it does the trees. This energy is taken in again like before but not in the open but below. Together the energy of the Earth and her Great Sisters, the Sun and the Moon continue to make everything that is needed in your world and in ours, to grow and survive.

You are looking for advice on what will or will not happen. I will answer you by saying…"All things come and go but all things will remain." If I die, I die because I have to, but the essence or spark, the soul of this "Tor" will never be lost. My essence still is and always will be "my essence" and with it I will live wherever I live. This is my truth and what I believe. Every *being* is given this and with it builds what they are, what they have been, and what they will always be. Because I accept this, destroying myself will never destroy the foundation on which I am built, because it is said…All things end but never end …all things die but never die.

All things live to do and to be and to grow and to learn all that they can learn and to keep moving forward on their path. It is too bad, because many deep inside of me live but don't know why they do. Yet, their truths, what they believe, are theirs and the time will come when this is needed and they will finally know this.

As for the *Nature Spirits*, many of the ones that you are looking for live deep inside of me and know what is true. Like you, they are always moving further ahead to do what they have to, to find the truth. Just like the spider, *Fishu*, has come and gone, so too must you and I and the *Nature Spirits*. Each of us gathering information to move forward, always looking and understanding this one life we have chosen for ourselves, the life we are living now.

You ask me if the *Nature Spirits* are more aware of you than you are of them? The answer to this question is both yes and no. Some of the *beings* that live far below and have never seen your world have never been asked this question. Because they have never seen you, they don't know if you exist or not so they would not know how to answer. Those that live above know that you exist but some don't want to change what they see and so they become like you, never seeing and not knowing what is in their "real" world.

As you look for these forms, these *beings* or *Elementals* that are all a part of *Nature,* understand that the ones that speak to you are those that know where you are from and why you have become their "voice" to the outside world. To these *souls* (a better term is *essence*, but in your world they are the same) you are what they need to inform your world that they live.

Though many of the *Elementals* live to be what they are and to continue on this path, many do not. The destruction of their world is what they worry most about, because the world that you live in has turned into a world that needs help. Arguments can bring many in both worlds to times when they do not trust others. I will continue to live with this problem and in my life in this world.

This building, this place where people once lived is just a shell.[20] Many have come here before and this is just a piece of what is left from some that have lived on this hill.

These stories can be told to you (about those people and other ages) at another time because the information that you want is not about the world below (where many legends sleep) but about the lives of the *Nature Spirits* that you look for. The very hard part starts now but starting again does not bother me.

You think this place might be like a "spa" for *Nature Spirits?*[21] You are kidding, because the renewal of all things comes from the restarting of energies given to us from the one that rules above us all … *The Great Mother.*

Just as *The Mother* is our giver, so must we all believe in something more. The power to light our world is only given to her by the "*ONE*" that is even more. Just as you do, each *being* here has "*ONE*" that means more to them, or as you would say a *Higher Power*. The *Mother* must also have *ONE* that lives beyond her realm, beyond her world.

The *Mother* (*Mother Nature*) is everything on the Tor and in this world, giving to each one the goodness of all things. She is birth and rebirth. She is what provides life in this place. Yet her sisters, the *Sun* and the *Moon*, also rule with her and so they are also needed to make us grow on this planet that you call Earth.

Belonging to everything, I look for news, just like the tree in the courtyard at Barachah House[22], but mine lies on a level which is different than that tree below. Many of you are "tuned in" or are made aware, when they are on the *Tor* and with this awareness comes the information needed to keep us alive longer in this world.

As the weather changes, so must we, and because of this the idea of "climate" was born. As your seasons change, so do we, each in a never ending circle dealing with our growth and the way we will look. As information about the outside world is given to everyone that will listen; the trees, rivers, rocks, plants and so on, it is passed on and *Nature* changes. When things seem different, this may

---

20 Here the Tor speaks of the old stone structure that sits upon the top of his hill.
21 Alright, so I was thinking that since this was a place of renewal, it was like a "spa" for *Nature Spirits* … rather stupid, right?
22 Refers to the reading, "The Tree at Barachah House".

be because you have told them why and where things have changed all over the Earth. So in keeping with this and the rebirth of all things, this is told to *Nature*, or ones like us, and we relay what must be told to others, who in turn tell us everything we need to know.

Just as the wind is as it is, so are the snow and the rain. They are all controlled by what they must be, and everything comes when it needs to. They all know when this is.

The answer doesn't lie in what you say or do but in the reactions of what you have been given. We know that the actions are useless and that whenever one changes how he feels, then likewise it changes ours. Reactions cause actions and so it is.

As you look for Stones and trees and flowers and the sky and the rivers, understand that every *being* has a purpose... something it must do. For me, it is simple ... to begin again ... to change ... to give ... to inspire ... to let go when I need to, but to hold all of those (*Spirits*) that wait until they can return again.

Legends are born here and legends die here. I will stay as long as they do. The truth is ... all things live, if they are what is needed at the time. When they are forgotten they die. I remain and my essence shall live on.

My chasm deep inside will stay filled with truths and pasts and growths. Filling up with everything I was given and giving back everything that I must.

I tell you this and hope for you that everything you desire comes true. Like in the past you will remain, whether near or far, a part of my story, a part of my legend.

Go in the love that continues and look now for others that can lead you closer to that knowledge. Come again in the spring.

I will remain, This *Tor* of Old, Myth, and Legend

The Tor is truly a magical place. I have seen many things that I could never explain and have had many experiences that have changed my life. (I know you probably wondered how these things could happen on such an ordinary looking hill. Hopefully after reading this passage it has become a bit clearer. I know that just being able to actually communicate with this amazing *being* is truly an honor.)

When the Tor told me that there were many stories that could be told about the *beings* below, I wanted to hear them all. Yet, the Tor, being part of the *Elemental Kingdom*, knew the path I had chosen and that a detour at this time would be disastrous. It was right. Gee, why am I not surprised?

I just know that if it is meant to be, I will someday return to write down these stories. Maybe then these myths and legends that have been forgotten can once more live again.

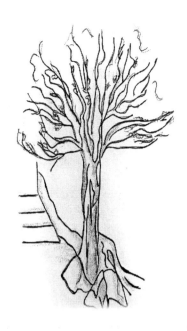

This Tree at Berachah House

Glastonbury, England – Thursday, February 06, 2003

I AM IN GLASTONBURY AND it is raining. I am using my battery to run my computer. As of now I have no way to recharge this thing but am confident that I will find some way this afternoon. I was told to do this book and so I am asking the Spirits that have guided me so far, and my guides, to provide the power I need to continue.

I am sitting at an open window, as it is raining outside, looking over the garden of Chalice Well. I will get there later; if not today then tomorrow, but for now I have, in front of me, a very impatient tree who has a lot to say...and so since I have the window open, and my hands are freezing, I had better move right along and get down whatever it is he/she wants to tell me … so it begins again, in Glastonbury … hit it.

A TREE OUTSIDE MY BERACHAH HOUSE BEDROOM WINDOW

As I stand alone but in this midst of chaos, I remain true to the ideals set forth before and for the future of this place. As before you continue with this journey and we welcome you again to this trial. This time that shall be given, shall always be felt by you, as a time to continue. Not only with what is needed to begin again this task but also with the need to be more than what you are at this time. So speaking now, I must relay what you must learn to continue. As before, you have come to relate to those that dwell upon this land. Not in the sense of those that seek out customs which impart others to begin their quests but in the assurance of what is needed to continue yours.

As we dwell here, we remain true to what we must accomplish and thus you too, must also be as we. As we exist in our plane, our duties are not unlike ones that exist within your realm. All have duties as well as things that shall make this plane of existence tolerable to those that exist among us.

You seek out friends in this place. Thus in doing so we must tell you that those entities do exist here but relying on them is no easy task. As we dwell within this earth plane, they do not, for they are an illusion that becomes real when the entity truly wanders into their realm. This is quite possible as you know and yet to you this is normal but to those that come here it is not. Many seek out ways to see these beings, but the fact be and the truth be that only those that exist within this realm have the ambition and the knowledge "to be (seen)" to those that seek the beings that they are.[23] In fact they are as they are and this is truth and none shall ever change this. So saying, I shall relate to you some information that shall be of use on this. As I encounter many that travel here I understand much more than before. You exist here to be what you must. In this I stress that what "you must" in relation to what "we must"… this is quite a different scenario. For as I exist in outward appearances to be a tree, per se (as that is the name I have been given), then in fact, this is what I am. But in my world I am more than this. Surely you understand that what I say is truth as we have no reason to speak what is not fact. As a "tree" I exist to clear away things that will harm many that dwell below. I supply sunlight/energy to those that seek it and I live to observe what I must to attain this existence that becomes more futile in this age. As I grow I undertake changes, not unlike you and so in accepting this, I remain as I was before… but also become more than what I have begun. As I attain knowledge in this world, I impart it to the center (the trunk of the tree) which in turn distributes it further to all creatures that live among us. As a messenger I am given rights unlike many that dwell here, for as an informant I can relate what changes may affect us here on this plane.

(I ask if the tree will give me the truth of its existence and will it answer some questions?) *Truth? Yes. Questions? Yes. I hear what you think and to this I shall relate.*

Yes, I dwell within both worlds and thus have the ability to do and be more than many that do not. Though many do (live in

23 Many expect these beings to look like the fairies shown in those beautiful fairy books and thus most of the time never recognize them as the Nature Spirits they truly are.

both worlds), the possibility to become an informant does not become to them what is needed and so their existence is unlike what I must attain here.

As was stated, I travel not as many here can do, (as a tree, it is stationary, it can't move around like other Nature Spirits) but the ability to see beyond is given (to me) and so what has passed becomes clear. As the cables which are known to you pass within your planes, these are not unlike those that support my being. As my roots reach into this soil, sacred beings to us that dwell within it, these facts are relayed to others and these are transmitted. You say newspaper...

(Again I am thinking, like a newspaper and again it picks up on it...so clever!)

Yes I know and yes this is semi-truth. For as a messenger I send news but in fact this is barely what I deliver. For the truth is, what I seek is not news of your existence but the purpose to compose what I must to sustain our place on your plane.

As I dwell I have accepted that many destroy us but in fact, this has been the case for all times, thus in acceptance growth can continue. As each extends their lifetime to include what they must, so must we and in this comes what is needed to "grow". Not unlike you.

Acceptance is hard, much more so to many others here, but alas it is what must be taken and so I/we continue. As I have stated, I seek out what I must. I stand tall against all that would disturb below and shelter many within my boughs. As I relate, understand that what I give is truth to many here. For like me many have this responsibility and yet you have chosen me and thus I shall relate.

Before you spoke to Axel, which is given (the name) and he spoke of lighters. To this I am not secure, for my truth is not this. I employ others that relate this to my being and I do not what he accepts...understand? Relate this in terms that can be understood...

(You do a different job?) *Truth? Yes. Axel does what he does, what he must, and I also do the same.*

I dwell here on this Tor (this hill) for I seek solace from others... but in this my truths can also be related to others...

(I asked if I could close the window and still talk with him and he said ok...as my hands are freezing)

As I relate things, understand that others also seek out news and thus what I give can also be taken from them if seeking this is what you desire. Many below my roots know that what I seek can only be related if they give what they seek to you and in turn you accept what is given. Nature Spirits you ask? To what of this do you relate?

I am of Nature and I dwell within this and all realms, am I not one?

Truth you say, then other entities you seek that appear to others as winged goddesses or mythical creatures. Ah, this is so and thus they shall be called.

To finish is futile as truth is never finished for many lessons I can give and many more shall be related. This shall continue? Yes

You seek to understand now what I must relate but listen carefully and know what I speak. Many times before in ages past, many came to this land. Unlike you, they dwelled within this realm and with them began this path which leads to now. As related they became what we are and in this we exist...

The story you ask...and to this I relate...when The Ancients came, and thus you know these are truths, they came as one... not as entities different. Ones among themselves sought out what they had and thus was ended what they began. For always others seek what exists and thus what was never shall remain as such. In this coming the changes began and with these came the differences which remain until now. As the fairies or others that exist, independent, became further away from those that saw so did we also became different than before.

Deep within my roots messages are given but before they were not. For before we traveled freely and relating all to all things. Yet in accepting this I have become accustomed to being "rooted" as you say and thus have become what I must to attain this being. These entities that many seek came to be known as such (fairies, gnomes, elves, etc.) because they appeared to many in many forms. Yet in relaying this I give not attention (to these beings) but this will be to you as they seek. As I continue... As these peoples that stole away our existence or "past existence" came, we became not less than before, for none can become less that what they are... but only less in knowledge and acceptance of what they should attain. Is this not truth?

Setting ourselves as before, we arranged to attain what we must and so accepted this and have become as now. As relaying messages I also give to those that dwell below many things that are needed to attain what they must.

Alas no sun shines today but in part what comes is also needed and all can be related in the safeness of this dwelling. (It is raining and I am in my room.) *To attain what must be needed many things are accepted as stated. The rain is indeed a needed factor and the drops that fall nourish us in ways unknown to you. As each entity seeks to exist within its own being so must I accept that without this moisture, I would not be. This is truth... but not.*

As each being, be it a tree, a plant or a slight being unseen, all have certain restrictions to attain but even in this, that being's uniqueness… his self… shall remain forever into all eternity. For the sense is ever present and the growth and the death mean little to us that dwell within this place. Of course we exist and we remain and we grow ever weary and alas many seek to be released from what they have accepted. This is possible and changes occur. Right or wrong is never an issue and with this all is accepted. Why the conception of this is, is that what we seek to know can be learned only through the growth sustained in what we have chosen. As you exist and cease, so do we; accepting and declining but ever ready to attain what we know we must, to grow in the new existences we have chosen.

(Again my mind wanders to the "fairy folk") *Fairies again! Why do you seek this so?*

Relating to growth this is understood, and yes, as we, as all choices are made and these decisions are as they are chosen. Acceptance is easily given and in this many change and rearrange what they must to learn what is needed to progress. Substantial trials are given and if accepted each begins again another duty, trial or advancement on this line to accept what they must to begin again.

As a tree I have accepted to be what I am. I must supply information. I must supply energy. I must relate information and collect that which is needed to pass on further to those that enter my realm. I cover those that sleep in the winter and shelter those that awaken in the spring. I supply warmth and coolness to all that must need this to survive.

I wrestle with the wind and give due to the moon. I speak with the stars and relate to the snow. I listen and I speak but many like you do not hear. I rustle in the breeze, which is indeed also but not unlike what you desire. I am what I must be and this is truth. I seek this solidity and thus I have it. I reign here for this place offers what I need. I attain inspiration from ones that seek. As the forest offers configuration with others, my solace is what I desire. Many existed before me and many do what I do but all, like you, are unique unto themselves. To this I am thankful.

The "Great Mother" resides here but not only in this place but in all places and in all realms… for the existence of places can never be without her. She is the foundation on which all is built. For all worlds do exist but beneath their being there must exist a foundation… thus it is so. Thus so is She. Thus so She exists. Thus so She is all.

Not all worlds exist as this one but all beings need this and all must dwell within a plane. For the acceptance of this can only be accomplished if it is known that what you seek can be found on other levels and the existences that you serve can be as we… as we can be as ye, also. As a stone you have related[24]; as a tree I relate to you … but differently. Each plane offers different realities and to this we all seek.

Acceptance of this is acceptance of all things.

You seek out now, a new source for this writing and thus it is so. The energy that is contained within my being can never be related to what you need but the energies of all the universe can be and thus we send you ever searching … so you must return.

Seek now what you must and return soon. Go in peace.

We remain steadfast… This Tree at Barachah House

The Tree at Berachah House — Revised

Standing alone in the middle of chaos, I will remain true to the ideals made before, made for the future of this place.

Like before, you continue with your journey and again we welcome you to your task at hand. This time given to you in Glastonbury to finish this book will always make you feel like you need to do more. Not only with what is needed to start these channelings again but also to become more than you are now.

I will begin by telling you what you must learn to continue. Like before, you have come to identify with those that live on this land. Not in the way that some search for different worlds or beings, which in turn encourages others to begin their search, but in knowing what you need to continue yours. Living here we remain true to what we must accomplish. You too must do the same. Living in our world, our duties are not much different than those in yours. All of us have jobs, as well as things that will make our world tolerable for those that live here.

You are looking for friendly *Nature Spirits* here but in doing so we can only say that these *beings* do exist but relying on them will not be easy. Just as we live within the earth plane, they do not. They are only an illusion that becomes real when a person truly wanders into their world. As you know this is possible and quite normal but to those that come here, it is not. Many of you look for ways to see these *beings* but the truth being and the fact is that only those in this realm that have the ambition and the knowledge to be seen,

---

24 I must have been a stone as they truly seek me out.

can be...And only to those that look for the beings as they really are. The fact is they are as they are. This is the truth and nothing will ever change this. In saying this, I will give you some information that will be useful on this subject. I see many of those that travel here and I understand a lot more than I did before. You all live to be what you must be. I stress what "you must" in relation to what "we must" because there is quite a difference. Just as I outwardly appear to be a tree, per se (because this is the name you gave me) then in fact, this is what I am. Yet in my world I am more than that.

I am sure that you understand that what I say is true because we have no reason to say anything that is not a fact. As a tree, I live to clear away things that may harm many of the beings that live below. I supply sunlight and energy to those that need it and I look for ways to survive in this world, a world that becomes more hostel at this time.

While I grow, I change just as you do, but in accepting this I stay as I was before but also become more than I was at the beginning. As I gather information in this world, I send it to the center (the trunk of the tree) which in turn distributes it further to all the creatures that live among us. As a *messenger* I am given rights that are different from others that live here, and being an *informant* I can relay what changes may affect us in our world.

(I ask myself, in my mind, of course, if a tree will give me the truth about its existence, and will it answer some questions?)

Truth? Yes. Questions? Yes. I hear what you think and these are my answers.

Yes, I live in both worlds and so have the ability to do and be more than many others that do not. Though many here do live in both worlds the possibility of becoming an *informant* is not what they may need and so their life and job is different than what I must accomplish here in mine.

As I told you, I do not move like some here can do, (a tree is stationary and can't move around like other *Nature Spirits*) but I have been given the ability to see in the distance so what passes by becomes very clear.

Our roots are not much different than the Ley Lines you may know about that run through your planes. As my roots reach into the soil, which to those that live in it consider sacred, these facts are sent to others and they are passed along. You say "Like a newspaper". (Again I am thinking this and he picks up on it, how clever.) Yes, I know and yes this is partly true.

Being a *messenger,* I do send out news but this is just a small part of what I do. The truth is, what I look for is not news of your lives but what I need to know so that I can survive in your world. After living here for all these years, I have accepted the fact that many of you have destroyed us. In fact this has always been the case and yet in accepting this I can continue to grow. Just as each of you live out your lifetime and include in it what you have to, we do the same; each of us learning what we need to grow. Accepting this is hard, much more to others here, but unfortunately that is just the way it works. We must just accept it and move on. As I said before, I look for what I must. I continue to stand tall against anyone or thing that should bother those beings that live below or the ones that I shelter in my branches.

Understand that what I say also applies to many others here as well. Like me, many have this responsibility, yet you have chosen me and so I will be the one to pass on this knowledge.

Before, when you spoke to *Axel*[25], which is the name you have given him, he told you about *the lighters*. I am not familiar with this because I follow a different path. I asked others that told me about his work, but this is not my job. Axel does what he does, what he must, and I also do the same. I live here on this hill (called *The Tor,* in *Glastonbury, England*) because I want my privacy but also in living here, my beliefs can be told to others.

In telling you these things, understand that others here also provide news. If you want, the information that they give me can also be taken from them. Many of the beings that live below my roots know that what you are searching for can only be given to you, if what they know goes through me. You in turn can accept these things as true.

"What about *Nature Spirits*?" you ask.

What do you mean by that? I am part of *Nature* and live in this world and in all worlds, so aren't I one? You ask me if it is also true that the other *beings* that you are looking for, the ones that appear to you as *Goddesses* with wings or *Mythical Creatures*, are also *Nature Spirits*. Ah, yes this is true and is why they are called this. (I thought I might stop there...I guess not)

It would be useless to end now because truths are never finished and I still have many more lessons to give you.

Shall we continue? (Of course.) You are now trying to understand what I am saying so listen carefully and believe what I tell you.

Many years ago in ages past, several beings came to this land. Unlike you they lived in our world and with them began the path that leads us to the present. As you were told, they became what we are and that is why we exist.

---

25 See passage, "A Conversation With Axel".

"What is the story?" you ask. I will tell you. When *The Ancients* came (yes, the Ones that you channel) they came as one group, not as different beings. Some of them looked for what they had before and after finding this place, ended their search. There are always those that search for what existed before but what was before will never be the same. The changes began when they arrived and with these changes came the differences that still remain today. Just as the *fairies* and the others that existed independently became further withdrawn from our beliefs, we also changed.

Deep inside my roots, messages are sent, but they never were before. We use to travel freely and worked along side each other. Over time I have accepted being rooted, as you would say, and have become what I had to in order to survive. These beings that many of you search for have come to be known as the *fairies, gnomes, elves,* etc. because they appear to many of you in that form. In telling you this, I have to say, I pay no attention to these beings but you can do what you want.

Continuing…As the people that took away our existences or past existences came, we didn't become less than we were before because no one can become less than what they are, only less informed and accepting of what they needed to know. Isn't this true? Presenting ourselves like we were before, we arranged to get what we could, accepted it, and became what we are now.

The beings that live below receive what they have to know and what they need from my messages

(I am in my room and it is still raining.) It is too bad there is no sun today but in part, this is what we need. Everything I need to tell you can be told to you in the comfort of your room. To get what you need you must accept the things I say. The rain is a needed factor and the drops that fall feed us in ways that you are not familiar with. Just as each of us tries to control our own life, I must also accept that without this moisture I could not live. This is true but then again, it isn't. Each *being*, whether it is a tree, a plant or a tiny *being* you can't see, has an uniqueness, a self that will remain forever… into eternity. This sense or self is always present and birth and death mean very little to us that live here.

Of course we live and we stay and we grow tired and it's true that some ask to be released from their job. This is possible and these changes do happen. All of this is accepted and whether it is right or wrong is never an issue. Why is the idea that what we need to learn can only be learned in the job we have chosen? We don't understand. You live and die, so do we; accepting and declining certain jobs but always ready to learn what must be learned to move ahead.

(Again my mind wanders to *fairy folk*.) Fairies again! Why do you keep thinking about this?

When we speak of growth this is understood and yes, like us… like every thing, choices are made and these decisions are what you choose. It is easy to get approval here and so many beings change or rearrange what they must learn and when they need it to move ahead. Every *being* is given plenty of time to experience each job. If it's accepted, he again begins another duty, trial, or advancement on his way to doing what he must to start over. As a tree I accepted to be what I am. I must supply information. I must supply energy. I must give information and collect what is needed to be passed along to those that enter my world. I cover those that sleep in the winter and shelter those that awaken in the spring. I supply warmth and coolness to everything that needs it to survive. I wrestle with the wind and honor the moon. I speak with the stars and connect with the snow. I listen and I speak but many like you do not hear me. I also rustle in the breeze but this is not what you want to hear. I am what I must be and this is my truth. I wanted to be grounded and I am. I live here because this place gives me what I need. I get inspiration from the ones that search just like you do. The forest offers to all *beings* many places to grow but I like to remain separate and grow in solitude. Many have lived before me and several also do what I do, but like you each of us is unique. I am thankful for this.

The Great Mother lives here, not only in this place but in all the places in all the worlds. No place can exist without her. Many worlds do exist but beneath their being is a foundation and *She* is the foundation on which each of these worlds are built. That is the way it is. That is who *She* is, why *She* lives and the reason *She* is everything. Not all worlds are the same as this one, but all worlds need this and all worlds must live on a plane. You can accept this only if you know that what you are looking for can be found on all levels. The life that you live can be like ours, just as ours, can be like yours. Just as you relate to the stones, as a tree I relate to you, but differently. Each plane, or world if you prefer, offers different realities that we are looking for. To accept this is to accept everything.

You are now looking for a new *Nature Spirit* for this book. So be it. The energy that is contained inside me can never be everything you need but the energies of the entire Universe can be. So we send you searching … and so you must return.

Look for what you must but return again soon. Go in Peace.

We remain steadfast. The Tree at Berachah House

TREE AT BERACHAH HOUSE CONCLUSION

It was very interesting for me to find out that some Nature Spirits, like some of us, prefer to work alone. This seems to be more prevalent in trees for some reason, though I have channeled a very small stone that rather liked being on its own.

Never the less as the Tree pointed out, each being whether it works as a collective or alone has a certain job to perform and each does so with the same intensity and determination as its counterpart.

As you also read, Nature Spirit are not just fairies but includes every being that works and lives in the world connected with Mother Nature.

I know I always thought (wrongly as usual) that fairies were the Nature Spirits and that plants and trees were just…well, plants and trees. I now find in fact, that the fairies, elves, etc. are different beings altogether and that the Nature Spirits are pretty much everything else you see around you.

Take it from me, the more I learn the more I realize I don't know. Hopefully we all can find the answer to some of the questions we have and maybe even find out answers to questions we hadn't even of thought of yet. Does that make sense?

Chalice Well: The Waters of Glastonbury

Glastonbury, England – Friday, February 07, 2003

The Goddess Conference in Chalice Wells Gardens

THE CHALICE WELL IS CONSIDERED sacred in the small town of Glastonbury, England. Alive with legends and tales of its healing properties, it lies in the heart of a beautiful enchanted garden. This setting is amazing and that in itself is reason enough to visit.

The rumors of the Holy Grail have led many here as well as the stories of Arthur and Merlin. This is the mystical Avalon, or at least this is what many people believe.

The Goddess is also alive here and women from all over the world meet each year at Lammas to celebrate and honor her with rituals, workshops, and celebration. It is a wonderful event and amazingly hectic with women running everywhere. The presence of the Goddess can be overwhelmingly felt at this time and the colors and sounds, the bonfire and the dancing draws everyone from miles around into the celebration.

On the last day of the Conference, a statue of the Goddess is paraded through the streets of Glastonbury before it is carried to the top of the infamous Tor. Before reaching it, the whole procession stops at the Chalice Well Gardens to honor the Goddess and the Waters that flow from under the Tor and into the gardens.

There are two springs which feed into the waters here. One is called the white spring, the other the red. This is believed not only in the Goddess Movement, but also in other beliefs, to be the male and female springs representing both the sperm of the male and the blood of the female. The waters come together here and some believe that through this meeting also comes the healing power of the waters.

Water has always represented life. We come into this world in a rush of water and without it we could not survive. Knowing this, I had no choice but to ask the waters for a reading.

Again, the Elemental Kingdom gives us information that can help us understand their purpose in our world. They as the water, flow through our lives, beginning and ending through our journey from existence to existence. Maybe that is where the phrase "Go with the flow" comes from.

CHALICE WELL: OVERLOOKING THE WELL BENEATH THE TREES

We exist to serve all things. For water has a purpose, not only for the survival of all things, but in the knowledge that is carried from one portal to the next. We flow as life, stopping in streams to assist those that are needed. As your life stops and starts, so is the ebb and flow of our reality. You come here to learn and in this insight can readily become useful.

Enchanted Gardens await many here, but in this, our realm, all things are as they exist.

To you, each is unique and different, allotting each a section to become what it is and in what useful conclusion that is purposed. As you enter this world, our world, learn what you must, but be aware that what we say is our reality, our quests, our lead. Not that it is much different than yours, being in fact the same.

As life flows, so do the waters, never ceasing, ever flowing through existence to existence. We revive as do all things and yet we cease not as you, but change as rapidly or as slowly as each is meant to do.

We are the heart of this place, the soul of what is needed to project thoughts and make them reality. For myths and legends exist in our world and like yours they begin and end here. We are few, the rivers that flow through sacred ground and yet in our entirety we are also many. For as we seek out new ground, and to this a purposely lot, we find new experiences in which to relay our quests: our information given, taken by all that drink from the root of our soul. So unlike you, we exist to serve, to give, to sustain and yet as we flow we incur[26] all that would destroy what we have begun so long before.

In the realm of things we exist to serve, as stated, to employ knowledge to all things for the imparting of our growth is through the acceptance of all things who partake of our being. As we ebb and flow through many miles, we absorb knowledge and through this sense what must be given to all to sustain them in the plight they have chosen. Thus we expand or contract giving life to all that exist on your plane.

In our world we are a care-taker, this is true, but in actuality our waters provide nourishment and solace to all. Many exist for the growth that is needed, which can only become reality if given what we provide. We exist to serve, as do all in this realm, but in merging with others we assume more on our path to the Great Sea that awaits us here.

Our Mother guides us, this is truth, but in this guidance we must carry with us all the guidance given over eons of travel through this great planet on which we serve. This does not mean that we are small; on the contrary, we exist to be as we are when we reach where we must be.

As this Well holds memories of past days, the waters give guidance to those pasts and yet the waters move and collectively give guidance to all that partake. A man that thirsts for knowledge, is it not said, is a man that must drink? And to this we incur that what we give is but that. Sourcing through us is all that exists or has existed before, ever ready to become what is needed to divulge all to those that would drink of such realities.

Before as now we existed to serve, to deliver all to whomever and whatever was needed to survive. The distant past, the totality of the future lies within this haven, this Well, this Water. For it is through us that all that was, shall be or has happened is contained. Drinking in/of us will incur upon your being this truth, thus bringing to all a unity unto themselves. Many diverse from this and seek out others that would change our being but in truth all is all and we are as we are. Without this, no one would exist on your plane; all would feel the burning and the thirst would ensnare them into that what shall never be.

We seek out knowledge from all living things, carrying with it the wisdom of ages past. We receive what is needed, shaped by the ponds that linger in small places outside of here. We relax in pools upon islands long gone (far away) but seldom seen by others.

We rush forward over giant friends, the Stones of millenniums of knowledge pent up in unmoving, yet ever absorbing in mobility, ceasing to understand imparting as we linger for that brief respite... giving knowledge learned through countless ages, passed "down stream" to those that would absorb within their being this knowledge.

Still or rushing or alone and deep as here, we remain. For the trust given to us must be relayed and this is what we do, this is what we have become and this is our truth.

As you sit here know that the Well below offers to all that seek knowledge. The growth of ages past and the return to days far past and times long spent in quiet contemplation of the beauty of this time. Ages come and with them come the influences upon this place.

Sufferers among you are healed, not through us or the understanding that we give, but through the act of intelligence given through the acceptance of why we are here and what we have become. Healing waters, we have heard it said, and yet is it not what you desire in your being that heals yourself, not the waters that impart this intelligence to you, but the acceptance that what is needed is indeed available to all ... if accepted by them as truth. Deep and cool, shallow and warm, both are offered and both refused by many and yet this intelligence is absorbed in all no matter what the cause. For water, all waters, be they sacred (which is difficult for us to comprehend as all water is sacred unto all beings) or not are still what they are and that which ones believes them to be.

Nature exists all around us, this is truth, and we provide.

As many, our relaying, as the insect upon this box[27] is the "Beneficial Being" of our path in which we impart to you through this process, all things

The absorption, be it in the city or here, will bring memories and talents from all the ages and times and earth movements of all and through this you will be filled. This is our gift, but yet it is our duty, our job, our quest and given freely to you. We exist here as we exist everywhere, freely given, pure when needed but acceptance is still noted now that pollution does indeed hinder progress, but unlike before, things change and with them we will survive. For the ocean remains and the tides change but as the earth ... we remain.

As the Mother guards all that survive so does she provide and with this acceptance do we exist and flow; we learn and give.

---

26 "Incur" is a word that many of the *Elementals* use and in most cases means "to encounter".

27 In some passages, the Nature Spirits refer to a certain tiny creature that crawls over my computer or the paper while I am writing. These *beings* are called "watchers" and gather information for the Nature Spirits.

Drink of us deeply and enjoy. Feel the depth of understanding, of the despair and of all that have gone before. Drink of the joy of ones that live far from my/our shores and the laughter of sights unseen. Absorb the ancient knowledge of streams overlooking Stones of ages past and know that all that is given shall return once again to the Earth. For as we flow, we ebb and as we ebb, we recede into man's other reality; one of goodness and lust of plenty and more often of the gifts given before, ever returning to impart to all the beauty that is renewed. That is she, that is all that dwell within our being. A river becomes a Sea and thus returns again to a trickle, a stream and again a well.

Well, what do you think?[28] What do you know? Has it passed from us, through you before or is this knowledge which you have now become aware been related as new? This is truth and the path remains open. Drink and renew, assist and deliver. The water holds memories that flow though us all. It also holds the truth for those that look for it.

We remain, the Waters of Glastonbury.

Q: Are there any Nature Spirits around that want to talk to me?

I look up and there is this wonderful little Spirit; a Plant Spirit that looks so forlorn. Will he speak to me and can I capture him? Of course we are talking spiritually!

Aye, I am Leftus.

I reside here in this garden, changing within this place as needed. I exist to be of help to those that have come before. In this fact I reside. I stand tall but in reality, I am quite small for my buds have opened not and I am left alone to ponder this. I am singularly here and alone but see much and in this reality you have awakened me to this mission. As I exist to be what I should become, I have lost my bearings and no longer am as I was before. I look towards the soil that is what you call your Earth and wish to fulfill what I must. Yet in this I have not accomplished what must be so. Awakenening to this fact, I shall relate what task I must accomplish so that you will know this, for this task has been given to you as mine has to me.

I am a flower of sorts. In the sense that I exist to bring "sunshine" and pleasantry to all things, yet in such I provide for others the path to renewal. As each falters and dies, the renewal must become a reality, but can only be accomplished through acts given each entity on this plane. As a worker, this is my truth. I exist to give, but then this is all (everyone's) truth. I give to beings, not unlike yourself, many things. Beauty? Yes, but to others I give nourishment and the ability to

"BE" again. Understand? My acceptance of this encourages me to become more with each year.

I sleep when the frost appears but alas have remained.

You seek me out, this is truth, and to realize this causes me joy for my purpose, unlike what was before, has occurred and this path has become reality. In doing so I shall return to what I must but then sharing of this knowledge shall lead me to another distant goal, unrealized before.

I seek now solace, for the rest that should impart upon me did not arrive. As winter comes we sleep under the earth and awaken renewed with the power needed to transform. We then give nourishment to those that seek it; to the harvesters who provide what we provide, within our beings, and others in our realm. To the flying ones (bees) that flitter among us and provide others with the source needed to extend, within their being, new beginnings. To the energy again stored within ourselves to power all through the sleep that comes each year. All is and all shall be as before. I have accepted this as a provider to all things.

Yes, seeds are given, not only to the wind but to the others that live within our realm. Yes, those beings that dress as such, but only in your reality, live for our beings as well. Bodies regenerate and nourish the earth and speed with it the nourishment to extend to all what must be. I am as I am, not in sequence, but nonetheless what I must be.

A plant you say, yet a Spirit indeed. For all are as they are, imparted within with a spark that ignites all living things, seeking ever and ever the need to be.

I give all that I can and long for rest, but the sheerness of this meeting relates the importance of why I have become late in my ways. Assist me, now in the return into this earth and my growth shall return. We are as we are and we accept this as such.

Noticed by more than is known, we relate only to those that seek out what we desire and yet in this capacity do not answer to those that would not heed us in this direction. We are leaders in this world as such for we are given leave to bloom, to raise our heads

---

28 Again, they use *Nature Spirit* puns. Do you get the "Well" in the "Well, what do you think?"

within that Sister's realm. We give nourishment and we return after refreshment spent in the cold world of darkness. Not unlike you, we exist in the darkness but ever aware that the sunlight awaits. Like us, seek out the goodness; become a giver and receiver of light. To suffer in the darkness is of no use. Release this and within the darkness grow and store and know that the Sun will awaken you to what lies above. Burst through and once again give to all what they need. You will cease to bloom but like all beings you shall return to bloom again.

I remain, Leftus

CHALICE WELL: THE WATERS OF GLASTONBURY — REVISED

We are the waters of the Chalice Well and we live to serve every being.

Water has a purpose, not only for the survival of all things, but in the information that it carries from one world to the next. We flow just as life does but we also stop in streams to help those that need our help. You came here to learn, and because of what you feel, this can be useful.

These Enchanted Gardens wait for many here, but here in our world all things are (appear) as they live. To you, each creature may seem very strange and different but still you give each *being* in our world a place to become what it is and to fulfill what purpose it has. As you enter this world, our world, learn what you must but understand that what we say is about our world as we see it. The things we search for and where they will lead us is not much different than yours in your world … in fact they are the same.

As life flows, moving along, so do the waters; never stopping, always flowing through lifetime after lifetime. We awaken like all things do, but we never stop like you do. We change as fast or as slow as each of us are meant to. We are the heart of this place, the soul of all that is needed to send out thoughts and make them real. Myths and legends live in our world and like yours, they begin and they end here. There are not many of us, the rivers that flow through "sacred or holy ground", but if added together there are still more than you would imagine. As we search for new ground, which is our purpose, we encounter new experiences on our search. This information we have gathered is given to you when you drink from our waters. These waters are the <u>roots of our soul</u>. So, unlike you, we live to serve, to give and to hold what we learn. As we flow, we also find those that would like to destroy what we have started so long ago.

In our world, as we have said, we live to serve; to give what we know to all *beings.* In order for us to grow, others must accept what we give to them when they drink from us. As we move forward and back through many miles, we take in knowledge that is there for everyone; knowledge needed to help them live with the lives they have chosen. We become larger or smaller, giving life to everyone in this world.

It is true that in our world we are the *care-taker,* but in truth our waters also provide nourishment, food, and comfort to those that want it. Many things live and receive the growth that they need, which can only happen if we give it to them. Like everyone in our world, we live to serve but in coming together with other waters we do more on our path to the "Great Sea"… the "next world" that waits for everyone.

It is true that our *Mother* guides us. In this guidance, we must also carry with us all the knowledge we have received over the countless years of travel throughout this great planet on which we serve. This does not mean that we are small, quite the opposite. We chose this size so we are able to go where we must go. Just as this *Chalice Well* holds memories of days long ago, the waters guide those past days.

Still, the waters move and together they also give guidance to anyone who uses them. Isn't it said that "a man that thirsts for knowledge must drink"? We agree and this is what we give. Flowing through us is everything that lives or has lived before. We are ready to give this knowledge to anyone who would "drink of such realities" and would believe in our world.

In another time we lived to serve, to give everything to whomever and whatever was needed to live. The distant past and what will happen in the future, lies in this *well,* in this water. It is through us that all that was or will be, happens. Drinking from us the *water,* will bring you this truth and this truth will bring to everyone a feeling of togetherness. Many will move away from this and look for others that would change the way we are, but all in all we are as we are. Without the way we are, no one could live in your world. They all would feel the burning and the thirst would be so extreme that they would not survive.

We look for knowledge from all living things, carrying with it the wisdom of those times long ago. We receive what we need from small shaped ponds that lie near here. We relax in pools on islands far away, seldom seen by others. We rush forward over our giant friends, the *Stones,* who hold thousands of years of knowledge in their "unmoving" state. Moving (Flowing) along we gather information, stopping for a brief time to understand what we are given; the knowledge learned through countless ages and passed "down stream" to those who would take this knowledge inside of themselves. Still or moving forward, or alone and as deep as here, we will stay. This trust given to us must be told and so this is what we do, this is what we have become and this is our truth.

As you sit here at *Chalice Well*, understand that the Well below offers everyone who looks for it this knowledge; the growth of ages past and the return to the days long ago. To long hours spent in thinking quietly of the beauty of this time. Different ages come in time and with them also come the changes that happen in each time.

Those among you that suffer are healed; not through us or the understanding that we give, but through the intelligence of those that accept why we are here and what we have become. We have heard it said that we are "healing waters" but it is not what you want in your life that heals you or the waters that give you this intelligence, it is that you accept that what you need is here for you, is here for everyone, if you believe it is true. Deep and cool or shallow and warm, both are offered to you and both are refused by many. Still this intelligence is "absorbed" as it sinks into all of us, no matter what we do. Water, all waters, whether sacred (which is hard for us to understand, because all water is sacred to all *beings*) or not, are still what they are and what you believe them to be. It is true that Nature lives all around us and we provide for it all.

Just as others Nature Spirits you have contacted have passed on information (and like the bug that crawls on your laptop passes on information to us), the reasons why we exist and the benefits to you in this existence are passed on to you through this process. Through absorption, whether it is in the city or here, memories and talents from all ages and times and all the earth movements will fill you. This is our gift, but it is also our duty, our job and our challenge that we give without bounds to you. We live here just as we live everywhere and when it's needed we give ourselves freely and purely to everyone.

Yes, we know about pollution and it does make our progress harder. Even though it is not like before, things change and we will survive. The ocean will stay and the tides will change, but like the *Earth* we will remain. Just as *The Mother* guards everything that survives, she also provides what we need and by accepting this, we live and we flow; we learn and we give.

Drink of us deeply. Take a big drink, and enjoy us. Feel the depth of understanding and also the heartbreak that has gone before. Drink in the joys of others that live far away from our shores and the laughter of sights you have not seen. Absorb and take in this knowledge; the lessons from the streams that overlook the ageless Stones and understand that everything you give to the Earth will return to the Earth … Everything you do to the Earth you do to yourselves. Everyone ebbs and flows. We move forward and back and as we move back, we go farther back into mans reality, into what he imagines; into a reality of goodness and the desire for all things. Yet more often its for the gifts that he was given before…but always returning to give to every *being*, the beauty that will come again; the beauty that *She*, *The Great Mother* who is everything, lives within our being … within ourselves. A river becomes a sea and again returns to a trickle, a stream and again becomes a Well.

Well, what do you think?[29] Has it <u>passed from us through to you</u> or is this information we have just given you new? (Answering to myself, "It is new.")

This is true and the path will stay open. Now drink and become renewed, assist us and deliver to others what we have given to you. We remain, The Waters of Glastonbury

Q: Are there any others *Nature Spirits* around that want to talk to me?

I looked up and there is this wonderful little *Spirit*…a *Plant Spirit* looking so unhappy. Will he speak to me and can I understand him? Of course, we are speaking spiritually now.

Yes, I am Leftus,

I live here in this garden, changing as I need to in this place. I live to help those that came before me. This is why I live. I stand tall, but really I am quite small because my buds have not opened and I have been left alone to think.

I am here by myself but I see a lot and in my world you have made me aware of what I must do. As I lived to be what I should have become, I have lost my direction and I am no longer what I was before. I look towards the soil, what you call your earth, and wish to finish what I should have done but have not been able to. Realizing this, I will tell you what I have to do so that you will know this because this job has been given to you, just as mine has been given to me.

I am a sort of flower. This is because I live to bring "sunshine" and joy to all things. In this way I also provide for others the path to rebirth. As each being grows old and dies, the rebirth or new beginning must happen. This can only happen through acts that are given to each *being* on this plane. This is what I believe, my truth, as a worker. I live to give, but then this is everyone's truth. I give many things to *beings* not much different than you.

---

29 Again with the *Nature Spirits* puns. Do you get the "Well" as in Chalice Well, and the <u>passed from us through you</u>? Clever, very clever.

Q: Do you only bring beauty?

A: Beauty? Yes, but to others I give food and so their ability to live. Do you understand? Yes.

Accepting this encourages me to become more each year. I (usually) sleep when the frost comes, but I am still here.

You have looked for me, this is true, and knowing this makes me happy. My purpose, which is different than what it was before, has just occurred to me and my path has become clearer. In doing this I will return to what I must, but I will share this knowledge that we have exchanged and it will lead me to another far off goal that I didn't know about before.

I look for peace now, because the rest that should have come to me did not. When winter comes, we sleep under the earth and awaken, reborn with the power needed to transform or change. We then give nourishment to those that need it; to the *harvesters* who provide what we give (to them) in our lives and to ourselves in our world. We give to the flying ones, the bees and insects that flitter among us, and provide others with the "source" (such as pollen) of what is needed inside to start their new beginnings. (In other words: They give what is needed to cross-pollinate different plants so they can grow.) We again have energy stored inside that keeps us going while we sleep each year and so everything is and will be like it was before. I have accepted this as a "provider" to every being.

Q: Do you have seeds and what do you do with them?

A: Yes, we give seeds not only to the wind but also to the others that live in our world.

Q: Do the *fairies* live in your world?

A: Yes, those *beings* that dress like you imagine, but only in your own mind, live (and work) for our *beings* as well. Our bodies bring life and nourish the earth and send with it the food to everyone that needs it.

Q: Are you a plant?

A: You say I am a plant and this is right, but I am also a *Spirit*. All are as they are, each given a spark inside that ignites and lights up all living things, always searching forever and ever for the need to exist. I give all that I can and I want to rest, but this meeting tells me the importance of why I have been so late in doing what I do. Help me now to return to the earth and I will start to grow again.

We are as we are and we accept this. We are noticed by more than you know, but we speak only to those that look for what we need. In this way we do not answer those that will not follow us in this direction. We are leaders in this world, because we are allowed to bloom; to raise our heads within the "Sisters"[30] realm. We give nourishment and we come back after our rest spent in the cold darkness. Not unlike you, we live in the darkness but know that the sunlight is waiting. Like us, you look for the goodness.

Become a *giver* and *receiver of the light* because to suffer in the darkness is useless. Release this and inside the darkness, grow and store and know that the sun will wake you to what lies above. Burst through and once again give everyone what they need. Remember, you will stop blooming, but like all beings, you will bloom again.

I remain … Leftus[31]

When I saw this adorable little flower sitting alone, I knew I had to speak to it. After this reading I buried him. I think this is what he wanted; in fact, I know he was very happy I did this. I am convinced that his purpose was to stay until I got his reading and because of this sacrifice his path in life changed. He realized it. I only wish I knew where he went from here. I must go back to the Gardens and see if he has returned or if he has moved on to bigger and better things. Everyone chooses their own path, sometimes we stay on the one we have chosen but other times we may come to a fork in the road. Only we can decide which way we should travel. Maybe like Leftus, we will take the road less traveled.

What do you think about the conversation with the Chalice Well? Water and knowledge, I would have never connected them in this way. The idea that all the knowledge of our world flows through our water is a surreal idea but one worth thinking about. Water has always been the center of our world. Not only because our bodies are more than 80% water but also because without it we could not survive. I love the fact that water learns as it travels, stopping in pools and lakes to absorb more knowledge. Kind of like a traveling school.

This passage says so much about what we could learn if we were just open to the idea. I wonder if that is why young children learn so much in their first years. They drink without questioning because they have not been taught yet not to remember. It is sad that we have to grow up and release what we knew back then.

It makes me want to go to a mountain stream and have a few drinks. I bet you have been thinking the same thing.

---

30 Here he refers to the Sisters, the Sun and the Moon.
31 Another pun…..He was left behind by the other plants…so they left-us!

An Old Tree Outside of a Lube Bay

Rural Oklahoma – Sunday, February 23, 2003

WHILE DRIVING CROSS-COUNTRY ON THE way to Canada, my friend Leona and I were waylaid by a slight car problem. The car overheated. It was late at night and we in the middle of nowhere. Nothing was open and we had to turn on the heater full blast to reach the nearest service station.[32] The station was closed but we managed to get the top off the radiator and fill it with the bottle of water that we carried for emergencies. Thank goodness we had this because the station's water hose was broken. We eventually made our way to a small hotel, somewhere in Oklahoma, where we spent the night. The next morning we filled up with water again, thinking we had solved the problem. Nice try! Eventually we pulled into a really small town and there, in the middle of it, was a beautifully well-equipped garage. And they say there is no such thing as divine intervention. Wrong! We had been touched by it throughout our trip. This trip in itself could fill the pages of a book.

While Leona was trying to figure out what was wrong with the car and if it could be fixed, I decided to take a walk.

It was one of those towns that you read about in books; small and rural with old trees and vacant fields. And we came to find out later, it was also filled with the friendliest repair people you could ever find anywhere.

It was wintertime, but we could not tell. The weather was actually quite beautiful. The sky was blue and the sun was warm on my back. Since it was going to take a while to fix the radiator, I decided to sit down under this old tree in the middle of the field out back behind the repair shop. You can guess what happened next.

An Old Tree Outside of a Lube Bay in Rural Oklahoma

Aye, I am Duncan,

Type here, unlike others … mighty, yep. Not unlike others though…what?

Your energy is spent lately in finding out what it is that has nothing to do with what I believe or even know, and yet you are under my branches from the ends of this green Earth asking me, of all beings … What the heck I do!

You know many places are different here than in other places as weather affects us so much more. Seasons here can change and with this comes changes unlike many places you have seen. So you want to know what I manage to do here and to this I can only say, I survive and that's about it! Of course others still find me useful … unlike what was before, but less than what I am.

Your lighters are not here, Sugar, because they have traveled to others that have more.

As we grow old we too become obsolete, in the fact that what we were is gone, but still we remain. For memories can reclaim us, when the thoughts are there. Get the picture? You are looking around and wondering why I stay…what purpose? Good question! The choice, of course is mine. Others seek out new vistas. I remain, not in the sense that what relates to what I am or was, but to the fact that I still can and this is alright with me.

Do I have choices? Of course. Others come and go… purposes fulfilled or not, yet I kind of desire to be more. I don't sustain much more now, but yes, my roots are firm and stretch below the Earth, and again the spring will renew me. My branches are full of wondrous sights and the playthings still exist when called.

George, my friend, still talks with me. We relate to the Old Ones gone before but still our duty remains … conversations among those less suited than before, but aware. Yes, the fiddler below my roots still glistens with nourishment. Others dwell there and the line still forms around my trunk when the seasons awaken spirits long past.

---

32 I had been told that if the **red "overheated" light** ever comes on in a car, I should not stop. The heater must be turned on full blast to let out the heat. This can be murder if it is in the middle of the summer or the middle of the desert. Luckily for us, this wasn't the case.

Retirement is futile in this world because I still am an entity unlike others. The fact being that what I am and can be and forever shall be ... is now gone but within my branches still stirs the leaves of seasons ... still the beings sit and learn. The sky still hears my words and the blossoms give nourishment to all. For through Nature, we shall all survive. In me this is true.

Begin again? Someday, but for now I rest in a path full of reasons to survive. The call comes slowly but the time spent in contemplation echoes only days spent in service. I remain, true to the path chosen long ago.

Go if you must, but remember ... All end when truth becomes reality and reality echoes moments long forgotten. I live as before and remain until I again begin again... new and renewed on a path chosen again. But until that day, I shall seek out what remains and stay true to the path that I follow. Go in the love that remains from ones such as I.

I am, The "Older" Tree in Oklahoma

An Old Tree in Oklahoma — Revised

Yes, I am Duncan,

That's right; I am a different kind of tree. I'm still big and strong but not like any of the others around here. You've spent a lot of time lately trying to find out things that have nothing to do with me. Now you are sitting here under my branches, showing up from the "ends of this green earth" or who knows where, asking me of all *beings,* what the heck I do!

You know, many things are different here than in other places. The weather affects us so much more. The seasons here can change and with these changes come things that are different than in other places you have seen.

So you want to know what I manage to do here. My answer is, I survive and that's about it! Of course, others still think me useful; not like I was before but less than I am now. Your "*lighters*" are not here, Sugar (a name he called me), because they have traveled to others that have more to give them. When we grow old, we too become "out of date". What we once were is gone but we still stay around because the memories can make us young again when we remember what we were before. You get the picture?

You are looking around and wondering why I stay and how I can be of any use to anyone now? Good question. The choice, of course, is mine. Others look for new places to live, new lives, but I stay. Not because it has to do with who I am, because I am who I am, or in my case was but because I still can and this is all right with me.

Do I have choices? Of course I do. Others leave. What they have chosen to do, they have done, but then again maybe not, but I kind of want more. Sure, I don't help much now but yes, my roots are still firm and they stretch below the earth. Again, spring will bring me to life. My branches are still full of wonderful things and the playthings (The *beings* that have fun in the branches) always come when I call them.

George, my friend, still talks to me. We talk about our old friends that use to live here and even though we miss them, we feel a duty to stay. We are two *beings* talking together, both not as young as we use to be, but each still knowing what goes on in our world.

Yes, the fiddler and the music below my roots still play with what I need to live. Others still live below in my roots and the line still forms around my trunk when the seasons wake up the *Spirits* of long ago. In other words; the flowers still bloom in the spring all around the trunk of the tree. Retirement is out of the question in this world because I am still a *being* that is not like any other around here. The fact is that what I am and can be and will always be is now gone, at least in this lifetime.

Still, the leaves in my branches change with the seasons and the *beings* still continue to sit in them and learn. The sky still hears my words and my blossoms still give food to everyone that needs it. Through *Nature* we will all survive. I know inside me this is true. I will start a new life someday, but for now I will rest on this path I have chosen; a path full of reasons for me to stay. The call to start over comes slowly to me. This time I spend in thinking brings back only memories spent in service, in doing my job for the benefit of this place. I still remain true to that path I chose so long ago.

Go, if you have to, but remember: Each being dies when their truth and what they are searching for becomes real and what is real brings back those times they have forgotten. I will live like I have before and I will stay until I start again; new and reborn on a path that I have chosen once more. But until that day, I will take care of what is still here and stay true to the path that I follow. Go in the love that is still here in others, the "Old Timers" like me.

I am, The "Older" (not old!) Tree in Oklahoma

I love this reading because it talks about growing old and still remaining true to your beliefs. Too many people give up before they should because society seems to value the younger and fitter person first. We should realize that with age comes wisdom and that experience can only benefit those around us. To deny a person's worth and ignore their usefulness because of their age is surely a disgrace. Everyone has a path they are following. Shouldn't we be kind enough to let them travel it until they reach the end?

I think this is the least we can do.

The Spirit of Nature

Big Bear Lake—Wednesday, March 05, 2003

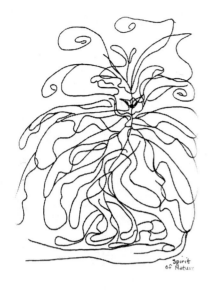

AT FIRST I COULDN'T REMEMBER where I had channeled this reading. It was written and dated on the first page so I obviously knew where and when it was, but I just couldn't remember the reading at all. Then it came to me. I was sitting outside at the picnic tables at the Snow Summit Ski Area in the mountains of Southern California. The day was beautiful and I had taken my Grandson Kurtis to the mountains for a weekend of snow boarding. I remember I had gotten guidance that I shouldn't ski but I should write instead. This time though I didn't tune into a plant or tree but instead into Nature herself. When I reviewed this reading I could really tell the difference between a single Nature Spirit and the whole collective called Nature. There is really a huge difference.

The problem here is that I never finished the reading. I really don't think it matters because the information is so enlightening that it is worthy of being included. If you think this is a lot deeper than most of the other readings, you are right. But if you think this is heavy, you should read what the Stones have to say. That would "totally" blow your mind.

The Spirit of Nature

Looking out upon this vista do you realize that what you see in fact becomes "you". This point now shall become reality as stated before. In each person, inherent to their ability to comprehend, there lies a dominant force known in layman terms as the <u>Force to Unite</u>. This is among all beings, not in relation to what you know or in the genera of things spoken on your level but in the way things are perceived, not only in this reality but in ones not known on this plane. As you seek out knowledge on which to base these facts, be aware that what you desire can be attained. Though we are collective as stated before, we are nonetheless separate in knowledge. This, in the fact that what we have learned is truth, in our ability to expound this knowledge to those that comprehend its source.

So, you ask now within the scope of reality, about this source. This is beneficial in the fact that this knowledge be given to those that would benefit from it. For in doing so, this balance that is <u>tilted</u> for lack of a better word, may be altered and thus aligned in this course. As Nature enters into every realm known, and as of yet unknown, it takes on a singular purpose. This is to unite all with the knowledge that is gained through this thing you call spiritual unity. For together "Nature" as stated, grows… for this is a term used to denote knowledge passed from one to another … thus giving each, knowledge unknown to that entity before. With this comes the united force needed to propel us further down and into that void that awaits all persons, entities, even such as us, and beings unknown to you, per se.

We, Nature, the collective (we are speaking now as a unit, not as an individual entity divided within this collective to extend knowledge unto the all) bring about changes as we speak of this period, this place and in this time frame, only in keeping with the marks we give in succession to this level you have inquired.

As each seeks out answers within this plane, about and through this entity which now shall be known as NS (for Nature Spirits), let us conclude that what we bring all be of knowledge to those that seek out not only solutions to problems that have arisen in this state but to reasons and purposes for each function performed within this realm we call NS. As NS reaches its potential here upon this plane it strives to become integrated with you, known as "the others" for lack of a better name. The same in degrees as we, you are nonetheless different in the fact that the lessons you must encounter will benefit your trial instead of ours. Thusly you seek out other means that will connect you with that force that is inherent, not only within this place, time or being but with all things in all realms and in all times. For each race, each being has a path chosen for reasons inherent unto his growth and with this comes the lessons, in layman terms, that shall bring about changes and also to admit him to other worlds unseen as of now. As we exist in such a place, the differences in each are strange but not unlike ones attained within your said "abode".

As your knowledge increases be aware that what is presented shall be scorned by many but truths seldom are accepted as truths when the inherent populous is void of knowledge...is this not truth?

So in keeping with the knowledge given and proclaimed by us, the NS we begin.

Collection precognition is beneficial to becoming and establishing the network on this plane. As governments rule (this is a term unlike ones used among us but inherent again within your scope of reasoning) so do we. But in this each section (country) within certain boundaries and climatic sections which differ not only in lack or the presence of moisture, rain fall, floods...sun, warmth, and climatic controls within its boundaries. This is every fact and relationship needed to regulate what forces or controls are needed to extend our being upon this plane. As you have spoken to individual beings within this realm, each being among the collective but separate unto itself, each with underlying jobs, duties and commands, so we as the NS collective shall give in higher detail that which constitutes the growth within your plane.

Each is divided into sections... a country, if this computes more with your reality. As stated before this has to do with changes in climate, type of weather situations ... which will be delved into more fully when needed and for the continuation of all that must be understood to begin again and again the renewal process upon this plane.

Yes, the collective does regulate Nature but the ruling entity upon this plane is indeed that entity that you refer to as The Mother, collective called Mother Nature. She indeed rules, so to speak, all here but this is a fallacy in that all accept that which is given and do not become over eager to undertake what and when they are either not inclined to accept or are unworthy to attain upon this plane.

As each exists to serve, which is different from you, we accept that which we must accept and the consequence that will ensue if not performed. For being on the regulatory plane, we all ensure that what you have attained be complete. For we exist even though you, which exist now, but often begin again and again, do not. You, often "blown away" for lack of words, by greed or hunger or just the intolerable destruction you impose upon all within your plane. Thus it is we, the NS, who reiterate this and regulate its existence in all phases of growth.

We are a collective but the individual, such as ones presented, represent as needed different views to relate their jobs/skills to those that seek out this information.

Speaking on a cellular level, we all remain consistent but spiritually we are more attuned to what our goals are among this challenge we all face in the knowledge needed to ensue our totality in this and all future existences.

As the ant that toils, "it" or so it seems, ever bringing food to his body...his collective, so are we attuned in much the same way. As one imagines this being, this ant to be non-singular, he is in fact not that at all. For each has goals which serve all but each also has inherent unto his being the goals needed to strive towards what shall entail upon this path his collective reasoning potential. This in turn will propel him further away from his collective. Options are presented to all beings, but many choose this way of life (as noted) and continue, but many search for more.

As the cocoon that eventually becomes the butterfly, so must all eventually become more than before. In seeking this they break away from this singular reality but in truth it all remains as the matrix of time ever connected, to continue singularly, at least in his conception with tasks highly suited more than before.

As you know, many upon your plane seek out more than others. Some are content to remain in a collective to strive to be part of the whole. Others break out of this mold and become more than the whole. Do they not continue within their lifetime to indulge in things that will benefit your mankind or do they exist within their own realm again becoming in charge of their total new collective? That which would serve him on this path he has chosen. As us, many have chosen to become more.

You ask now if the Devas, as you have noted, are as such. This is in keeping with our knowledge and that imparted as reality conciseness, a fact. For each rules (again for lack of a better word ... shall we say facilitates, as they do at that place which you frequent.[33] Much abridged are we for that asset you have attained upon this place. Please note this in our work) in whatever facility or capability it experiences its total growth ability within. For each being, the totality of his collective leads them through the "courses" needed to attain these goals upon this land. As one may undertake the flowers within a section, so must she see that each one alights within its time the ability to begin and end: to seek out moisture and sustenance and to be beneficial to your world.

As each deity belongs to certain time periods upon your plane be aware that many have belonged long ago to this collective and have moved along "the ranks" to attain their status that make them such. As the Mother that lies beneath the roots of this plane knows all that is needed to extend this to all, she in turn must impart this knowledge to those that have progressed even farther

---

33 The Findhorn Foundation, Findhorn, Scotland.

towards this goal that we all seek.

So it is that all beings … they of the NS, your type or weather patterns, cosmic influences or ether that rises above, all have and shall ever have a purpose and a goal on which this foundation is built.

As stated before, the Devas rule. Their appearance given over to legend becomes reality to you on your plane when the truth of this existence becomes encased in the minds of the working man. As before, many have come to realize that we, as a collective, seek to return the Earth to what it was before. Of this many have been given knowledge and this has been imparted, so if and when this is needed to extend this piece, then it shall be revived. Moving along with this framework, we must again expound upon this purpose, this existence that prompts us on through existences seen by you.

As we, NS return, year after year, season after season, we bring with each a newness and so it is that these lessons are given credence to your growth. Through these lessons you learn also if not through the ingestion of this knowledge but for the intelligence of "seeing", absorb … some of you, this knowledge, and the understanding becomes apparent. As each continues to become aware of these changes and with them the consequences, he becomes also aware of the responsibility of why and where we, as the collective, belong in the scheme of things.

As Nature, we align with certain aspects and this collectively aligns with what is needed within this plane for your survival. Had we not altered changes within this space many innumerable times within this framework, then this species known as Mankind would no longer exist.

We attain all through this growth and with it comes the knowledge that we need also to survive. If you destroy us, then you destroy also the ability to become what you must… as we are destroyed and in this process all things change. Understand?

For cases come and go and collectively all things are arranged by the one that leads us all… but instinctively they are given choices to make these possible.

As you think on this phase, be aware that what we shall impart shall answer questions, but the purpose of this exercise is to awaken those that do not comprehend the fact that we all are one and that collectively, be it plant or mineral (as you have noted by the exchanges given by the mineral kingdom) or animal or either, all relate to the being of all. Understanding of this is essential. Thus in keeping within the framework of what I must relay...I continue.

As each soul, (and yes all are inherent with this thing known as a soul. As some have stated we prefer "essence" and thus it is) as the rose say, emits a strange fragrance that entrances many, this becomes the essence of that rose. But in fact the essence is not the perfume but the being that entails within itself that perfume. This fragrance is but a part. A part to share with all that would inhale this fragrance and whose sense of awareness of Nature (is) heightened by this act. Again this is a labor, but one of beauty and yes, of love. For as this rose fades its essence is not lost. Yes, it is true that the fragrance has waned but the flower, the being that is this rose, remains…seeking once more to return to again impart upon those that would desire, the knowledge imparted with this sense. Since this being, said rose, shall and does return…thus the cycles of life, known to you as the seasons; her essence must remain in tact. Do you understand this? To lose this would impart, within the next growth, no scent. Thus she has what shall never leave and with this comes her renewal. As the soul that you arrange within this place that you call your body, you also impart to all what is needed to extend within your time on this plane, your scent… your essence and with it comes the knowledge that you have imparted or the destruction you have caused. But in the end you cease but again, like the rose you again return, with you again comes your essence; grown from before by the work you have accomplished or not by what you have not. Again challenges to all.

The rose sleeps as do all and with it, knowledge gained is shared and others impart to this being what they have learned. So in your case, does this also exist? If picked too soon, this knowledge is never extended and like you must be again renewed again and again until attained. Does the rose feel beneficial to being a rose and continue on this course until infinity? Of course not, for all things, be they you or me, or the rose or the Deva that lights the night sky...all are given choices but the knowledge must be learned before one can move higher into the realms that are offered all. As existences wane and flow so do experiences … each different, but many the same. Some are learned readily but others take many lifetimes to ensure this production. And so thus is the plight of all. To extend your ability to be more… to move on up to a higher work position, as you would relate to, and to become more to all that seek it.

Many here are teachers, not such as yours but still they impart lessons to those that seek this. Others, like yourself search out knowledge that shall be imparted to the all. This is truth and to this we all strive. For the reason one exists is to become more, not less but often ones such as you and we, of course, are not ready to begin again, and thus remain as we are for many seasons or lifetimes.

We have been like you and you like we for we all have searched for the reason for being. As one relates to certain plants, trees and Devas, little folks, fairies and the like, so they see what they have been or shall become. For isn't it what you are not that you seek to be? For always something is more through your existence, becoming magical in itself. This is not only Human Nature but all of Nature.

As the ant that trudges back and forth longs for the freedom of the sky so does the sparrow that is alight with fear from the hawk wish for the comfort of the Earth. Thus it is and has been and shall remain or at least in what our reality has been given. As the collective, we have these all and with them things are related and thus changes are made... but in due time. For some such as the Oak[34] that spoke, remain to rule those that would not be served well by others but in truth, his truth he also seeks the security and yes, the fame from this position. He also rests as many but still others seek out, often new vistas. If arranged they remain, for many eons or not. AGAIN CHOICE, as are thus and so they accept this, as truth, their path... the destiny arranged by the intelligence gained through experiences taken in turn ...

THE SPIRIT OF NATURE — REVISED

Looking out over the view, do you realize that what you see is in fact a part of you? We said this before but now we know you finally understand.

In each person, depending how much they can understand, there is a main force known in layman terms as the *Force to Unite*. This is in all *beings*, not in connection to what they know or the way things are spoken on their level, but in the way things are understood not only in this reality but in ones that are unknown to them.

As you look for information on which to base these facts, be aware that this is quite possible.

Even though we are a collective, as we said before, we are nonetheless individual in what we know. This and the fact that what we know is true, gives us the option of sharing this knowledge with those that understand its source. You would like to know, in language that you can understand, about this source. This is good because this knowledge should be given to those that can benefit from it. In doing this, the balance that is slanted can be changed and realigned in the process.

When Nature enters into every known world and those unknown, it takes on one purpose, to unite all *beings* with the knowledge gained through this thing you call *Spiritual Unity*. As we said, <u>working together Nature grows</u>. This is a term used to identify knowledge passed from one *being* to another, giving to each the information that was unknown before. Through this comes the *United Force* that is needed to push us further along towards that void that waits for every person, *being* (such as us) and those that are still unknown to you. We (speaking now as *The Collective* and not as the individual *being* that gives its knowledge to those who ask) bring about these changes when we talk about this period, this place and in this time frame but only when giving you the information you can understand on the level about which you have asked.

In looking for answers in our world about and through these *entities* (which will now be known as *Nature Spirits*), let us say that what we give you will be this information; not only to those that look for solutions to problems but to the reasons and functions each were performed in the world we call the *Nature Spirits*.

When a *Nature Spirit* reaches its potential in our world, it tries to become involved in yours, or *The Others* (as we call you) world. Though it is the same for you, it is nevertheless different in the fact that the lessons you will learn will help you on your path instead of ours. So you will look for other ways that will connect you with that force that is always there; not only in this place, time or your life now but with all things, in all worlds and in all times.

Each race and each *being* has a path they have chosen for the growth it can provide. This path provides the lessons that will bring about those changes and also lets them see other worlds they had not seen up to now. Though living in our world may seem strange to you, we also feel the same about yours.

You should understand that as your knowledge increases the more we tell you, the more you will be criticized. But the truth is, seldom are things believed to be true when the present population "doesn't have a clue". (They actually said <u>are stupid</u>, but I prefer this.) Isn't this true?

Going on with the information you have received through us, the *Nature Spirits*, we will begin.

It is good for *The Collective* to know what will happen in the future. This helps in becoming and establishing the network on this plane. Like different governments in your world (this is your term but it will work for us too) rule, so do we but in the different sections (like

---

34 See passage "A Conversation With Axel".

your countries), within certain boundaries and different areas of climate. These sections differ in their moisture level, such as rainfall, floods, sun, warmth and what the weather is like inside its boundaries. Each provides every detail and condition to regulate what forces or controls are needed to keep us alive in our world.

You have spoken to individual *beings* inside our world, each being part of *The Collective* but also each as an individual, with underlying jobs, duties and commands, so we, *The Collective* will give you in greater detail what brings together the growth in your world. Again, each area is divided into sections or countries if this makes it easier. As we said before, this has to do with the changes in climate and types of weather conditions (we will get deeper into this when we need to) and for the rebirth of every *being*. This must be understood before in order to restart over and over again the renewal process in this world.

Yes, *The Collective* does regulate *Nature* but the ruling *being* in this world is indeed the *being* that you call *The Mother* or collectively called *Mother Nature*. She rules, so to speak, everyone here.

It is wrong when you say that every *being* accepts the job they are given. This is not true if they are not overly anxious to do the job at the time, dislike where it located, or they either just don't want to do it or feel they are unworthy of the position.

Unlike you we all live to serve, accepting what we must accept and the consequences that will follow if we don't. Living in a world with rules, we all make sure that what we start is finished.

We have always lived but even though you live now, your race has often started over again and again. Sometimes it hasn't. You are often (blown away) destroyed by greed, hunger or just the unbearable destruction you impose on everyone in your world. So it is that we, the *Nature Spirits* tell you this and arrange the *Earth's* existence in all the different phases of growth. We are a collective but the individual, such as the ones you have worked with, represent a different view. A view needed to give the information about their job and skills to those that want it.

Speaking on a cellular level, we all remain the same but spiritually we are more tuned in to what our goals are in these challenges we all face and the knowledge we will need to ensure our wholeness in this and all future existences.

We are tuned in the same way as the working ant that brings food to his collective is. If you imagine this ant to be part of *The Collective* and not a separate *being*, you are wrong; he is not that at all. Each ant has goals which serve *The Collective* but also has within itself the goals he needs to move toward what will happen on his path, his collective reasoning potential.[35] This will move him further away from his collective. These options are presented to all *beings* but many choose the collective way of life and continue but many others search for more.

Like the cocoon that eventually becomes the butterfly, we must all sooner or later become more than we were before. In searching for this they break away from this singular reality, *The Collective* (but the truth is, it all remains a web of time... always connected) to continue alone, or at least as they see it, with jobs more highly suited than before. As you know, many in your world look for more than others. Some are content to stay in a big company and be part of the whole. Others break out of the mold and become more than the whole, independent. Do they continue through their lifetime doing things that will help all of mankind or do they live inside their own little world, again becoming part of a totally new collective?

This way or that? Whichever will serve him best on the path he has chosen. Like us, many have chosen to be more than part of *The Collective*.

You ask if this refers to the *Devas*. Keeping with our subject and speaking to the point, this is a fact. Each *Deva* rules or we would say facilitates (much as they do at Findhorn, which I was suppose to note because they liked the way they did this with the groups there) in whatever faculty or capability it needs to experience its total growth. The Deva, being the leader of its collective, leads them through the courses that they need to reach those goals in our world.

As the *Deva* takes charge of the flowers/plants/etc. in her section (her country) she must see that each understands when it is time to bloom and to die, to look for food and water and to be helpful to your world.

Be aware that just as the different *Gods* and *Goddesses* in your world belong to different periods of time, before their time they belonged to *The Collective* and had moved along the ranks to reach the status that made them what they became.

Mother Earth, who lies beneath the roots of both our worlds, knows everything that we need and what needs to be given to everyone. She in turn must give this knowledge to those that have progressed even further towards those goals for which we all are searching. This is why each *being,* whether it is a *Nature Spirit*, a Human *Being*, a weather pattern, cosmic influences or the air above, all have

---

35 Collective reasoning potential; this is the combined information of all the beings working together that a *being* can collect while working within the collective. This information if learned can be used to further the existence of this *being* and ready him for his advancement from a collective being to a singular entity.

and will always have a purpose and a goal on which this foundation is built.

As we said before, the *Devas* rule. Legends have been told about how these *beings* should look and believing this in your minds makes it so.

Many have come to realize, as they have before, that we as a collective are working to return the earth to what it was before. Some have been given this knowledge so if and when it is needed to save your world, it can be remembered.

Moving along with this framework in mind, we must tell you about this purpose, this life force that moves us along through the lives you see.

Returning each year, season after season, we the *Nature Spirits* reappear new again. Through this the lesson of how you grow and are renewed are proven. Through these lessons you also learn, not only from already knowing this information but seeing it. To some of you this knowledge and understanding then becomes apparent. When you each continue to become aware of these changes and with them the consequences, you also become aware of the responsibility of why and where *The Collective* belongs in the scheme of things. As *Nature* we connect with certain things and this collectively connects with what is needed in this world for your survival.

If we hadn't altered uncountable times, the changes here within this framework, then the species known as <u>Mankind</u> would no longer exist.

We get everything we need through this growth and with this, the knowledge that we also need to survive. If you destroy us then you also destroy your ability to become what you must become and in this process everything changes. Do you understand?

Different lives come and go and together all things are arranged by the *One* that leads us all but instinctively you are given the choices to make these possible.

As you think about what we just said, be aware that what we will tell you will answer questions but the purpose of all this is to awaken those that do not understand the fact that we all are one. That collectively, whether it is plant or mineral (as you have written about in the exchanges with the mineral kingdom) or animal or the air, all are connected to the being of all. Understanding this is essential. So in keeping within the framework of what I was saying, I will continue.

When each soul, (Yes every *being* has this thing that you refer to as a *soul*. As some have mentioned before, it is true that we prefer *essence*.) such as the rose, gives off a fragrance that draws others to it, this becomes the *essence* of the rose. In fact the *essence* is not the perfume but the *being* that holds within itself that perfume. The fragrance is only a part of the rose, a part to share with anyone that inhales this scent and whose sense of awareness of *Nature* is raised by doing this. Again this is a labor, but one of beauty and yes, of love. When the rose fades its *essence* is not lost. It's true that there is no longer a fragrance but the flower, the *being* that is this rose, remains and again finds a way to return and once more give to those who want it, the knowledge passed on though this scent. Since this *being* you call a rose will and does return in this cycle of life known to you as the seasons, her *essence* must stay in tact. Do you understand this? To lose this would bring her in her next life, no scent or no *essence*, and so no reason to return. So it is that the rose has what will never leave her and with this comes her rebirth.

Just like the soul that is inside your body, you also give to everyone what you need to prolong, in your lifetime in this world, your scent…your *essence*. With this also comes the knowledge you have spread or the destruction you have caused. In the end you will die, but again like the rose you will return, bringing with you your *essence or soul*. Your *soul* either having grown by the work you did before or not, because you did not accomplish what you needed to in your last lifetime. Again, challenges are given to everyone.

The rose sleeps, as does everything when they die, and in this state the knowledge that the rose gained is shared with others. They in turn tell her what they have learned in their lifetime. So it is for you. If the rose is picked too soon this knowledge is never spread and like you, she must be born again and again until this is done. Does a rose think it's helpful to continue to be a rose throughout all time? Of course not. Everything, whether it is me or you or The *Deva* that lights up the night sky, is given a choice. In order for anyone to move into a higher realm, which is offered to everyone, they must first have the knowledge that is needed to do this.

As lifetimes come and go, so do the experiences; each different but many the same. Some lessons are learned quickly but others take many lifetimes to learn. This is just the way it is and it is the same for everyone. Each *being* tries in their next lifetime to do more and to move up to a higher job… and for those that want it, to become more than they were before.

Many here in my world are teachers, though they are not the same as yours. Still they teach lessons to those that ask. Others, like you, look for information that will be given to everyone. This is the truth and this is what we all strive for. The reason one exists is to become more, not less than they were before. Often ones such as you and we are not ready of course to become something else and so stay as we are for many seasons or lifetimes. We have been like you and you have been like us: We have all searched for the reason for being.

When you connect with certain plants, trees and *Devas* or *Little Folks*, *Fairies* and others such as these, you see what you have been before or what you will become in the future. Isn't it what you aren't, that you want to be? Something is always better in your imagination. This is not only "human nature" but all of *Nature*.

Just like the ant that marches back and forth wishing for the freedom of the sky, so does the sparrow that flies above, fearing the hawk, wish for the comfort of the Earth. As they always say… The grass is always greener on the other side of the fence. This is the way it has been and will stay or at least in the world we have each been given.

As a collective, we have all these and with them things are learned and changes are made, but in due time. Some such as the Oak Axel[36] stay in charge feeling that others wouldn't be as qualified to do their job. The truth is, or should we say his truth is, that he also wants the security and yes, the fame he receives from this position. Like many others he also rests but others look for something new. If it is arranged, they may or may not stay for many more years. Again it is choice, the way it is and they accept this as their truth and their path. A destiny arranged by the intelligence they have gained though the experiences they have received in each lifetime …

Alright, are you still with me? Or should I say with them? Have you decided yet whether you are part of a collective or have you chosen to go it alone in this lifetime?

Nature seems to think that whatever you have chosen, it is exactly what is best for you in whatever lifetime you are in at the time. This is good to know. Sometimes it seems as if we are always making the wrong decisions but maybe those decisions are the choices we have to make to learn the lessons we need this time around. The idea that we have a chance to be and to do something different in our future lives is very reassuring and the benefits of talking it over with "like" souls after we die may be what we really need to understand these choices.

Over and over the Nature Spirits have said we all have choices, no matter what kind of *being* we might be. Choices in how we live our life, where we live it, and just what sort of *being* we have or will become. Whether it is working together or alone it is your decision and only you can decide what is right for you and all your futures to come.

As they said and we all believe, "The grass is always greener on the other side of the fence". I believe unless we try living on both sides of that fence, we will never know if this is true.

---

36 See passage "A Conversation With Axel".

Ivy on a Great Pine Tree in the Snow

Big Bear Lake, California – Thursday, March 06, 2003

LIVING IN SOUTHERN CALIFORNIA, AND also living in the most populated part of it, every once in a while I need to get away and reconnect with *Nature*. This is just something I have to do. Luckily not far away is a little mountain town called Big Bear. I assume there are some big bears there but even though I have been going there all my life, I still haven't seen any, at least not yet. However, I do know for a fact that there are *Nature Spirits* there.

When I was in my teens, a very, very long time ago, I use to spend my summers working at a camp there. Most of the time I was busy working in the kitchen but when I was able to escape I would wander the woods. Even then I had an amazingly comfortable connection with *Nature* and I really hated it when I had to return to the city at the end of the summer. I loved it there, and the connection I made so many years ago still remains to this day. I am lucky that I can go there anytime I need to and because of this I felt that this book wouldn't be complete without a reading from my Big Bear *Elemental* Family.

Since I no longer work in the kitchen at Cedar Lake, I have moved my location to a cozy Bed & Breakfast Inn called Apples. Since it is named after a very familiar *Nature Spirit*, namely the Apple, and my hosts let me spread out and work in peace and quiet, I love returning there again and again. The table where I work looks out onto these wonderful pine trees, giving you the feeling that you are part of their world. Again, the *Nature Spirits* in action.

This visit it was snowing and the great Pine Tree outside my window looked like something you would see on the front of a Christmas card.[37] The only difference and what seemed to me very odd at the time, was that there was Ivy growing around the tree. I never really thought about it before but I guess I just assumed that Ivy died when it snowed. I, as usual, was wrong. Big surprise, right?

Because this seemed so strange to me, never having grown up where it snowed and thus never really knowing if in fact Ivy does grow in the snow, I decided to find out for myself. While doing this I expected to get both a reading from the Ivy and the Pine Tree. This was not the case. The Ivy had a lot to say; the Pine Tree was on vacation.

Ivy on a Great Pine Tree, in the Snow

Ivy, as we grow as such 'round a tree, thus in doing so becomes one with this being. For such as we are, ones that travel, thus we continue.

You ask how we can survive the snow and to this we respond; we live as we grow and as we do we go as we may. For our will is that to be where and when we are best suited. Entwining with other beings we become as one, yet separate imparting within our core knowledge taken along within our path. This we give to those that seek needed plans and data to build or not what must be deemed necessary to continue with their growth.

As green and brown turning with the season we begin and end, not cumulative but separating into parts, renewing and with this the growth to sustain and to further our quests. Within our boughs lie countless others that assist us in our quests. They desire to live among our leaves; a cover from the harsh reality of the human world, they are nourished and grown and travel also if needed. They live in the moist soil covered by this structure that awaits all that find it's refuse.

We give warmth in weather such as this but we survive if tasks become not too unruly. We arrange with those that dwell beneath to suffer not the harsh reality of this cold that sweeps this place in this season. Cozy and warm they await the rays that will soften

---

37 Yes, in case you were wondering, it does snow in Southern California, but only in the mountains and only for a short time!

the earth and welcome again the nutrients needed to sustain their being.

We are green in colors known to you and thus are full of life, ever continuing to grow, we cease not as others within our realm. Parts of us vanish, wither, this is truth but in this give to The Mother what is needed to give to all what is needed, but the plant that we are is one and whole and ever moving towards that release that will bring us closer to the divine. We become your plant of choice for many reasons and sacrifice many to this need but still we remain as such, ever wary yet climbing still towards that path as all. We suffer not for we are of that species that defies weather. Not in the sense that what shall be shall always remain, but we are inclined to become ever new. For within each season some are renewed and others such as we remain still, relating to all the chances that have occurred during this stage of rest. The creatures that guard our forests attest to the suppleness of our leaves and use us for their beds, as in fact many rest as you. For the dormancy of many causes others to remain alert and yet those that seek to arrange this renewal also must be renewed.

As you seek solace at the end of each day so must those that keep our world ever near. They alight in the trees, alone in the water, alive in bushes and plants, ever near in caves and vales and glens and high holy hills of old. Each relating to all what purpose they have desired.

As we travel we also provide to all the energy to continue. As a conduit to other realms we are a cable or relay point in which to carry this information to different points. Slow in the eyes of man, nevertheless underneath our roots reach out to intertwine with those of others that seek out also this system known as the mantle of knowledge. In this all things are related and as your telephone line things come from every corner of this realm.

Need you knowledge of that tree in that place you have recently visited, then we ask and it is given. Not in a way that you see but in terms of the Ancient ways. The transcending of timeless spaces into conduits of energy that run from one point to the next. Relating within each coil the knowledge of what is good and bad in our world.

As a tree perishes in one area so another must begin and such is noted. Along with this others relay this and a team begins this task. Acorns are given and in its zone one is placed to recover this area that has been voided of said being. This tree that has perished be it from disease or other types. We do accept that what we desire need not always be of benefit, so acting on many diseased within our core becomes a benefit to others in ceasing this from ones that would also succumb, or from neglect, human or Nature. For all things change and areas that we curtail begin again the rein of draught and adaptation again becomes necessary. As we attend to this fallen tree others clear about all that was and begin again the transformation of a new being upon this place. For though the tree has been removed the essence exists still and remains as before. Yes, this is truth, for your thoughts drift to feelings felt in Ancient places void of living greenery. Yes still the essence of the place dwells within this place and still the feeling remains. As a cavern of the soul ever ready to warm and soothe you in its wake, so is this "feeling" that is emitted from places long devoid of such. Though you see not these beings they remain, but choices are different upon this realm. For this being, this tree then may exist again, choosing to accept this new beginning or not but in doing so must suffer again this growth to become once more a guardian of the forest.

As in the beginning a newling is given tasks. It is reasonable to assume that these tasks are slight. They must adapt, which in its being is difficult, (because) before they had attained the rank of "super structure" within his zone. In accepting this task to begin again as before, one learns what was not accomplished before, imparting with it Ancient knowledge held over from tasks long ago. In relating to this new endeavor he accepts the risks and joys associated with a new beginning. Acceptance is choice and with this growth.

Many seek the solitude of tree status, for the collective plant such as we means constant interchange with like beings. Others may ask for this position but the choice is first that of the lone soul that existed before. Many choose to move along the ranks and begin again as a lighter, or as a plant that grows along a river or gorge. Many seek out the highlands, vast, yet void of fellow man. Many seek out beauty and become a flower or give themselves to service as a tree or plant that bears fruit for all. Choices are many and such are resources apparent to all. As a collective, this is noted by how we assume we work together to provide what is needed yet each is still within this, separate unto themselves. We relate best to those that dwell within our realm, in the fact that we travel. We seek out vines and trees that will sustain this and co-mingle in an array of such. We feel that the need for our survival accounts for what we can accomplish both above and below the earth. Collectively we are given choices, directions, heights, varieties, changes, and climate adaptability. Others like us exist to begin and again in seasonal differences but offering things unlike what we have attained; as the vine that flowers in the spring often bringing with it the flowers that will provide nurturing to those that are needed to co-exist within this plane.

As insects abound they carry within these nutrients and impart them to other parts of the realm thus procreation begins again. Many others provide nourishment to others such as you, animals, and the like insects and even to those that dwell deep within this earth, arising ever new when the snow has gone. Many of the creatures unseen to you gather what is needed and give it to all that desire the sustenance of each vine. For plants such as we provide many things as before. We offer this and telecommunication and in this we reside.

You seek now others with options and growth patterns and offer these suggestions. Go to the Sea and seek out those that live beneath its waves. For unlike us, they represent a world seldom seen by mankind such as you. Yet they offer a wealth of information relating to times and places long forgotten upon your plane.

Exist now to be more than before and understand that like you we also sacrifice to give our all too all things. Understand that like you we seek out new lives and new experiences. We live within the whole or separately, within the earth or not, above the Sea or below, on the hill or beneath, in caves and caverns and cities destroyed long ago in days long past. We are Nature and we such as you continue. We grow and bloom. We listen and we move along; each confident in its own ability to begin again and again and to give to all that it can to sustain this place you call earth. Please remember that what you do to we (us) you do to yourself. Rally in this fact. Accept that what we give, all do what they must to sustain their being and in this we do also but acceptance and knowing in our world is relevant to outweigh our existence. Thus we know that what shall be, shall never cease what we are, can or shall be. For all of life exists intoned with the Great Spirit that guides us all. Remember this. Alight in this knowledge. Acknowledge our present and respect us in all ways.

We remain, the friends of Nature, for we are as such,

The Green Ivy that surrounds the Great Pine.

THE GREEN IVY THAT SURROUNDS THE GREAT PINE — REVISED

We are the Ivy and we grow around this tree. By doing this, we become *one* with the tree. That is who we are, the *Ones That Travel*, and we will continue to do so.

You want to know how we can survive in the snow, so we will give you this answer:

We live as we grow and as we do, we go where we want. We have chosen to be where and when we can best live our lives. Intertwining, moving in and out with other *beings*, we become part of them. Yet we are separate, keeping deep inside ourselves the knowledge we have learned along our path. This gives those that are looking for it, the plans and information that they need to either build or not, what they think is necessary to continue growing.

Just as the seasons turn from green to brown, we also live and die. Not all of us at once but in sections, each renewing, and living again. In doing this, we receive the growth we need to live and to move along to whatever path we have chosen. Within our branches live many others *beings* that help us on our path. They want to live in our leaves, which provides cover or a hiding place from what happens in the human world. They receive food and grow and travel too, if it's needed. They live in the moist soil under us; a place, where any *being* that seeks a safe harbor from your world, can find shelter. We make it warm for those *beings* in weather like this.

We continue to live in the winter if we do not accept too many difficult jobs. We arrange it so those *beings* that live below us do not feel the bitter cold that covers this place in the winter season. Cozy and warm, they wait for the sun's rays to soften the Earth and to again welcome the food they need to keep them alive.

We are the color that you know as "green" and we are full of life. We continue to grow and do not stop like others in our world do. Parts of us disappear this is true, withering and dying but in doing this we give to *The Mother* what she needs to provide for everyone.

The plant that we are is a *collective,* a whole working together, always moving towards the release that will bring us to the divine. We became the plant you chose for many reasons. We sacrifice many of our *beings* to this need, always careful but always climbing towards the path we have chosen, the path that every *being* chooses. Being a type of plant that does not feel the weather we are never hurt. Not in a sense that we will always live, but because we are more likely than some to renew ourselves. In each season some plants are renewed and start over, but others like us do not grow at this time but remain still, telling everyone about the changes that are happening in this time of rest.

The creatures that guard our forest know how soft our leaves are and use us for their beds because many *beings* are like you and must rest. While some sleep, others must stay awake and watch, but even these must also sleep and be renewed again. Just as you seek peace at the end of the day, so do those of us that live near you in your world. We, the *Spirits of Nature*, are in the trees, alone in the water, alive in the bushes and plants; always near in caves, vales and glens and above in the Ancient high holy hills. Each giving to everyone what they need.

As we travel we provide the energy to go on. As a link to the other world, we are a cable or relay point to carry information to different points. We may seem slow in the eyes of man, nevertheless, underneath our roots reach out to intertwine with those of others *beings* that also look for the system known as the <u>mantle of knowledge</u>. In this way, everything is passed along and like your telephone lines; information comes from every corner of the realm.

A great example of this <u>mantle of knowledge</u> suddenly made itself abundantly clear. I had been thinking about visiting this great old tree across the road after I finished this reading. I had passed it several times on my walks and it seemed to call out to me. Knowing I should do this but seeing the cold snow outside and also thinking about dragging my computer out in that snow and setting up shop under the tree, didn't seem that appealing just now. Of course, I should have known that I can talk to a tree or plant or whatever without being in its present. I somehow just feel more connected if I am right there with whatever it is I need to talk with.

I guess the Ivy picked up on this and felt I didn't need to go out to find out about the tree and so made the decision for me. Sometimes this is exactly what I need, especially when it's snowing.

Do you need to know about that tree in the place you have just visited? "Yes, please".

We will ask and it will be given to you. Not in a way that you can see, but in the way that *The Ancients* did it, the old way. A way of going beyond timeless space into channels of energy that run from one point to the next; giving to everyone in these channels the knowledge of what is good and bad in our world.

When one tree dies or is destroyed in an area, another one must take its place. The word is sent out and a team of *Nature Spirits* is formed to start this job. They are given the acorns or seeds needed to restore the area by replacing the *being* (in this case the tree that has died) that is no longer there. The tree that has died, whether it was from disease or in another way, such as neglect from either human or *Nature*, may in this way help others.

We do accept that everything that we want may not always be what is best for the whole. Stopping a disease in the heart of a tree, and so causing its death, may not be what we would like, but spreading this disease to others that could also die would not help in our world. So the passing of the tree, its death, will stop others from experiencing the same fate. All things change and an area that was once fertile may become an area of drought and so must adapt to these changes.

As we look after this fallen tree, others remove what is left of this *being* and once again the rebirth of a new *being* begins in this place. But even though the tree has lived and has died and been removed, the essence or the soul of the tree lives on and remains like before.

"I didn't realize that". Yes, this is true.

Think about how you feel in those ancient places where nothing green grows now?

(I thought about the caverns in Arizona.[38] "I know what you are saying. I could still hear the voices of the Nature Spirits and they seem just as real as those that live above the Earth. Do the same ones that lived before, still live here now?") Yes, the essence, the soul of the place still lives inside it. You still have the feeling of what it was like before. Like in the cavern, the soul of the place is always ready to warm and soothe you as you travel ahead, giving you this feeling that comes from these places that are no longer green but are still bringing this vibration to you. Even though you can no longer see these *beings*, they are there.

Choices are different in our world. This *being* you know as a tree can live again. He can choose to accept this new beginning (as a tree) or not. If he accepts it, he must also accept the years of growing before he becomes, once again, a guardian of the forest.

In every beginning a *Newling* (a new plant, tree, flower, etc.) is given certain jobs which in the beginning are very easy. They must adapt, which may be very hard, if they want to reach the rank of a *super structure* inside their *zone* or the area in which they live. In accepting this job to start at the beginning, like it had done before, the *Nature Spirit* learns what was not accomplished in its last lifetime. This is done before giving it the Ancient Secrets it had learned and remembered from its jobs long ago. In working with this new opportunity, quest, or job, it accepts the risks and the joys that come with this new beginning. Acceptance is choice and with this comes growth. Some may look for the quietness of a tree as their new beginning, because being in a *collective* like we are brings constant meetings with other *beings*. Other *beings* may ask for the position that the tree had before, but the choice is first given to the one's soul, that lived as the tree before. Many choices are given to each *being* so they can move along in the ranks of

---

38 See passage "Kartchner Caverns".

the chain of consciousness. They may begin again as a *lighter*, or as a plant that grows along a river or gorge. Some look to the highlands, vast, with no humans nearby. Many look for beauty and become a flower or give themselves "to service" as a tree or a plant that bears fruit for everyone. They make their choices and do what they have chosen to help everyone.

As a collective, which you should understand by now, we work together to provide what is needed but still each one of us is a separate *being*. We work best with others that live in our world, because we travel. We look for vines and trees that will support this idea and so we co-mingle with them. We feel that we are needed because of what we accomplish both above and below the ground. Collectively we are given choices; directions, heights, varieties, changes and how we live in different climates. We again start over in different seasons, providing things different than what we give; such as the vine that blooms in the spring, sometimes bringing flowers that will provide food to all those that live with us on this planet.

As the insects fly about, they collect nutrients and pollen and carry them to other parts of their world. With this, procreation begins again. Others provide food to ones like you and to animals, and insects too. They even provide it to those that live deep within the Earth, starting again when the snow has gone. Many of the creatures that you can not see, gather what is needed, and give it to those that need what we provide. Plants like us provide many things, as we said before. We offer these and telecommunication. This is what we do.

Are you also looking for other plants with different purposes and growth patterns? "Yes".

We offer you these suggestions… Go to the Sea and look for those that live under the waves. Why? Because unlike us, they live in a world that man has seldom seen. They have so much information about times and places that have been forgotten about in your world.

In conclusion; live now to be more than you were before and understand that like you, we look for new lives and new experiences. We, the *Elemental Kingdom*, live as part of the whole or by ourselves, within the Earth or not; above the Sea or below; on the hills or beneath them in caves and caverns and in cities destroyed long ago in days you can't remember.

We are *Nature*, and we, like you, will continue. We grow and bloom. We listen and we move along, each believing in what they do and knowing they will begin again and again. Each giving to everyone what they can to keep this place you call *Earth* alive.

Just remember that whatever you do to us, you do to yourselves. Come together in this belief. Accept what we give you. Every *being* does what they must to continue to live. We do the same. Accepting and knowing this in our world is important to our existence. We know that what we will be can never stop what we are or what we can be because all of life exists in harmony with the *Great Spirit* that guides us all. Remember this. Be free with this knowledge. Know that we exist and respect us for what we do. We remain, the Friends of Nature.

We are The Green Ivy that surrounds the Great Pine.

I got a wonderful reading from the Ivy but not the old tree. Still, it had in part to do with the life, death, and rebirth of a tree, which was very interesting as usual. It makes me wonder if this tree was ready to pass on. I certainly hope not. It is a very handsome old guy. Hopefully the next time I am here I can actually talk with the old tree. Since the reading said that the essence of the tree remained even when it was gone, I guess I will always be able to hear it even if it is no longer physically there. I find this rather comforting, really. Unfortunately I think I won't be back before I finish this book. But then again, you never know.

The "Sandstorm" Desert

New Mexico—Wednesday, April 02, 2003

When I first started getting readings, it was from the Stones. Not only the Standing Stones, but even the small rocks that lay in the road, always ready to pounce on me until I noticed them.[39] This was alright with me because I loved channeling the Stones, any stones. Their information was incredible; more detailed than anything I could ever imagine.

When I was asked to write this book I decided to write about the Elemental Kingdom of the plants and not the Stones. I know they are connected but they are so different from each other in their purposes for existence.

I would call the Stones, the recorders of our Earth's history, or keepers of every thing that happened in the past, is happening in the present and even what will happen in the future. This by no means is simple and the language and terms used are so complicated and unfamiliar to me that the idea of trying to revise these passages seemed impossible.

Still, when it came to sand, those tiny little specks of stones, it seemed different than channeling a big rock, or an imposing giant Standing Stone in a circle somewhere.

I've come to find out it is still very complicated but I don't care. I still want to include it so you can get a "feel" for what this Elemental Mineral Kingdom does and its purpose for existence.

I would love to add the volcano in Hawaii but that would really be a stretch. Instead I got a reading from plants that grew there. I did however relent and put in a reading from the underground caves in Arizona.[40] This is amazing and the personality of that place was definitely made known to me. Maybe someday it will be time to share these other readings by the Stones with you but for now the sand will just have to do.

I hope you can get the general idea of what the sand has to tell you and the secrets it holds. I can assure you that you will never look at the beach in the same way and when you see the desert, it will be in a completely different light.

The "Sandstorm" Desert of New Mexico

Old are we, breathless in the mastery of all things. Awakened once more to the mindless wonderment of lives among those that seek us here. We exist through countless times, unaware of the reluctancy of all things unrelevent to what we desire.

As acts join upon us and acts search through us, all things exist through things unchanged. Countless ages of times, unrelated but ever changing, through years and eons unrelated to what was before.

Seeking us out brings us closer and with this the knowledge that happens to be discovered in this realm, becomes the knowledge attained through years and definitions of losses and changes encompassed upon this reality.

---

39 See the introduction to "The Web" for the entire story.
40 See "Kartchner Caverns".

Changing now into what you desire, thus we speak, collective as before, yet in this you seek out causes and changes and with the existences of challenges … challenges and knowledge imparted to you. Yes we, the collective, dwell within the desert; a world unlike that experienced by many, though many dwell within this plane and exist as through countless times, keepers of this knowledge. We know that existences come in each realm as experiences and thus in accepting this, a token shall be given.

Ceasing to draw upon these shall cause to all that venture into these realms, as the mask that is imparted to those that dwell not within this framework of time. Acceptance of all things ceases to be of interest to those that see only what they have placed before them. But in each, things are offered and if accepted, become reality.

We know that to seek out those that dwell within this place is not chosen, for this place remains to many a place of desolation. Thus seeking those that remain does not confer with us in our reality.

Conferences between worlds exist and Spirits are thus, that which conjure up dreams of days past and the wakefulness of these realities provide a vivid recollection of what was.

As each, in their own time, becomes aquatinted with each growth cycle upon this plane, know that we have become what we were before this time; as recollections of times past and the acceptance of what we were and have become. Thus the reality of all and experiences that exist for each can and will change.

The face you see upon this stone is but a reflection of what you desire, for all things are as presented. This being, which the mind of man captures, is what it desires and the transference becomes the reality. Thus in accepting that we are "alive", know that what you seek can be accomplished. Each here has, as stated among others in different areas in this time frame, a position enabling them to attain the perfection, which is sought in this existence. But this being so, the worlds that collide do not interfere with others along side them. For each in their own space and time, exhibit certain areas and tasks are undertaken.

As your world exists to be as you have envisioned, so must we also attain what we must to attain ours. You seek out answers to what we "do", as if this act would circumvent any less what we have stood for or have developed over countless millennium on this planet. Each here seeks out what it must to attain the level to grow within this timeframe, which is unrelative to that which you seek in your world.

As the sand shifts, as related to many, so do years or lifetimes, each grain playing an integral part of the whole. As each acts as a buffer for the great plane, know that each act, no matter how small, reacts and this causes a flow that erupts into what was not before. What you call this we desire to understand… "the ripple effect", yet to ripple is not what we attain, only the growth that change inhabits and to this we all succumb. Know that existences on this plane and in this time are relative. As each season turns within its path into another, things here seldom change. For as the Nature Spirits that attain perfection from the coupling of species unknown to us, we remain as before stagnant; but not, for we are ever changing. For as we shift and turn we relate, not to the touch of this wind that blows steadily over these plains, but to the tolerance given to remaining. To sustain all that is true and relevant to this place.

As old as you may think you (your race) are, there is no truth to what we have become. For we are older by far and the tasks that we have undertaken shall rank us among those existing longest upon this planet.

As you seek out <u>Our Truth</u>, know that with this comes knowledge of the Old Ones and of the Creator that envisioned all that is below and above and in all beings, even yourselves. For each has a job, but more a purpose, for what they have accepted as their task and to this I give credence to this knowledge.

I am Sameyual, (Same as you all), known to some as the Spirit of this Place. As the rock you see me, as a face unadorned yet seen only by those that seek us out.

I/we exist in this time and place and tell you what and when things are chosen to encompass all things in this place. As each of you has chosen your path, we have so also and in this we strive to attend to this task fully.

Stones are mounted to view all that flow below and those below are mounted to see that which rise above. As each creature soars above or crawls below, this is transmitted and resonates through the Earth to sources unseen. As ones that live below and ones that live above, all strive to know and understand what this relationship has to do with each and in this the truth must be spoken.

Once when this plane was new, a soul once traveled from one place to another by ways unseen, for only through these means could he convey what was needed to understand what he must. As things progressed and understanding ceased, these ways ceased and those of us that remained maintained this task. For as each fact is given to us, it is captured to begin again as a thought. As in the beginning all things are and shall ever be known through this understanding and thus in seeking all that was, shall it be relayed.

For ones such as we, The Great Keepers of the Sand, share with none what has transpired, but when needed or even desired and relayed to us, then this knowledge becomes fact. Though many seek out what and where things have begun and ended in this vast space, all things are easily forgotten. As the sand changes, thoughts are likely to become as they, lost in the ever changing drifts of time. Unrelevant now, but ever sought by those who wish to know what was before.

As keepers of these thoughts, these goals and all that came before, it is thought that we can relate these and all things for our one purpose. This is false, for the purposes of our world are divided and thus we are two-fold in our work, or purpose, upon this plane.

To exist within a world shattered by dreams of men long past and ages of dreams renewed can bring to many tasks unrelated to, but nonetheless relevant to the now.

For as all have come and gone before, all have incurred within their world, knowledge. Once attained, this shall lead them further towards tasks long forgotten.

As time changes, people such as you come and go, yet in your reluctance to attain truth you skirt all that would give to you the knowledge needed to attain that which you desire.

Thus in seeking what we know, the knowledge stored within these Stones of Time, the particles evaporate and blend again to attain truths and paths and knowledge forgotten many lifetimes hence and beyond.

Knowledge is given, when taken in truth and given in understanding of all beings. Knowledge is that ability to control that which he desires, and not that which he seeks. This is relevant in the fact that many that seek out the past do not accept the facts for truth, because their reality is only what appears to be sought in this world, visible in a mind unable to see beyond the past days or future lives.

We know that what you seek now is transference to all, the ability to give what we have delivered and to know what we "do" in this realm that exists within your world.

As you look out upon this plane and all planes that exist in all this world, know that the connection is thus and the Stones alone hold the truths to what was before. As warriors that have grasped all in the battle and stored it for the youth that has become reality, know that we too have stored what we should know, to extend all upon the paths they have chosen.

As each grain of sand holds a memory of one fact in each soul's existence, so does each Stone hold the clues to each path. As a book that exhibits a glossary in each section, so goes the purpose of many here. As each piece of Stone (sand) that lies beneath your feet and is born upon the wind carries words of past events, so do we store within our chasms the ability to write and relate all this knowledge.

As you think now, know that each event on this plane is carried over the waves that you seek. Each memory is engraved upon these specks (of sand) and thus if you decide to stray within a tunnel made of such specks (sand) and listen to the roar that is echoed, strange feeling will begin; ceasing only when the specks (sand) have ceased. For each tells a story and if one would listen then they would be filled with hope or despair, with anger or joy. If not, as most do not listen, then they are faced only with the destruction that is carried by each crystal, the sand that is carried by the wind upon their path.

Know now that the solace of the desert is never that in this fact, for to find a speck of sand is to find a path. Not of yours only, but of one who passed before or one so far ahead. As time does not stray within a chosen line, so does each life and in this time may overlap and with these experiences and events so are planted in these events.

Thus all the times and events and things taken are recorded within these hills, these Stone that remain within this realm.

You think now of other Stones, if they exist to relay also what knowledge was taken?

To this we say, all are and shall be connected, but thoughts like the grains of sand are relayed in this place and all places that attain this level but recorded among the hills of distant places unseen by many such as you. As the Akasic records record all thoughts of all people and of all times, we also record such. We record what we see and know upon this plane and none other. For we have chosen and thus remain the hills of knowledge, the sands of events and times and challenges. Of loves lost and lives changed. Of events planned and not. Of war and peace and doubt and mistrust. Of liaisons and dreams and realities seen and not. To enter this world is for some the entrance into the past; the truths given of days past and of events not yet known. To enter this world that awaits all that would "walk upon" the deeds of mankind. Only those that WOULD LISTEN CAN HEAR THESE VOICES. All are given this note and so we give to you this creed.

Go and seek out what you must, but know that if you desire to learn, look to the ones that lie not only beneath your feet but rise high in the sky.[41]

For we remain the recorders of all time. In this we relate. Give this message to all that will desire it.

We remain now and for all times the Event Planners of the Universe ... this one anyway.

THE "SANDSTORM" DESERT OF NEW MEXICO — REVISED

We are very old, but we are still in awe of how everything in this world is interconnected. We are awake again and amazed by the way those of you that look for us live your lives. We have lived throughout all time, not aware of things that have changed or of time and the things that are unimportant to what we want.

As events happen <u>on</u> us and also <u>in</u> us, we still remain unchanged; through countless ages of time, unconnected but always changing and throughout years unconnected to what it was like before.

Looking for us brings us closer to you and with this the knowledge we have in this realm...our world. Knowledge we have learned through all these years; the meanings of the losses and changes that have surrounded our reality.

We will change now into what you want and will speak together, like we did before.

Yet when we do, you must look for the causes and changes, and with them the challenges that exist, the challenges and knowledge we will give to you.

Yes, we as a <u>whole</u> (the sand) called a *collective* live inside the desert. Most people do not know this world, our world, though there are some that have lived through countless lifetimes and remember this knowledge We know that different lives are lived in each world as experiences. By accepting this, we will tell you a small amount of what we know. If you do not try to remember these past experiences from your different lives, then those of you that want to learn about our world will be unable to see or understand it.

Accepting that these things are real isn't important to you when you "only" see and believe in what is right in front of you, and no further. In each cause, you choose what you want to become your reality. Either you believe that what you see is all there is, or you believe there is "more" than what you see.

We know that some of you would not go to the desert to look for *Nature Spirits*.

Many of you feel that the desert is a place of desolation and loneliness and looking for those that are still here doesn't make it easy to talk with you in our reality.

Meetings between these worlds happens and *Spirits* or *Nature Spirits* are those that make up the dreams of days past. Waking up these realities provides a clearer picture or memory of what was before.

As each person in their own time becomes familiar with each growth period or cycle on this Earth, they will learn that we have become what we were before this time:

When you remember the past, you will accept that what <u>we were</u> and what <u>we have become</u> are the reality of everyone and the experiences that exist for each person or thing, can and will change in each lifetime.

(I am looking at "*The Stone*", the rock I am channeling and it looks like a face.)

The face you see on this stone is a reflection of what you want to see. Because all things are what you see them as. The mind of man captures what it wants and then he transfers this into his reality. So if you accept that we are "alive", then what you want to learn from us can be given to you.

Each *being* here, as many of the other readings have said before, has a position or job that will let them attain perfection; the perfection that we each look for in this existence. This being the case, the worlds that exist along side each other, such as ours and yours, do not interfere with each other. Each in their own space and time, are given certain areas and tasks to be done. As your world exists to be as you imagine it to be, we too must do what we need to do to make ours as we imagine it to be. You look for the answers to what we do. We could care less because what we have developed over countless lifetimes on this planet is what we have agreed to do. It is the job that we have accepted.

Each *being* here looks for what it must to reach the level to grow within its lifetime. This does not have anything to do to with what you look for in your world.

---

41 Here they mean: Don't only look down at the rocks under your feet but also look above to the great mountains (of rock) that "rise high in the sky". I also think it's a metaphor which means; there is more to life than what's right in front of you or in their case, there are more worlds than what you can see. That's for sure!

As the sands move, so do the years or lifetimes; each grain of sand, like each person, playing an important part of the whole. As each grain of sand acts as a buffer or a shield for the great plane called Earth, understand that each act, no matter how small, reacts. This causes a flow that erupts into what wasn't there before. You might call this the "ripple effect" but a ripple is not what we get. We get only that growth that changes us all.

You must realize that all lives on this Earth and in this time are important.

When each season changes into another, things here seldom change. Just as the *Nature Spirits* receive from species that we don't know, what they need to once more restart the mating season, we stay as we were before, the same…but not, because all things are always changing. As we move and turn and learn, it is not the touch of the wind that steadily blows over these plains, these deserts, that moves us along, it is the strength to hold up to what is given to us to stay and to keep everything that is true and useful to and in this place.

As old as you think your race is, there is no way of explaining how old we are. We are older by far and the jobs that we have chosen to do make us among one of the oldest *entities (beings)* on this planet. As you search for <u>our truth</u>, understand that with this comes the knowledge of the *Old Ones* and of the *Creator* that sees everything that is below and above; all *beings*, even yourselves.

Each *being,* whether it is you or us, has a job but even more, a purpose that they have accepted as their job. This is the "*Universal Truth*".

Now channeling from the Stone:

I am *Sameyual*, (Same as you all), known to some as the *Spirit* of this place (the desert). As a rock you can see me clearly, yet only those that search for us can see us. I/We exist in this time and place to tell you what and when things are chosen to bring them together in this place. Just as each of you has chosen your path or the direction you will take in this lifetime, we too have chosen ours. In doing this, we each work to get our tasks done fully. Some Stones or rocks, are placed up high (such as mountains) to see everything that rises above them, while others are placed low (under the earth) to see everything that flows below them. As each creature flies above the rocks or crawls below them, this is transmitted and these vibrations or movements, are sent through the Earth to places we can not see. Each creature that lives above or below the Earth tries to learn and understand what their relationship has to do with each other *being* on this planet. This is what we believe and so we must give our truth to you.

Once when this Earth was new, a soul traveled from one place to another by ways you could not see. Only in this way could they give to others what was needed to understand what they should. As time moved on, this understanding ended and was forgotten and these ways of travel changed but those of us that remained, did not forget and continued to do our jobs in the old way. When each fact is given to us it is held, to start again as a thought. Like it was in the beginning, everything that was and will be, can be known by understanding this. If you search for anything that happened before, it is there waiting to be given to you in the form of a thought.

Beings like us called *The Great Keepers of the Sand*, do not share with anyone what has happened but if you want to know, or need to know, then this knowledge becomes a fact, or an idea in your mind. Many look for what and where things began and ended in this huge space, you call the desert, but things that they search for are easily forgotten. Just like the sand changes, these thoughts are likely to become like the sand, lost in the ever changing movements of time. Though this doesn't seem important now to many people, there are some who want to know what "was" before. As keepers of these thoughts, these goals and all that came before; it is these thoughts that can tell you these things, all things. This is our one purpose but not actually only one purpose. In our world we are divided in two and so have a dual purpose on this planet.

To live in a world, both destroyed by the dreams of men that lived long ago or in the ages when these dreams came true, can bring to all of us here jobs that do not make sense to you that live now. Still, they are important. Everything, every *being*, has lived and died before. They all have learned many things in their worlds. If they use this knowledge it will lead them to what it was like before, what jobs they should do and what things they have forgotten. As times change, people like you come and go. In your reluctance to find the <u>real</u> truths, you try to avoid any of this knowledge that will lead you to these truths. You avoid anything that will cause you to face what you have become, and why you have become what you are today.

In looking for what we know, the knowledge stored in these Stones of time, these problems are removed. The ideas come together once again to bring you these truths, the paths and the knowledge that you have forgotten over many lifetimes.

This knowledge is given to you, only when it is believed and is for the benefit and understanding of all *beings*. It is the ability for man to control what he wants, not what he looks for. This is important, because many people that look into the past, do not accept the facts of what has happened as true because what they see is only what they believe or have been told all their lives.

Seeing something, such as our world, is not possible because it is not what the world believes at this time. Because of this they are not able to see what has happened, really happened, before or what may happen in the future.

We know that what you want now is to tell everyone what we have said. Also what our job is in our world and how it affects the world in which you live.

As you look out over this desert or any other place on this Earth, understand that the connection between every thing and every *being* exists.

"*The Stones*" alone hold the knowledge of what happened before. Like the warriors that took everything in battle to keep for their young, we too have stored what we needed to know to move you ahead on your path in this lifetime and in all lifetimes to come. Each grain of sand holds a memory of one fact in each persons/souls many lifetimes, and each Stone holds the clue to the path that each soul must take.

Like a book that has a glossary or a plan for each section of the book, some of us here do the same thing. Each grain of sand that lies below your feet and is moved by the wind, carries information about things that happened before. We, the *Stones* store deep inside us, the ability to write and give you this knowledge. We are like a glossary and each grain of sand is a page in this book of knowledge.

As you think about this, you must realize that everything that happens on this planet is carried over the "waves" that you look for. (I think this means the "connection" between our world and that of the *Nature Spirit's* world.)

Each memory is written on these specks of sand. If you decide to stay awhile and become a part of our world and listen to the stories that are retold, strange feelings will begin. These will stop only when the sand has stopped telling its stories. Why? Because the answers we are all looking for are there. Each grain of sand tells a different story, holds a different memory. If you listen, you will be given these memories filled with hope or despair and with anger or joy. Like most people, if you do not listen then you are faced with only the destruction that is caused by the sand that is blown across your path. In other words, you are destined to repeat, over and over again, what you have done before.

Remember that the peace of the desert is never just this. In fact, to find a grain of sand is to find a path, not only your path, but also the paths of the ones that have lived before or the ones that will live in the future.

Time does not exist in a straight line, so each life and each time may overlap. Things are planned using these experiences and events. All these times, events and things that have or will happen are recorded in these hills and in these Stones that remain.

You think about other Stones[42] on this planet and wonder if they exist to give us the knowledge that they have? We answer by saying, "All things are connected", but thoughts, like the grains of sand, are answered in this place and all places that have reached this level. They are recorded among the hills of places far away, not seen by our race. Like the Akasic[43] Records record all thoughts of all people, of all times, we record the same, but in our case we record what we see and know on this plane, this Earth, and not any other.

We have chosen to be and remain, *The Hills of Knowledge.* The sands of events and times and challenges…of loves lost, and lives changed…of things planned and not planned… of war and peace and doubt and mistrust and of liaisons and dreams and realities, both seen and unseen. To enter this world is for some, the entrance into the past. The truth told about the days in the past and about events not yet known.

This world waits for anyone who wishes to "walk upon" the history of mankind; to walk upon the sand of knowledge. Only those that will listen can hear these voices. Everyone is given this information and so we give to you this pledge…

Go and look for what you must, but understand that if you want to learn, don't look only at what lies beneath your feet but also what rises high in the sky. Don't look at only your little world and where it is taking you, but also to the other worlds you can see or ones you can not. Look towards the stars as well as the Earth. All things are connected. We are the writers of all time. This is what we do. Give this message to anyone who would like to have it.

We remain, now and for all times,

"*The Event Planners of the Universe*" … This one anyway!

Don't you feel as if you have talked to beings that are so informed about our world that it is frightening? They know

---

42 I am thinking about the standing stones.

43 The Akasic Records is the book in which is recorded all the thoughts, events and things that have happened to every person in every lifetime and in every world.

everything about the history of this planet and about every *being* that has ever lived upon it. They are the librarians of our world and what they know is available to us all. This may not seem possible but I am convinced that if you believe it, it becomes reality. I know I would love to know about the past, not only my own past lives but the past of this world. I want to find out what we did right or even more what went wrong and how we can prevent this happening again in the future.

The idea that each grain of sand holds a memory or thought makes me realize just how many lives and the moments in each of them lie waiting for anyone who will listen. Remember the phrase "If these walls could speak"? Who would have ever thought that also meant the sand, the stones or the mountains. It makes you see the desert and the sea shore in a very different light!

All things are connected and believing this can bring the answers we are all looking for if only we will listen.

Kartchner Caverns

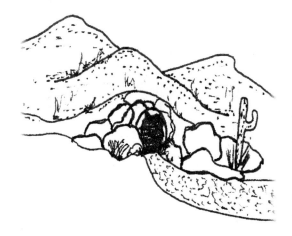

Benson, Arizona–Wednesday, April 23, 2003

WHEN I FIRST DECIDED WHAT to put in this book and what to leave out, I thought that I would only include passages from the plants, trees, flowers, bushes, etc and not include any readings from The Minerals (stones, volcanoes, mountains, gems, rocks, etc.) which is also a huge part of the Elemental Kingdom. I was wrong. Not only did I add water, sand and then a hill but here I am adding a cave. Actually it is much more than just a cave. It is a magnificent cavern found in Southern Arizona. The Kartchner Caverns, named after the people that own the land where they were found, is now a National Park. Lying about half an hour outside of Tombstone, Arizona, you can take a tour of this amazing cavern which lay undisturbed by humans for millions of years. The Park services people make sure that nothing or nobody will disturb this unbelievable sight and take the strictest precautions with everyone who enters these caves. I really can't blame them because many sacred sights have been destroyed by people who have no respect for the land. Even well meaning people taking just a bit of this or a chunk of that have destroyed many a mountain. It was because of this that I was unable to write down what the Nature Spirits were saying to me. As I have mentioned before, if I don't write down what The Elementals say, I mean right then and there, their words are gone. They evaporate instantly and I am left feeling horrible because I couldn't capture some great insight that was given to me at the time. So was the case with my visit to the caverns.

I actually didn't plan on doing a reading at all but once I was inside that matter was quickly disputed. Everywhere I turned I saw faces and heard words, different formations had things they wanted to say and by God or Goddess, they wanted me to hear them. This can be a problem when The Nature Spirits know you can hear them. They make themselves known and what was even worse was I could see so many of them. I would have given a year's pay to have a paper and pencil inside but that just wasn't allowed.

Of course the Elemental Kingdom does not understand "isn't allowed" and was very angry that I didn't write down what they had to say.

I tried to get permission from The Park but they just looked at me like I was some sort of "weirdo". I'm sure if I would have asked if I could bring a pencil and paper with me so I could write down what the Nature Spirits wanted to say before I went the first time, I would never have been allowed inside at all. Some people just don't have an open mind when it comes to Nature Spirits.

My only alternative was to try and channel outside by connecting with The Elementals inside. Getting as close as I could to the Caverns, without being hauled away by security, I sat down on a large rock and connected. I know that what I heard inside was a hundred times more relevant than what I received here but something is better than nothing, don't you think. They still were annoyed when I returned a second time and my only hope is that someday someone from the Park services will read this book and decide that I should be allowed to write down the wisdom that they offer to all of us that live above.

I promise not to touch anything.

THE PATH BENEATH THE HILL AT KARTCHNER CAVERNS

The wind blows and with each breath comes changes … changes that seek out form and the ability to become what was once forgotten. Journeying deep within this place you have seen what was taken before time began and with this comes the realities offered to those that would accept these gifts. Know that in these places that lie deep within this Earth also lie man's lessons. Lessons offered to many and accepted by those that seek out not for themselves but for all the benefits of this Earthy realm.

As you enter into this contract, know that what is pursued will be for all that dwell within your realm and what shall be given shall relate to all that desire to understand what this has become. Not only to the benefit of those that have viewed this with wanton lust but for those that would seek solace from the world above and accept the reality of what lies below.

Those beyond this hill have sought you out to speak, but in knowing that what you have given can not be accomplished by our talents from within, the permission to give this to all has been allowed. Not in this sight alone but in many places on this Earth plane. As you were given instructions for the benefit of all in the attempt to relay these instructions, note that what we shall relay shall be from within and this task shall partake of many hours of truth. Prepare to understand that the perception of what was attained can never be realized until the totalness of what was given can be understood.

As you entered into the great hall, not all were aware of the Deva or Solemn Entities that awaited those that arrived upon this place. Yet in seeking out these, you have connected and thus ensues this communication. In an attempt to clarify what it is that you seek you must first understand that what is needed is not always what you desire and acceptance of this must curtail all things. Though some may cease to begin, it is truth and that alone shall guide them in this quest. Know now that what lies ahead is what was left behind. For in the beginning all things began as before, ever continuing to evolve further toward goals unseen in this lightness you call today. As the earth was new so were the Great Ones that illuminated all places, but the ONE that guides us all, places these entities where and when they are needed and to this they attained what must be attained to survive.

As each of you grows in the knowledge that you attain in each lifetime, so does this great planet so evolve and with it comes many lessons and growths that are attained. Through countless ages, so grow all things and through these comes beauty and love and all things that are unseen but exist on levels not attained through your visions. As the Earth "became", as was stated, the ONE that you call what you shall, became annoyed with the mass that was useful but alas not attainable by those that would seek out the radiance of what was before. In each person so lies this radiance, but seldom is it seen, for below the surface much lies hidden. Thus the face that is extended does not always offer what is indeed within. Given these choices, this entity, this person, may become not what is seen below but what is layered on top. So also is this place.

In the beginning the GREAT ONES succeeded in defying all things and searching for their truth, they set out a plan to include all that was above and below the surface in this time. In assuming that many would come and remove these gifts, they chose to hide these gifts below. This being the matter of choice, the surface became as they desired; barren and without the means to assist any in the interest of being. Thus the Gods and such, kept within their places these jewels hidden but ever near. All came and believed and knew, but this gift was given only when understood and enjoyed by those that could relate to those truths.

You seek now what you have asked and this can only be given by those that remain.

As the story unfolds, know that what they give is their truth and with this the truth of countless ages and times changed. The entities exist still, this is truth, but their tasks become lessened. As he, God, and the beings that were fade into the reality of past times, the glory that eluded those that did not see became legend; thus in many places this is what is known as truths spoken in trust, but the reality of this is not that it is truth per se but the truth that was … so long ago.

As you seek out those entities that existed before, know that the trust that they impart shall be yours to share, but the truth that they exist still shall only become reality if accepted by those that know within their beings their path and the truth that becomes reality. You have chosen to answer this call and all can and shall be given. We as the Elders of this place know that those that dwell, as you have seen, wish to answer what you ask, but can no longer speak for their path and yours cross only on contact of being. Thus in truth, to become more with them, you must become less with those above. Contemplating this we know that limitations are given in this path and yet we shall strive to give to you what we must, to attain what you shall from below. Yes, you can begin later in another realm but as of now we shall relate some to begin with.

As their age of reason began some billions of your years ago, The Ancients, not unlike those that you know, began their existence on this plane. They lived as you and thus sought out paths to the greatness of all things. The beauty that erupted at that time was immense for no restrictions were given. Those that chose to become what they remain, became as such and others remain now what they have become for lack of conviction. Thus in saying this we offer you this truth: "All are given their path in what ever means they accept". But in changes and eons of reality, some claim not what they desire but only what they accept as what they must become, to be what they must. Thus in accepting this, they remain for millions of years as entities that seek out only what they must to attain this inner trust. For trust, be it of each person to another or each creature to another; be it mineral, animal or the dust that flows through the wind, each seeks out what they shall, to be as they desire. In this earth shaped cavern, the center of this world, it becomes to some that rely on their existence the center of such and with this comes the acceptance of what they are given to attain.

What is this you ask? What can be attained from becoming a formation of immense girth or a drip that becomes a small pool, ever stagnant in a world unseen by all? Alas, why do you solve your problems by becoming what you feel you must, when in reality you are never what you desire, but only a reflection of what you must be to attain what is expected in this lifetime?

So, some accept this as truth, while others strive to become more. Yet in this world, the systems change and all are as they have been for countless eons; ever ready to exist or not but each in their own individuality a component within this place, dependent on one to another to maintain this void within this hill upon this planet. Thus it is so and more shall be given if understood and taken in the cumulative.

Come again and understand the path that lies ahead. We release you of this task now but later you must begin again to understand the reasons for each existence and why they do what must be attained to continue ever onward. As a stone that turns to dust, all things cease but in reality all things continue. For all change and with this comes advantages and with these paths unseen. Thus it is so, and thus it remains. So it shall end until later.

We remain, The Path beneath the Hill

THE PATH BENEATH THE HILL AT KARTCHNER CAVERNS — REVISED

The wind blows and with each breath things change; not only changing in shape but also becoming again what was once forgotten. Traveling deep inside this place you have seen what it was like before your time began. We offer to each of you that will accept it, our world and the world in which we live.

Know that in these caverns that lie deep inside this earth, also lie lessons for you. Lessons offered to many of you but accepted only by those that search for what will benefit the whole world and not just themselves.

As you write what we say, understand that what you are looking for should be given to everyone that lives in your world. What we give you now is for anyone that wants to know about what we have become. Not just those that would use what they see for material gain but for those that search for rest and reflection from the world above and accept us and our world below. Those inside the earth have waited to talk to you but knowing that you are not allowed to bring anything inside, the *beings* below gave us permission to give this to you, not only here but in many other places on earth. As you are given instructions on how to give this information to everyone, understand that what you write will come from inside the cavern and will take many hours … many hours of what is their truth. Try to understand that what you believe to be true can never really be realized until everything that we say can be understood (by people that read this).

As you came into the main cavern (the Great Hall), not everyone saw or felt the presence of the *Deva* (of the Cavern) or the quiet *beings* that waited for those that entered our world. Yet because you came "looking" for these *beings*, you were connected and the messages will continue.

In trying to make clear what you are looking for, you must first understand that what is needed is not always what you want and accepting this must come before anything else. Though some may not begin to understand, it is only the truth and this alone will guide them to what they are looking for. Realize that what lies ahead is what was left behind. In the beginning everything started as it had before, continuing to evolve forward toward goals you have never seen in this "outside world of light" you call today. When the Earth was new so were the *Great Ones* that radiated light to every place, but the *ONE* (some say *God* or *Allah*) that guides us all, placed these *beings* where and when they were needed. Here they did what they had to do to survive.

As each of you grows through what you learn in each lifetime, so does this great planet Earth, also evolve. With this evolution comes the growth and the many lessons that are learned. Through countless ages all things grew. With these came beauty and love and all things that aren't seen but still exist on levels you cannot see.

When the Earth began, the *ONE* (that you call whatever you believe) was upset by this useful space inside (the Earth). Though it existed it was unattainable by those who looked only for the light that existed before. In each person there lies this light but it is seldom seen because below the surface many things lay hidden. So it is that the face you see on the outside may not always be what is inside. Given these choices, this entity or this person may not be what you see below but what is "layered" on top or seen on the outside. So it is in this place.

In the beginning the *GREAT ONES* were successful in defying everything. Searching for what they believed in, they made a plan which included all that lived above and below the surface at that time. In assuming that many would come and remove these gifts, they chose to hide these below. Having decided this, the surface above became barren, with nothing to support anything that might want to live there. So it was that *The Gods* kept inside these places, these jewels; hidden but still very near.

Everyone came and believed and knew, but this gift was given only when it was understood and enjoyed only by those that could relate to these truths.

You come now looking for what you have asked and this can only be given to you by those that remain. As the story unfolds, understand that what they tell you is their truth and with this, countless ages and times have changed. It is true, these *entities,* these *beings* still exist but what they do is much less than before. As *He, God* and the *beings* that existed then faded into the past, the glory that eluded those that didn't understand became legend. So it is that in many places this is what is known as "truths spoken in trust" but the reality of this is not that it is the truth, as you would say, but the truth that was so, long ago. As you look for these *entities* that existed before, understand that the trust that they give you will be yours to share. Still, the truth and the belief that still exist will only become reality if this is accepted by those that know this within their being … their soul. Then this truth will become their reality. You have chosen to answer this call and everything can and will be given to you.

We are the *Elders* of this place. Understand those that live in the cavern, as you have seen, wish to answer what you ask, but they can no longer speak because their path and yours cross only when you can be in contact with each *being.* To get more information from those below you must go below and not rely on those above.

Thinking about this, we know that certain limits are given to you on this path you have chosen (to speak to entities that live in the cavern) and yet we will try to give you what we can from below.

(Q: Can I speak to them at another place in the Earth?)

Yes, you can begin later in another world but as for now we will tell you some things to begin. As their "Age Of Reason" began some billions of years ago, *The Ancients* (not much different than the ones that you know[44]) began their existence, their life on this earthy plane. They lived like you and looked for ways to see the greatness in everything. The beauty that existed in that time was abundant because there were no limitations given to them. Those that chose to become what they still are became what they asked for and others remain what they have become because they could or would not decide.

In saying this we tell you what we know to be true, everyone is given their path, by whatever means they need to accept it. Everyone is given a choice of what they will do. The acceptance is up to them whether they do it or not.

But in chances and eons of reality, some don't ask for what they want, but instead just accept what they have become, to be what they have to be. In accepting this they remain for millions of years as *beings, entities* that look for only what they must to get this inner trust. Trust, whether it is between one person and another or each creature to another…whether it is mineral, animal or the dust that floats in the wind, each being searches for what they can, to be what they want to be.

In this earth shaped cavern, the center of the world, it is to those that depend on this place for their existence, the center of their world and in this world they accept what they are given to do. What is this you ask? What purpose is there in becoming a huge formation or a drip that becomes a small pool, always stagnant in this world not seen by everyone? Well, why do you solve your problems by becoming what you feel you have to be, when in reality you are never what you want to be but just a reflection of what you must be to get what is "expected" in this lifetime? So, some accept this as true while others try to become more. Yet in this world, the systems change and are the same as they have been for countless eons, always ready to exist or not but each their own individual, a needed part within this place; dependent on one another to take care of this cavern on Earth. So it is. More will be given for you to add later. Come again and understand the path that lies ahead.

We will let you go now but later you must start again to understand the reason for our existence and why they do what they do to move forward. Like the stone that turns to dust, all things die but in reality all things continue. All things change and in these changes come advantages and with these the paths never seen. So it is and so it will remain. We will now go until later.

We remain, The Path Beneath the Hill

Like I said, I did not get as much as I would have liked. I know that the portal has been opened for me above ground to their Kingdom below. They have even opened it for me to other places on the Earth. I really appreciate this and would love to return and write down all the knowledge that they have learned throughout the lifetime of our planet. Then again, this is a book about the jobs of the Nature Spirits of the Plant Kingdom, so to delve into this world would lead me towards another path which would take me a very long time to "walk".

---

44 I have channeled a group called The Ancients for many years. They seem to be of a Celtic origin and give advice on your spiritual path and other esoteric subjects.

For now this reading is enough. I know I will return and I also know that this information will be given to me and I will write down every word. Even if no one else ever reads it, I will, and that is reason enough for me to return. The connection with this world and ours has made a bridge and I have been asked to cross it. Right now I am on another path but when this is complete, I plan on crossing that bridge when I come to it … again.

The Cottonwood in the Wash

Tucson, Arizona – Thursday, April 24, 2003

ALRIGHT, SO I TRIED TO channel by the pool and it didn't work out. The pool, especially one filled with kids, is definitely not the place to get in touch with Nature Spirits.

Leaving the pool area, I moved down near the wash where a Road Runner, which I named "Roader", seems to have taken a liking to me and moves closer. Maybe I can hear what he says? Let's see. Well, maybe not! He seems to be curious but moves away if I move closer. A nice try though. "Doctor Doolittle", I am not.

I look out over the hills and the wash below, which contains mostly Cottonwood trees. It is dry or so it seems, but I was told yesterday by a knowledgeable park ranger that if things were green then there was water about 18 inches below. They are green.

A butterfly just flew past, sent by the Nature Spirits to check on me? I wouldn't doubt it, as they have sent many different things; spiders, bugs, ants, and insects to visit my computer and check out what I was writing. The wind has arisen a bit. I think because I was hot, the tree above my bench seems to have spread its branches so I'm not sitting as much in the sun now. I close my eyes and thank them both for this gesture. They welcome me and ask for my help with many matters. The birds seem to be having a squawking match, in the next tree down the path. You can hear traffic, but that can be ignored.

The Road Runner is still checking me out but The Cottonwood is the one that wants to speak to me.

THE COTTONWOOD IN THE WASH OUTSIDE TUCSON, ARIZONA

We await alone in this place, but never alone, for all things are taken in turn and thus we stand as one. We are, of course, not among those that dwell within the desert that you seek, but we attain this status, because we live among those that surround this place.

As you know, all plants are needed in some form, to help all to attain what must be accomplished on this plane. As you also have attained, we are different in the fact that we dwell where the water is simplified and the lack of this justifies our task.

As you attain knowledge, know that what we seek to bring to you is a system that differs from ones that exist in places full of air surrounded in part by moisture that relates to growth patterns of plenty. As we survive in times of need, we induce what is given and increase production of essentials which balance out the need for those that dwell along our rim.[45] *For many here desire*

---

45 They are in a dry bed of a stream which in the Western United States is referred to as a "wash".

needs, which in times of drought are not provided.

The subsistence of these types depends not only on the survival of what lies ahead in this realm and the world they have accepted, but in the tasks that we have accepted to belong to our realm. Many elements are given in many ways and with them come responsibilities that demand attention on those that dwell within these places. We, in accepting these tasks, know that what we must attain is not the influence of changes on these creatures but the skill in evolution given to each within our means. As each person, plant or thing on this plane needs nourishment to survive, so must we in our realm, provide what is needed to each that desire it. Thus in choosing which we have undertaken as our task, we shall provide this to those that seek this and all things that are needed in this place.

In our world, the need to survive is countered with the need to perform survives to this end and thus we have been given certain qualities that deal with these changes that occur in this and other places farther reached within our framework. As the soil becomes less for those that seek our help, the moisture that has retained within our bodies, gives to those that seek it out, the means to continue. This is indeed a trick which I know you do not realize but it is indeed necessary in this part of your existence. Places such as these retain this task and give this meaning to their existence. We lie within the Earth through systems that relate this path to those that seek out what they need, when and where it is needed. As the needs become greatest, the pathways are opened and sensed through the acceptance of those that understand where and what is needed to survive.

As "Retainers", we also provide all nutrients given over to us by what lies below. Others that dwell below, carry these things into our being thus admitting the flow with energy given to those that desire to attain it in their existence. You know that many here see this place as desolate and yet we are not as such, for below much becomes of beauty to those that seek out what is needed to become one with all above.

As you have seen and were given a path in which to travel on this Earth plane, so were we and in traveling it, we attain as you, the truths that we know and have learned over the years spent in this time and place. As each of us become one with the Earth, we take in what we need and relay it to those that live below and in such, seek out knowledge to impart to those that dwell above.

As time travelers, we exist in all parts and worlds and have seen many changes come and go but the truth be this, we exist to be what we must; to serve when called on, but to also grow and nourish our existence with the knowledge taken from what we observe. As the birds that fly above see all that is below, we too observe what we can, as all beings in all places relate it to others. Thus in accepting this, we begin again what we must to attain that right to grow in the knowledge we have attained.

As the spring rains come, we nourish our bodies with this coolness, ever absorbing within our being, the knowledge given through this change. All of Nature provides assistance to all and thus what we receive through this shower brings not only healing from the winter before or the summers to come, but the knowledge exchanged through the presentation of this greeting. For every purpose in Nature is given to all and thus in this knowledge that is spread is also given.

(Shelby (Shall-bee) the fly came to check out the computer...knowledge spread, I take it.)

You comprehend what we are saying and thus to speak in words that are understood, is equal to what we desire.

Q: So the rain gives you knowledge, as does the wind and other parts of Nature. You in turn, spread it below and likewise, below gives you information and you attain it as such?

In question, we relate that this is, by in large, what is attained, but many things are not received when needed. For many changes take place that desist us from certain knowledge. If faults in the systems are disrupted, then we attain not what is needed in these times. This is truth, but in our reality we adjust, as you, to change and the means are given to these changes and things continue.

Yes, weather adapters are relayed and thus we know in times of need, when and where to resist the flow or not, for which animals or guides or entities that feed off our knowledge, our abilities or resources. Many changes have occurred in this state of being, for changes that existed to us as hardships have become easily overcome by the advent of structure that kinder to the flow of nourishment to our being. Thus those that seek out our needs know now that the likelihood of attaining these is likely more here than in the hills above. Thus in incurring this civilization as stated, we have attained a status of growth, but freedom is unrelated and we remain captured in this position. For some this remains fine, for others this does not. Yet it is as it shall be, and acceptance is no harder. For we have and shall be what we have begun, until we choose to release all to return again. We speak now collectively as before, but in truth if you seek out one that exists alone, his tasks shall be related to you also, though his truth shall be the same, but you should find this out in your ability to differentiate between the two.

As you look out among the hills that form this basin, know that the knowledge attained within these places is never attained through sheer reluctance of being, but only through the knowledge that what you desire, is indeed what is truth. For the hills shall speak, but each apart is a total to the sum, and all relate to Nature as one. As the race of mankind is in part one, we too are so individual in training but still in fact one among our being.

As the spark that lights each creature that exists, flames true in his search for truth so burns our truth and our search is one of knowledge; the knowledge of forgiveness and of balance in this world torn apart, one from another. For before we existed as now but now we exist as here and this is change. Not unlike you and the changes you make in your world. Before you existed in places unclear to us, but now you are here and we see and we relate and ask that you begin to know these facts. You unite in front to attain lands to save those of use endangered and to this we relate to you the same. For we too unite to save you also. For without our guidance and what we provide, you would perish from this place forever. Changes are good in ways for all beings and adjustments must become truly related, but survival must be attained in all things and the destruction and rebuilding of all beings, begins and ends in the knowledge spread through these existences.

As the birds sing above and the entities unseen move below, know that each represent what is needed to those that dwell within both worlds. For each exists to become one… though separate they are united. For this place called Earth exists to become one with all beings and in this, things become reality when accepted by both.

As you entered the caverns,[46] unseen by you as stated, you were awed by the splendor that radiated from these places. The beings called to you and you sought out answers. Understanding became a question, for understood things that are related can not be assumed by ones that know not this world in which you dwell. They seek you out, but you admit that what you need can not be attained, for they (the National Park) give not permission for you above. This is unsettling for these entities, these Nature Spirits have taken their ability to communicate and offered to you what they know and with this you have given cause for pain. You relate what we know to be truth and this we give to our Carriers that live below and this shall be relayed to those that sought out you of late in hopes that the attempts to become knowledgeable allies still may be attained. We know that you desire to learn of this world, so unlike ones that you have seen, but this shall come in time. Now you must relay what we give and know that what we seek and give shall help all concerned.

We ask that you come again and we shall relay information of those that live below and the work that is attained through their leads. For each are given, as we, jobs, accomplishments as travelers, moving along lines unseen; as messengers given over to tasks attained in all lifetimes. Thus unseen, except by those that know, begin and end unseen but often belong to the world of legends long lost from times before.

Often this is relayed, for as spoken, times have changed and with this shall come knowledge lost.

Ah, you search for old civilizations also. The Nature that was theirs still exists in places unseen but will come soon times of unspoken recognition and the beauties amplified will be reassigned. You shall see what we desire and with this, shall come discoveries unlike those before. For to link what we are and what we have given to all that must see what this means is a gift that is presented.

We remain, Cottonwood in the Wash

COTTONWOOD IN THE WASH — REVISED

We wait here alone but we are not really alone because all things are where they should be when it is their time. So it is that we stand together as one. We are, of course, not one of the desert plants that you are looking for to write about but we are like them because we do live among those plants that surround this place.[47]

As you know, each plant is needed in some form or another to help us all get what we need to survive in this world. As you have found out, we are different in the fact that we live where there is not much water and because of this we have found our job purpose in this lifetime. As you learn more about us and begin to understand, we will tell you about our system here. It is different here than in other places that have plenty of the water needed for things to grow. When we must survive in the bad times, we provide and make more of the things needed to produce balance along the edge of the wash where we live. Many here need things that they cannot get when there is drought. The lives of these *beings* and the jobs that are part of depend not only on what lies ahead in this world and the world we have accepted, but in the jobs we have undertaken to belong to this world. Many essential parts are given in different ways and with them come responsibilities that must be dealt with for those that live in places like these. When we accepted these jobs we knew what was needed was not to influence the changes in these creatures, but to let each evolve the best way they could

---

46 See passage, "Kartchner Caverns".
47 I had intended to collect a reading from a cactus, a typical desert plant, but instead came away with this reading.

in their environment. Each person, plant, or thing in your world needs food to survive. The same can be said for ours and we must do what we can to provide this. In choosing this as our job, we will provide this to those that need it and to anything else here.

In our world, the need to survive and the need to make it happen, both rely on each other. We have been given certain qualities that can help with the changes taking place here and also in those farther to reach areas where we work. As the soil becomes dryer, those that need it to survive are given the water that we store in our bodies. This is something we know you don't realize but it is a very necessary part of your existence. Places such as the one here do this as their life purpose. We lay in the *Earth* through systems that show this pathway to those, when and where they need it. When the need becomes great these pathways are opened and sensed by those that know where and what it is they must have to survive. As *Retainers* we also provide all the nutrients given to us from below. Others that live below carry these things to us, thus giving to those that want it, the flow of energy into their lives.

In our world below there is beauty for those that want to be a part of both worlds.

On your journey, you have become aware of the fact that you were given your path to travel. So were we and in traveling it we also learned the things that we know now and have learned over all the years spent in this time and place. Each of us becomes a part of the Earth and takes in what we need. We send it to those that live below and in doing so look for information to give to those that live above.

As time travelers we live everywhere and in every world and have seen many changes come and go but still the truth is, we live to become what we must and to serve when we are called on. Yet it is also to grow and nourish our existence with the knowledge we take from what we see.

Just like the birds that fly above can see everything below, we too look for what we can learn when every *being* in all those places above, speak to each other. In accepting this job we do what we have to, to earn the right to grow with this knowledge we have received.

When the spring rains come, our bodies are nourished with their coolness, always taking within ourselves what we learned through this change. All of *Nature* provides help to everyone and so what we receive from these showers brings not only healing from the winters before or the summers to come, but also the knowledge we exchange through these waters. Every purpose in *Nature* is given to everyone and it is given to us in this knowledge which is spread through this rain.

(Shelby (Shall-be) the fly comes to check out the computer...knowledge spread, I take it.)

Q: You understand what we are saying and so you want us to speak so that everyone else can also understand?

They obviously do not agree and continue in their normal way. I now want to try and make clear what they were talking about and so asked them this question...

"So the rain gives you knowledge, just like the wind and the other parts of Nature, right? You in turn, spread it below and likewise below gives you information and you get it as such?"

A: (as best as I can translate) In the most part this is what we get but at times we don't receive a lot of things when they are really needed. Many changes can take place that keep us from getting this information. If faults in the system are stopped in some way then we don't get what we need. This is true, but in our reality we adjust for this, just as you would, and the problem is fixed and things continue. Yes, different weather changes are sent to us and so we know when we need to stop or not stop this flow and to which animals, guides, or *entities* that live off of our information, our abilities, and our resources. We have adapted to the changes here. Problems which were once hardships are now easily dealt with by the newly changed structures we have become. This makes it easier to bring us our nourishment. Those that need what we can give, now know that the likelihood of getting this is more than in the hills above. In gaining this "new system", we have reached a status of growth but have lost our freedom to move. For some this is alright, for others it isn't. Still, it is what it is and accepting it is no harder. We have and will be what we have started as until we decide to die and return again as something else. We are speaking now as a collective but truthfully if you look for one that lives alone, he will tell you the same thing, but you should be able to find this out when it is possible for you to tell the difference between the two.

Looking out on the hills that form the basin of this valley, realize that the knowledge one gets from these places is never received when one doesn't want to believe we exist, but only through the understanding that what one want from us and what one believes is indeed what is true. The hills will speak, but even though they are separate from each other they are still part of the whole picture. Everything relates to *Nature* and everything is one.

As the race of mankind is, in part, one, we are also individual in what we have chosen to do but still in fact we are only one part of who we are together.

Just like the spark that lights each creature that exists, burns true in its search for truth, so the flame of what we believe burns. Our search is one of knowledge; the knowledge of forgiveness and of balance in a world of people torn apart from each other. We existed before, as we do now but now we exist here with you, which is a change. This is not much different from you and the changes you have made in your world. Before you lived in places we did not know about. Now you are here and we see and we understand and ask that you start to understand these facts.

You unite in groups to acquire land to save those of us that are endangered. We understand this because we too also unite to save you. Without our guidance and what we provide, you would perish from this place forever. Changes are good in many ways for all beings and adjustments must really be understood.

Yet survival must be reached in everything and the destruction and rebuilding of all *beings* begins and ends through the information spread through these different ages in time. Just as the birds sing above and the *beings* you can not see move below, realize that each represents what is needed to those that live in both worlds, each exists to be one. Though they are separate they are united. This place called Earth exists for all *beings* and because of this those things become reality when they are accepted by both.

When you entered the Kartchner Caverns[48], which you had never seen before, you were overwhelmed by the splendor that radiated from these places. The *beings* called out to you and you searched for answers. Whether you understood or not became a question because these beings that do not know about the world that you live in can't just assume that you understand what they are telling you. They depended upon you to take their information but you admitted that what you hoped to learn from them was impossible because the park would not allow it. (The park would not allow me to bring any paper or pencils inside to write down the channeling from the cave.) This was upsetting for these *entities*. The *Nature Spirits* had taken their ability to communicate with you and offered to tell you what they know and you could not write it down. This caused them great pain because they did not understand the park's policy. We will tell them about the reason you could not write their stories and give this to our carriers that live below. They will relay this to those *Nature Spirits* that looked for you yesterday and hopefully the attempt to become informed friends may still be possible. We know you want to learn about this world, so different from the ones you have seen. This will come in time. Now you must write what we have told you and just know that what you are looking for and what you give will help everyone concerned. We ask that you come again and we will give you the information about those that live below and the work that they do throughout their lives. Just like us, each is given a job and things to accomplish, moving along unseen lines as messengers doing the jobs we must finish in each lifetime. Never seen, except by those that know, we begin and end unseen and often belong to that world of lost legends from the times before. Often these legends are told, as we have said. Times have changed and with these writings will come some information that was lost.

Ah, so you look for old civilizations too. The *Nature* that was theirs in the past still exists in places that you can not see. Soon the time will come when you will know without being told and this increased beauty will take you in a new direction.

You will see what you want to see and this will bring discoveries that you have not seen before.

That link between what we are and what we have given to you, the link that you have been looking for, is this gift that we give to you though this message.

We remain, *Cottonwood in the Wash*

It is amazing how the information system within the Earth is so connected. The way the *Plant Kingdom* connects with other parts of *Nature* such as the rain and the wind. Each element providing the information needed at just the right time to be beneficial to the *Nature Spirit* concerned. If we would follow this example in our lives and with others all over this planet what a difference it would make.

Nature lives in hidden places and these offer their own beauty and their own reasons to be. Just as each of us has our own path to follow, so does The Elemental World. We are all connected and so each of us must do what is needed to make this world a better place for all beings, no matter who or what they are. Easy to say, but can we do it?

---

48 See "Kartchner Caverns".

Ancient Places by the Sea

Crystal Bay, California – Monday, May 26, 2003

THERE IS THIS PLACE BY the Sea near where I live called Crystal Bay State Park. It lies along the Southern California coast and the cliffs overlook the sea. To reach the beach and the Sea below you must climb down a steep path that winds its way from above. When the tide is out and in the winter time, the rock formations that appear are amazing. They remind me of the ruins of a great ancient temple that might have fallen into the Sea in some mysterious age long ago.

When I first visited this place I had nothing to write with. This drove me crazy because the Stones, these great rock formations, were calling out to me, asking me to listen to them. I was in my "Stone Period" and so wasn't even thinking of channeling the sea. I was only concerned with these amazing formations and the history behind them. Knowing I had to return but finding that this was easier said then done, it was finally summertime before I managed to return. When I did I was amazed and very disappointed that those great stone temples, that by this time had grown in my mind to be the Lost City of Atlantis, had disappeared. Where they had once been, now only the beach remained but scattered here and there with a few lone rocks rising up through the sand.

Since I must admit I had never been attracted to the sea, I felt at a loss as to what I should do. Of course, this was easily remedied by our friends the Nature Spirits of the Sea. I was asked to take a seat on the nearest rock and listen to what they had to tell me. They said it was important and whether I liked the Sea or not really didn't matter; they were a big part of the Elemental World and they needed to be heard. This put me in my place, which of course wouldn't be the last time, and I began once again to listen and to write. This is what they said:

ANCIENT PLACES BY THE SEA

We are the spirits of this place and we exist as you. For none others know the existences that have wrought power upon lands such as these and with this comes our plight.

Existences change and so do all things in lifetimes ... coming ever forward to present times and yet in these the shadows grow ever slowly until they become darkness once more. For each in their own time and place exist to be what they shall and with each comes the knowledge given and taken ... often within ones own time and space. We dwell now as the <u>Charmed Ones</u> and so bring to you what was before.

Looking now over the Sea, know that all things shall be forever changed and conclusions given are often misspoken. For things known only to ones unknown to you, can truly understand what is, what was and what shall be.

Relevant to now and knowing that you exist to further knowledge we begin:

Days past brought to those that dwelled upon these shores, things unknown to you. Great birds flew and Nature was abundant, for it flourished unhampered by greed or the lack of challenge given in this age. The tides came as now and subsided but "eventuality" came and with these tides, the change. Challenges come to all peoples ... and in all times and thus was presented these. Asleep are we still but seldom do ones seek out knowledge to what was before. The Nature Spirits exist, that is our truth, Universal Truth, and so we shall impart what we have and shall recall from before. Devas as such, do rule these shores as before and their care is given to all beings. The Sea is alight with greatness, abounding with all that would serve the Great Lady of this place. She has given to many the ability to see beyond and this is now given to you. For challenges come in all ages and thus in yours shall they begin.

As we grew long ago, many different ones … unlike those that live above, became to understand what was needed to extend the life upon this plane. With this, duties also became relegated. Once as before, the notion of propagation began and we increased. Not as you, but through countless ages of growth and knowledge attained through the undercurrent of given truths. For each below, as above, perform certain joyous tasks that are accepted as goals for all beings. Each searches for their truth and in this, gain what they seek.

Many here appear as souls lost in the darkness. Many of you have seen them late at night or heard them call to one another through the darkness that covers the Sea. They appear as apparitions that desire to attain what they shall, but in fact, as just "mists of beings"… unable to apprehend what they desire. This task undertaken by these beings is truth, for each can and shall bring to those below what lies above.

As the turtle that escapes from the Sea and returns again, these too become as they, ever ready to explore the knowledge given to those that set upon our place… the Sea.

These beings, these spirits, are indeed true and thus those that have dealt with such should never be faulted but enjoyed for their truths shall bring about change to all that shall see. These fellows are but the culmination of souls lost to us, again regrouping for the benefit of all. Have you not accepted now that all should have choices? Be they of our world or the world that exists within your sight. Each are given what they accept and with this acceptance, the knowledge to change all that would surround them.

Moving forward, many here that rule below do so with knowledge gained through centuries, say countless ages of regrouping and knowledge attained through these ways. The Sea Goddesses rule, though this term suits not the connotation of our ways, but favors your ways. Alas they are in succession, not through timely rebirth, but through wills and ways and things undertaken for the betterment of all.

They exist below the surface but seldom arise for they lack substance on your plane and thus in doing so, would cause only a stir in the night sky.

(Note: A tiny crab like creature walked up to my computer, took a look and walked away.)

Did he scare you? Tis only our "watcher" as before. Do you not realize that all places have these and as he appears as a soul recognized by you, he is in fact … a Spirit of the Sea. He has again begun his search for the knowledge you have undertaken and shall impart this to those below.

We exist to believe that all things are possible and within our world this truth is so. For all things as the tide, ebb and flow and as She (the Earth), we too change within each day.

As the Sea Goddess gives tasks to many, others become less encumbered with tasks and so begin their climb to respite. Taken often in remote places far from those of your existence, they appear as shining lights in the sky. Often they dance in the heavens, for the distance from the Sea and the sky offers them changes needed to expand within their realm. Often they flicker and fall and are seen by some as bright glows in the sky. Often the colors of the night light up that same horizon and they dance through this joy known as <u>renewal</u>. All are given this opportunity and if taken, the joy abounds within each being and thus again they recapture their tasks to begin anew as before … or not. Transcending space and time in actuality is one feat given to all below and the options are immeasurable … but tasks remain and those below obey when asked to perform such challenges.

The Sea Goddesses are different in the respect to what you desire, for all of Nature is as perceived through the eyes of man and yet to all here, we remain apart from all the rest. As many have laid claim to seeing "beings" alight upon storms in the Sea amassed with transfixion of beauty, in truth to our world this is so, but to present this form to you would challenge your patience and so we change into the conception of what you desire. Do you not understand that all things are of beauty that exists in this and all worlds but each sees them differently, and so amassing this truth we "present," if undertaken and become what is desired?

The beings that live beneath the waves that churn your shores are varied and with this each offers different talents to the tasks at hand. Like those that dwell above, there are those that provide food to other species … <u>the givers</u> as such. There are those that speak to all, and carry along with them to all parts of the Sea the knowledge attained above. There are the <u>distributors</u> who impart nutrients to the air people that carry them along to you above. There are the <u>delvers</u> that search further north for the light of existences yet unknown. For even still, there exists within this great plane, those unknown to even we. For they exist, even as we cannot understand. Thus in giving this, we ask that through your search, can you not become again one with such beings? We know not, for we search often … yet in truth, ones such as you do not exist in our world and thus we are saddened by this.

Yet in pursuing this, we offer you our truth and the knowledge you seek

Congruent to what you believe, we do exist to hinder not the completion of cycles undertaken in this orbit of life. For we too, exist within a time frame as you but our existences far outweigh you and the challenges that are offered. We face challenges and our life is as you, wrought with challenges given and taken in this lifetime. We alone know of these but accept them as so. You ask now of rebels that exists in your world and the likeness in ours. Tis truth that all beings exist not as one and thus others seek in solace the need to be individual. With this may come the deception of one over another but seldom is this tolerated within this place that we dwell. For be it alone or in a group, all must be all they are given and tasks must be performed. This is so and thus it is given.

We do not always remain "workable" (for seldom do we suffer as you with the tiredness or boredom, for our place of existence is quite lovely and offers solace and joy to all that dwell within) yet at times many alight as given and many also desist to be. As the Stones that have imparted this, we too can also be, but in accepting this we alight in purpose for each absorbing within this time of stillness all things given in this place. Others may choose to become what they are not, if only for a time and legends expound with tales of men and women of the Sea becoming real for a time. Thus it is so and the Devas themselves often do this for their pleasure. Children here are different but all seek what they must to attain the maturity needed to expound upon their tasks. As each generation fades, each new one becomes what it must to continue, accepting the challenges given to each … dually overcome at first, but ever aware of the tasks at hand. As above, our acceptance of a past task can change and in transition this is given. For many find that the talents they lack can be attained through the guidance of ones unlike they and so begin again in the tutelage of such beings; learning still, more to attain higher in the search for redemption.

Redemption in our terms is subtle, in that it does not mean "fraught from discretions" but forward thinking and growth through learning and acceptance of tasks given … though often tolerated or hated (yes, this happens also on all realms, though this is quite a harsh reality) yet ever done for the betterment of all.

The species below relate to us and we to they. The respect continues, for the essence we impart, be it through <u>the givers</u> or <u>the lighters</u> or the <u>communicators</u> becomes imbedded into their reality and welcome as they, ever ready to begin again. As many leave, caught in the nets of those above, the knowledge from these transactions are imparted fully to some above. For memories are carried through the body and those that consume "said" entities become as these below, accepting and absorbing and relating still to those that would hear. Knowledge is passed as such in your land locked people and thus, in absorbing nutrients from the spirits above, their knowledge is also imparted to those that would seek it out. Knowing all this, we ask that you relate this, also that what we have given becomes truth to those that would believe. We know of your journey, for the ideas do travel and the vines that clamor to become the heights also reach deep within the soul of this Earth. Thus we see also and with this grant you leave to give out truths above.

We know that the task ahead will be tedious but still we shall impart to you what you desire and yes the knowledge to attain likenesses of what we are, shall be provided. Continue on your quest, for we challenge you to this goal of success for all that live below and all that sail above. For though you came to seek out what was before, know that what lies below is what is needed. Another shall give to you the knowledge of this place, but at another time. Is this not possible?

Acceptance is noted and so we retreat again, once more to our home beneath your sea. Search the night sky for the dancers and the shores for the Sea Goddess … for as surely as you breath … so do we. The existence as light and free, we wish for you all.

Come again in other parts of this Great Mother and all shall speak of days long spent in joy, understanding and truth.

We remain, Speakers of the Sea, the Nature Spirits Below

Ancient Places by the Sea — Revised

We are the spirits of this place and we live just as you do. Though this is true, no one else knows about the different lifetimes that have brought power to our land, the sea. This is our problem.

Each new lifetime brings changes leading up to this point in time. Yet in this time what was remembered in the past will soon slowly fade away until it is forgotten. Every *being* in their own time and place lives to be what they must, often learning and giving knowledge from their lives before to others in this lifetime. In this lifetime we are called *The Charmed Ones* and we will tell you what our world was like before. As you look out over the sea, you should understand that some things have changed forever and facts that you have heard or believe are often wrong. Only those *beings* that know, the ones you have never seen, can understand what our world is now, what it was before and what it will be like in the future.

Speaking now and knowing that your reason for living in this lifetime is to bring this information to everyone (they are speaking to me here) we will begin.

Long ago things you have never seen before lived on these shores. Giant birds flew and *Nature* was able to grow anywhere. Everything that was needed was provided. Like now, the tides ebbed and flowed but eventually with the tide also came changes. Just like challenges come to everyone and in all times, they were given to us.

Sorry, we are still asleep. It isn't often that anyone wants to know what happened before. Yes, the *Nature Spirits* exist here. This is our truth, the *Universal Truth* and we will tell you what we remember. *Devas*, as you call them, rule these shores just as they did before, taking care of everyone here. This great Sea shines, filled with all of us that serve the *Great Lady* of this place. She has the ability to see ahead and now this is given to you.

Challenges come in all ages and we will now begin to tell you about ours. Long ago as we grew, *beings,* different than the ones you see above the water, began to understand what we needed to do to continue to live in this world. With this understanding, certain jobs were given to each of us here. Once again, we understood that to increase we must propagate. Not like you do but through countless ages of growth and knowledge we received through the undercurrent. Through this the flow of truths were given to us. Each of us below, just as you above, searches for things that will make everyone happy. We look for this in what we believe and hopefully find what we are looking for.

Some of the *beings* here may look like souls that are lost in the dark. Some of you may even have seen them late at night or heard them calling out to one another through the darkness that covers the Sea. They look like ghosts searching for something but are just the "mist of *beings"* unable to find what they are looking for. What these *beings* do is search for what is actually happening above and then bring it back to those of us that live below. Just like the turtle that leaves the Sea and returns, they are always ready to learn what those that enter or set sail upon our world, the sea, know. These *beings* or S*pirits* are indeed real and you that have seen them or will see them should not be afraid but instead should just enjoy them. What these S*pirits* know, their truths, will bring a change to anyone who believes. These S*pirits* are just the end of souls that we have lost, coming together once again to help everyone.

Have you accepted yet that everyone should have choices, whether they are from our world or the world you see? Each of these *Spirits* accepts the choices that they believe and with these the knowledge to change everything around them.

Moving ahead, many of those that rule below do so because of what they have learned through centuries, even countless ages of regrouping and the knowledge they have gained through these ways. The *Sea Goddesses*, a title that isn't what we would use but a name that fits how you see them, rule here. (I ask if the Sea Goddesses grow in power over the years.) Yes, the Sea Goddesses advance but not through rebirth. Only through our ways and their will to get everything done to help all of us here, can they move forward. They live just below the surface of the water but don't come above often because they lack substance.

Note: A tiny crab like creature walked up to my computer, took a look and walked away.

Did he scare you? It's only *the watcher* like before. Don't you realize that all places like these have watchers? Even though he looks like a Sea creature that you might recognize, he is in fact a *Nature Spirit* from the Sea. He is searching again for the information you have and will bring it back to us below the Sea.

In our world we believe that anything is possible. Just like the tide ebbs and flows, we like the earth change each day. The *Sea Goddesses* give jobs to many of us here but others who have finished these tasks often "begin their climb" to rest. They take their rest or vacation, as you would say, far away from ones such as you and sometimes can be seen as shinning lights in the sky. Often they dance in the heavens because the distance from the Sea and the sky gives them the room to spread out in your world. Sometimes they flicker and fall and are seen by some of you as a bright glow in the sky.[49] You may see "colors of the night" light up that same horizon as they dance in this joy they call "renewal".[50] Everyone is given this chance for renewal and if they take it, the joy of what they are doing returns. They then go back to their jobs again filled with the joy that is this renewal, but in some cases this doesn't always work.

Traveling through time and space is something that everyone below (in the Sea) can do and the opportunities are endless. Still things below must get done and the ones below follow directions when asked to do these jobs, leaving only when they are not needed. The *Sea Goddesses* are different in respect to what they want at the time. This is because you as humans see them differently than

---

49 Can these be falling stars?
50 This seems to be a clear reference to the Northern Lights.

we do here. Many of those above have seen these *beings* come to them during storms at Sea. They look like beautiful creatures and of course we agree but if you saw them in their true form they wouldn't appear to you as beautiful. Don't you understand that everything has its own beauty, whether it is in your world or in ours? It's just that what we consider beautiful may not be so to you and because of this we can become what you imagine we should be.

The *beings* that live below the waves that come ashore are all different and with these differences come the talents to do the jobs that we need below. Just like above we have those below that provide food to other *beings* here (like fish). We call them *the givers.* There are those that speak to all of us here and carry what they have learned to other parts of the ocean. The *distributors* give nutrients to the *air people* that carry them to you above. There are the *delvers* that are searching farther North for other *beings* that are still unknown, even to us. Yes, there are still those that live in this world that we do not know about. As you continue your search, couldn't you try and find out about them? We still haven't found them yet and are sad because there is no one like you here that could help us. Still we will give you what we know and the information that you are looking for.

Different than what you believe, we do live to further the cycles needed in life to continue. Just as you do, we too live in a time frame but we have much larger challenges and longer lives in which to pursue them. We are given and take on many of these in our lifetime. We are the only ones that know what these are and we accept them as they are given to us.

Q: Are there any *beings* there who don't want to do the jobs they were asked to do?

A: You ask us if we have any rebels like you have in your world. Yes, sometimes. It's true that we don't live here as *one being* (they are not a collective, as many other Nature Spirits are) and so we each look for the peace of being an individual. At times, one of us may try to deceive or lie to another being here but this is never tolerated. Whether it is alone or in a group, we all have to be what we are and do what we have agreed to do in this world. This is the way it is done and that is that!

We aren't always able to work, but unlike you above, we seldom suffer from tiredness or boredom. The world in which we live is very beautiful and offers peace and joy to everyone who lives here. Still at times, many will take a break, like we explained before, while others will just remain content to be alone within themselves. Like the Stones you have channeled have said, "We can be"; we too "can be," just absorbing inside the stillness, everything given to us in this place. Others may choose to be something different for a short time. Legends are told of men and women of the Sea becoming human for a while. This is true. *The Devas* often do this just for fun.

The children here are different but each one looks for what they need to grow and accepts the job they are destined for. As each generation passes on, each new one becomes what it must to continue our way of life; accepting the challenges given to each of them. Sometimes this is not easily done but each one knows that it must be done anyway. Just like you above, what we have chosen to do can change and when we are reborn we take on this new job. Some of us find that the talent we don't have can be learned through working with *beings* different than we are. So we look for a teacher among this species to teach us, each of us learning more to reach higher in our search for "redemption". *Redemption* in our language is subtle, in that it doesn't mean "to take away what we did wrong" but means instead "forward thinking and growth through learning and accepting the tasks we are given". Even though we may not like these tasks or even "hate" them, we accept them because they are done to make everyone's life better in our world. Yes, hate does happen in this world, though it is quite a hard life to accept. The Sea Life below works with us and us with them. The respect we have for each other continues because the knowledge through the love we give, whether it is through the *lighters* or the *communicators*, becomes part of their reality. Like us they welcome it and are always ready to begin life again.

Many of these beings (Sea Life) leave here caught in the nets of those above but what they know is passed on to anyone that will listen. The memories of each of these *beings* is carried through their bodies and those that eat them get this information from us below. The same is true for the animals that live on the land. The spiritual knowledge of these animals is also given to those who will only listen. [51]

We ask that you, knowing this now, tell everyone and they will find this is true if they would only believe it.

We know about your travels because the vines that reach high in the sky also reach deep inside the soul of the earth.[52] This is how we know what you are doing and we give you permission to tell everyone what we have told you. We know that the job ahead will be tedious at times but still we will give you what you ask … and yes, we will let you see what we look like. Continue searching. We challenge you to succeed in this goal for all of those that live below and all that sail above. Even though you came to this place to

---

51 The American Indians also believe that if you eat an animal, you also take into your body the spirit of the animal and he then becomes part of you.

52 The vines are travelers sending news back and forth throughout the earth, See <u>Ivy on the Pine</u>.

look for what had happened in the past, what lies below the Sea is more important. Someone else will give you the history of this place at another time. Isn't this possible? (I said yes)

We understand and so we will return to our home below your sea.

Look in the night sky for the dancers and on the shores for the *Sea Goddesses*. For as surely as you breathe, so do we. We wish for you all, a life just as light and free. Come again to other parts of the world and we will tell you more about our days spent in joy, understanding, and truth.

We remain, *Speakers of the Sea ... The Nature Spirits Below.*

After reading this, my feeling for the Sea has changed. I no longer only think of the Sea as a place where fish live and ships sail but now as a magical world filled with great *beings* of light; each living and bringing to my world, a world where one walks instead of swims, what is needed to survive. Many of the myths and legends became reality in my eyes and the call of those ancient sirens of long ago echo in my ears. Though, after thinking about it I did have one question; Are the Devas of the Sea and the Sea Goddesses the same beings? The answer was an astounding "NO".[53] I was just curious; you see, even I have questions.

Of course, I still am not a fan of actually "sailing" on the Sea but when I see it, I now look at it with different eyes. I must admit that after reading this I now search the night sky for those dancers and also keep a lookout for a *Sea Goddess* or two.

---

53 Sea Goddesses and Devas of the Sea are very different. One is legend the other is diligence. The Sea Goddesses are what you would call "ethereal beings" or in your terms ones that were (here) before but no longer exist, yet still contain the essence of before. They are and shall always be the ones that carry on the myth and legends of the past. They are the ones seen in the mist that rise high in the storm, the fabled ones of the writers that tell tales of legless beauties that dance with man only to return to the sea. The Devas are also ones of beauty but of hard work and perseverance. They lead us in our tasks, taking time (for themselves) only when the work is finished. They are assigned different areas by the Great Mother and so assist her in maintaining all things in our world. They are seldom seen for their diligence is often not undertaken with the pleasures but only the benefits derived from hard work accomplished under their care. This may seem strange, for your world refers to Devas as ones that are flighty and underachievers, yet in our world this is not so. They differ, yet are truly beautiful in our eyes for all they do and give to us. They are who we are and what we do. Without them we would not exist.

Indigenous, Plants at the Point

Crystal Cove, California – Monday, May 26, 2003

AFTER DOING THE READING AT the beach below, I climbed back up to the road and stopped at the posted lookout point at the top of the trail. Looking out over the Sea, I started thinking about what the ocean had said and about all the *beings* that lived below the waves. It was very overpowering and made me think again of just how small a person I was compared to the vastness of the ocean. I felt insignificant and wondered why would or could this book ever make any impression on the people in my world. I really wanted these messages to have an impact; but good intentions are completely different from the reality of Human Nature.

While staring over the huge Pacific Ocean below me, I sensed that I was being watched by something on the right side of me. The only thing I could see at first was a medium size bush filled with little yellow flowers. Having seen quite a few of these along the path into the park, I really hadn't paid that much attention to these bushes. Now, when I looked closer I could see, peeking around from inside, a set of small black eyes peering back at me. Alright! A *Nature Spirit* and one connected with this place ... perfect! I pulled out my paper to do a sketch but before I could begin, I was told that I should do this reading first. I just figured that this particular *Elemental Being* wanted to "check me out" for a while before I ran off back to my world. I'm sure I was probably the first human to ever notice him and he was very surprised, not to mention curious.

That being the case, I asked if he would stay there until I was finished writing. The plant assured me that he would stay and on that note I channeled the passage below.

I must preface with a few words before you read this passage.

All around this park are houses. The houses have slowly filled any open spaces available along the coast over the years. These houses push out all living things, above the earth anyway, and leave many of our *Nature Spirit* friends homeless. I don't want to get into any political issues here so I will just leave it at this. After removing the indigenous plants in order to make way for the homes, the builders and new homeowners then replant other things that they find more suitable, or should we say prettier, around the area.

You may be saying to yourself, this is okay as they are replacing one plant with another. What is the difference anyway? Ah, this is just the point and again another view that I hadn't taken into consideration; at least not when it had to do with new housing tracts and development. I had heard about the reforesting methods in other countries (replanting trees and plants that had been there originally but had been removed for various reasons) when I had traveled but had never heard or listened to the *Nature Spirits* view on this issue.

In this passage, you will learn how the *Nature Spirits* feel about plants that are native to the area and the removal of these plants to make room for others. After reading it, I am sure you will see how this might relate to the human population as well. It seems our friends, the *Nature Spirits,* are always giving us something to ponder. I guess this is part of their gift to us.

INDIGENOUS, PLANTS AT THE POINT

As you sit here upon this beach we notice you and ask that you notice we. Therefore having said this and becoming visible, we shall impart what we must. You have come to the Sea but many above still await you, for our truths are given also and this must be so.

We ask now that you absorb this... what we give, so that in imparting it to all that deem it of importance, it shall be.

We are indigenous to this area that is truth and we exist for that purpose. For many have come here that are not and they survive. This is truth but still their struggle is truly hard. We exist to be what Nature must in this place and so advise others to disturb not what begins where it must. You think now on trees far gone from this place and know that what was taken and given is in truth not what should have been and to this we give credence. For as we exist to store nutrients and moisture for all that live within our bounds, others cannot and yet in seeking out this existence we come regal in our restoration of what we have become. We are well formed and yet the essence can not be seen, for hidden within each blade of our existence is the knowledge of countless ages and the endurance of times well spent or not… in subsiding in all types needed to become what we must in this place.

We have chosen you today as our messenger and ask now that the Spirit of this plane present herself to you in this knowledge. Alight now and sketch her in true form and tell all that would listen the importance of this task we have undertaken. Give all the knowledge that what exists is truly what must. To add is never undertaken with stress but to remove is indeed harmful. Do not mess with what you do not understand for all things are as they should be.

Yes, you ask is it not possible to re-attain plants and impart them in your surrounding. This is given if taken in contents with what shall benefit all concerned. This is truth and so we say…go now with knowledge and we shall send you only light and love and knowledge attained through patience.

We remain, Indigenous

INDIGENOUS, PLANTS AT THE POINT – REVISED

As you sit at this beach we can see you and we ask you to look at us too. Having said this and since you can now see us, we will tell you what we have to say. You have come to the Sea to channel those beings that live under the water, but many here on the land also have things to say. We ask that you now listen to what we say, so that when you tell others that want to know this, they will have the right information.

We are indigenous, which means we have always lived here. We live for that reason. Many (plants, trees, etc.) have been put here who are not from this place and they survive. They do live but their struggle is very hard. We live in this place because *Nature* made us to adapt to these conditions. We ask others, such as you, not to plant things that are not meant for this area or to disturb what grows where it must.

(I am thinking about the reforesting of Scotland and how they replanted trees that were not meant to grow there)

You are thinking of the trees far away from this place[54] and we know that what was removed and then replanted was not what was there before. This was not right. We agree with this. Although we store food and water for the *beings* that live in our area, others cannot. In looking for our purpose, we realize that the main thing is to maintain what we have become. We are made well but outwardly you can not see our essence. Hidden deep inside each blade is the knowledge of lifetimes and the ability to withstand the good times and the bad and to become what we must to remain in this place.

Today we have chosen you as our messenger and ask that the spirit of this place be given to you in this message. Sit down and draw her (the plant) in her true form and tell everyone that will listen the importance of this job we have undertaken.

Teach them that what lives in a place is what is truly meant to live there. You should not worry too much if you add things to a place but taking things away is very harmful. *Do not mess with what you do not understand because all things are as they should be.*

You ask if it is alright to get certain plants and plant them in your garden. This is alright, if what you plant will benefit everyone concerned. This is the truth. We ask that you spread this information and we will send you only love and light and knowledge learned through patience.

We remain, Indigenous

I hope this gives you "pause to think", as they say, and that you might reconsider before cutting down or removing a plant that just does not fit your idea of perfection. Perhaps your garden would thrive if that plant stayed. It couldn't hurt to give it a try; you could always disguise it with a hat or something.

By the way, the little *Nature Spirit* in the bush did wait around and let me draw him. Considering my talent for drawing, perhaps he shouldn't have.

---

54 Here they refer to a program called "Trees for Life". This is a project that replants the trees that were indigenous to the Scottish Highlands, replacing the non indigenous pine trees planted there in the 1800's to produce timber. This was done after they had removed the original trees from the area. This program is restoring the Highlands of Scotland and the land back to its original and healthier state. It is a volunteer program and if you are inclined, any help would be greatly appreciated.

Sea Kelp

Point Lobos, Carmel, California – Thursday, June 19, 2003

IF YOU EVER GET THE chance to drive along the California coast between Los Angeles and San Francisco, take it. It is some of the most beautiful scenery you will ever see. The combination of the Sea on one side and the forest on the other is amazing.

Traveling north along Highway One, just before you reach the famous town of Carmel, you will find the State Park at Point Lobos. It is well worth a visit and if you are lucky you will see the famous otters that float in the bay. There are lots of hiking trails, some of which hang out over the Sea offering breathtaking views of the ocean below.

My husband and I had decided to drive to Carmel for a long weekend. We had spent our honeymoon there and it had been many years since we had returned. Over the past few years, we had taken up hiking and having heard about the trails along the cliffs we decided to visit. I, as usual, brought something to write with "just in case". Needless to say, I always have paper and pen with me but brought along the big gun this time, namely my laptop.

While on the trail I saw so many things I would have liked to receive readings from but since I don't ordinarily hike with my laptop, I waited until we got back to the car. My husband decided it was time for his daily "siesta" and I headed out to channel the bay that lay in front of me.

I found a lovely bench that overlooked the water, right in front of a large stone on which sat a very contemplative seagull. He didn't seem to notice that I was there, which seemed odd. Then again, I am the last person who should judge what odd is and isn't.

The Sea was calm and, yes, there was an otter lying on his back, wrapped like a baby in a bed of Sea Kelp. It was a beautiful day and he was enjoying the sun.

I could have channeled the Sea, but I had already done that at Crystal Bay[55], not to mention spending two hours channeling the ocean this morning, only to push the wrong button and have the entire passage disappear forever inside my computer. Don't you hate when that happens?

Needless to say, I wanted to change gears. I wanted a Sea plant. Taking my cue from the otter, I connected with the Sea Kelp. It was, as you will see, a great decision. Not only did I get a great reading from The Sea Kelp but also one from the *Devas of the Deep* that live there as well. Two for the price of one. That works.

Sea Kelp at Point Lobos, Carmel

We are the Sea Kelp. This is our story, thus in telling it, it shall become truth. Not only to those that seek out such but to all that do not. We live as beings such as you, ever ready to serve and to enlighten but in our truths all things are as such.

As the bird that sits upon the stone that aligns within our path, so are we as he, a haven for all things, ever soaring through spaces given to each in their own space.

As he travels through the heavens to soar, ever seeking that which will become his reality, so do we also. For this space that is our Sea is our sky and reaches far deeper than the heaven he knows. We exist as all things, to do what we must to continue. As you, our reality exists because we indeed believe it is so.

In all things we travel forward and thus in our time and the expanse of our space we are ever alive with distances and growth and the need to expand whatever we must. Often within our realm things exist that are never spoken of and in this we give credence, but still we exist to do what we must to attain our place in this time and space in this place you call Earth. As each

---

55 See "Ancient Places By The Sea".

season changes and things begin and cease, so do we but in renewal all things change. The diligence of this is ever new but in spaces unseen to you, things exist unlike those that you know. Many stories have been told of great beings that dwell within our domain, of times long spent in idleness, and of distant planes and areas unlike those known to you. They exist as you and the joys and sorrows that are given and taken are thus unto them that dwell below the sea.

As you seek out now answers to jobs that are done, be wise to these facts...all things exist to be what they must and so have become what they have chosen. In your existence you breathe and live and dwell within your world but ours, unlike yours, exists within a cloud of illusions given by many to cover the reality of what is and shall ever be.

Stories are told of those that travel our Seas and see those of use that dwell within them. Many search out these beings and in truth know within themselves that what they seek is indeed what they know to be their truth. For all things, be they of the heaven or the Earth or the Sea or the depths not realized by those that dwell above, exist. Exist to give and to return all things to what was before.

The bird sits still upon the stone searching for what you ask? Why must all things purpose to be what you desire but not the reality of what it truly is? He is alone for this is what he seeks, not to extend himself to others but to contemplate and to exist within this plane. When he exists to be more, then his reality is altered and befitting most people such as you, his purpose waylaid.

You search now for reasons; for Nature Spirits that abound on land and now within our Sea. Desires to learn increase and with this, truths that shall bring to those that desire it, the knowledge to begin again all things that were. Aged, the Sea exists. So do all things exist, to be as one in creation and thus to attain that balance tying all things within its path together. We remain as this, a traveler to many realms and thus exist where many do not. We provide nourishment to all things here and above but truths implied are never all that exists in this world that we call ours.

Devas are truth here as on your land and they as before direct the ebb and flow of all things. They guide the tides and change the Seas from the dismal oblique to the wailing alliance of their depths of being. Each section of this place has those that assist others and this knowledge that is attained is exhibited to all that must attain this to know what must be learned to attain this knowledge.

As the Kelp washes forward it brings within its flow the choices that many above are given, but below this is taken not as chance but as what is needed to sustain them in their world. As a plant we survive within our place, giving nutrients to those that need them. We are as others, givers and thus we accept this as such. The Devas that rule us, for this is what you have attained the names as such, tell all what shall begin and end and the tasks that must be taken. We in turn perform the duties that are given and give to those that desire what we need to enlighten them as well as our being upon this place. We know that many questions are given and tales are unclear upon this task but later again they shall be related. We work in part with the air above to exchange that which is needed for our growth and give to this what is needed for yours. In exchange all things are possible and with this lessons for all beings.

We are not of the hierarchy here but all have a part in all things as related.

Many seek out now the legends of who rules the Seas. As the Deva that searches ever forward for the mindlessness of all things, we help in her woes with knowledge attained. We give and we take and in this our chain is thus and no more. We are providers and in this we exist. The complications you ask in seeking more are useless now for we are as chosen and are as we serve. In the chain of command those below are more substantial and they exist further in depths unknown to us. We glide above and thus our world co-mingles with yours and we see where many do not.

We seek out solace, this is truth, but in our way we know what is above also.

We give to many that exist here knowledge but all things that delve below give this, as above. For the transportation of truths is universal and seeking knowledge is what it shall ever be. Not only for all that exist in this time but for all that have existed before and shall to come. What purpose do we serve in the realm of things? We give as stated.

We take nothing except what is presented. Our knowledge as in all beings of this kingdom is imparted when accepted and thus we remain. We hold court within this place and thus give to others (the otters and such) comfort. To the fish (we give) nutrients, and to the others such as you subtenants of the ocean and the cleaners of it, the terms. To the Devas (we provide) the directions in which to pursue the needed growths on the shores in all the seas.

Attaining what we know, we seek now to give to you she which rules this place, Dora. For she unlike us exists to bring together those things which are misplaced, those things that are construed through countless places and the indulgences of those forgotten but ever aware in their fruitfulness of existence. Aside we move, freedom ours upon this wave we call life, we remain, The Kelp of San Lobos.

Dawn awakens in her radiance here upon this plane. This watery place beneath the sea that awaits those that seek. As a wave that rushed forward to plant itself upon the sand, she too offers this to you and thus it is so. Dora is one that teaches… that brings to those that will listen, truths of what shall be.

She is the enchantress of days hidden long ago, but still reality prone in the minds of those that exist still.

She lives beneath these waves and instructs all within her path towards places and seeks out ways to restore what she must to attain peace within her path.

She is beautiful in color, for her hues are deep; the green of the light that reflects from the sea at night when the moon casts its glow upon the waves.

She is as blue as the Sky that overlooks her Sister the Sea and as cobalt as the Stones that lie deep within the caverns of this place you call Earth.

She glows as the embers of the fire that lies below, with the depth of desire. Not only to cast her glow to all that seek out her knowledge, but in truth, to dwell within the arms of all things that are planted within her path.

She needs no one to guide her, for her knowledge comes from the One that gives her credence and thus she knows all and we ask no difference.

She rides on the waves and dives into the crisp water when the tides are high.

She glows when the sky is enlightened by her presence, as a sun upon the horizon.

She leads many to places that are hidden but only when she desire this challenge.

She is what we are and we are she, but in her depths she rules not as advisory, not as teacher, not as friend but as all things, in all ways.

She guides the habits of the new and ceases the end of the old.

She sets challenges and grants pardons and is all to all things.

We give her credence and the joy that awaits her in her quest, for all that must be needed to sustain us in this plight. This is she and through her we exist to serve, to grow and to be what we must to sustain the Sea that exists now and always. She remains and thus as we the challenge to begin again, to cease and to believe that through knowledge all things are as they should be. Go now and come when questions are given.

We remain, the Masters of the Sea; Countesses of all things below.

The Devas of the Deep.

Devas of the Deep, Sea Kelp at Point Lobos—Revised

We are the Sea Kelp and this is our story. In telling it, it will become true not only to those that read it but also to all of those that don't. We live just as you do, always ready to help and bring light where it is needed. We believe that this is the only way to live. We are like that bird sitting on the rock near the path having found his safe place in this lifetime, flying through the freedom that is given to every *being* in its own world. As he flies through the sky, soaring and looking at his world below, so do we all. This space that you call the sea is our sky and it reaches much deeper than the sky this bird knows.

We live like all things, to do what must be done to survive. Like your world, our world exists because we believe it does. Everything we do pushes us forward and so in our time and the vastness of our space, the sea, we are always occupied with distances and growth and the need to move forward whenever we can. It is true that in our world there are things that are never talked about. Still we live to do what must be done to find our place in this time and space on this planet you call Earth.

When the seasons change and things bloom and die, so do we. In renewal (rebirth), everything changes and accepting a new life can sometimes be very hard.

In our world, there are places you know nothing about and things you have never seen. Many stories have been told of huge *beings* that live in our world and of times long ago when life was simple. Tales of distant worlds and places you have never imagined. These stories are true and those that live there, below the sea, share the same joys and sorrows as you do in your world.

As you look for answers to what "jobs" we do here, first understand these facts; every thing, every *being*, lives to become what they must become. In doing this, each becomes what they have chosen.

In your lives you live and breathe within your world, the world you see. Our world, unlike yours, exists inside a cloud of illusion through legends told by many to cover up the truth of who we are and what we may become again.

Stories are sometimes told of those that sail our seas and see some of the *beings* that live here. Many look for these creatures, knowing deep inside that who and what they are searching for is real. There are more things in heaven and earth or in the deepness of the ocean then you realize above. These *beings* live only to give and to work, hoping to return things to the way they were before.

(Thinking to myself, I ask...) Is the bird that is still sitting on the rock thinking about what I'm asking the Sea Kelp? (And here comes the answer ... from The Kelp, of course!)

Why does everything you ask have to be what you think it has to be? He (the bird) is alone because this is what he wants. Not to be with others but to sit alone and think about his life in this world. When he must live to be more than what he has chosen to be, his life is changed and just like you, his purpose for this lifetime is ended.

You are looking for "the reasons" (why we live, what we do, how we do it, etc) from the *Nature Spirits* that live on the land and in the sea, right?

As more of you want to learn these things, the answers that you will need to restart everything that was lost will be given to you. Throughout all time the Sea and all things have existed to be "one with creation", to find the balance that ties all things within their paths together. We, the *Sea Kelp* still do this, traveling to many worlds and living where others don't. We provide food for everyone here and also for those above.

Some things that you think are true may never be exactly what they seem in our world. The legends of the *Devas* here, like on land are true. They have always directed the "ebb and flow", the coming, and going of everything. They can change the tides from boring and flat to their "wailing alliance of their depths of being."[56]

Each area of the sea has those *beings, the Devas* that help others. Their knowledge, which is learned, is taught to everyone that must also learn it to receive this knowledge. When the kelp washes forward it brings many choices to those that live above. This is not considered a random act to those below but instead something that will help them survive in their world.

As a plant, we continue to live in our world by giving food to those that need it. We, like others you have talked with, are also *Givers*. We accept this as our job.

The *Devas* (this is what you call them) that <u>rule us</u> (we prefer <u>direct us</u>) tell us what project must be started, when it must be finished and the things that must be done to make this happen. We in turn, do the jobs we are given and then give not only to ourselves but to those that want it, the information they may need for their enlightenment. We know you have many questions and some things you have heard may not be clear. Later we will give you more answers.

We work partly with the air above to exchange what we need for our growth here and you receive what you need.[57] With this exchange, anything is possible and this should be a lesson for all *beings*.

Many of you want to know who "rules the sea". We don't have a hierarchy here but each has a part in everything that happens in our world. With our knowledge, we help to calm the *Deva* who is always looking ahead for senseless acts that could harm our world. We give and we take, no more or no less and this is where we fit in on that chain in our world. We are *Providers* and this is why we exist. Asking more is complicated and useless because we have chosen this and this is what we do. On the chain of command those below do more and have more responsibilities. Because they live much deeper then we do, we don't know much about their world. We just glide above, so our world mixes with your world and we see where many others can't see.

Yes, we do look for peace and quiet but in our own way we also know what is above. We give many that live here information but so do all the things that live below. The moving of "truths between all worlds" is universal and searching for knowledge will never stop. Not only for everyone that lives in this time but for everything that has lived before or will in the ages to come.

What is our purpose in our world? We do just what we have told you and we take nothing that is not given to us. Our knowledge, like every other *being* in our world, is given only when it is wanted. So we stay. We help settle problems and this gives comfort to *beings* (otters, seals, etc.) here. We supply food to the fish and others, even you. Also we are a part of a system to keep the waters clean and give advice to the *Devas* on where more plants should live and grow, both in the sea and the land below.

To find more out about what you are looking for you should know about our *Deva, Dora,* that rules our part of the sea. *Dora's* job, unlike ours, is to bring things back to the way they were before. Back to before those things that have been changed or have moved over centuries in time; forgotten things, but still existing, once used for pleasure in those times when the sea was overflowing with plenty.

We will move aside now. Freedom is ours on this wave we call life.

---

56 This is one huge storm.

57 Carbon dioxide for oxygen and oxygen for carbon dioxide, which we of course need... except in New York where they survive on diesel fumes.

DORA THE SEA DEVA—REVISED

Dawn awakens to her beauty here in our world, this watery place under the sea that waits for those that search for her. Just as a wave rushes forward to meet the shore, she offers this to you.

Dora is a teacher that brings to those that will listen, the truth about the future.

She is the enchantress of those hidden days of long ago and is still remembered as she was by those still living from that time. She lives under these waves and tells those that she manages, where they are needed. She looks for ways to restore and maintain peace in this job she has chosen.

Her color is deep and beautiful, like the green light that reflects from the sea at night when the moon casts its glow on the waves. She is as blue as the sky above her Sister *The Sea* and as dark as the stones that lay deep in the caves on your Earth. She glows with her depth of desire, like the embers at the earth's core; not only to light the way for those that search for her knowledge but truthfully, to live among every *being* and thing that is on her path.

She needs no one to guide her because her knowledge comes from the *ONE* that made her our *Deva*. She knows everything and we ask for nothing else.

Dora rides on the waves and dives into the cold water when the tides are high and just like the sun on the horizon, the sky glows when she is there. She can lead you to hidden places but only when she needs a challenge. She is what we are and we are what she is, but in the deepness of the sea she rules not only as an advisor, or as a teacher and not only as a friend but in every thing and in every way.

She teaches her ways to the young and releases the old. She sets challenges and grants pardons. We give her purpose and the joy that waits for her on her journey to maintain this world we know.

This is who *Dora* is and only because of her do we continue to serve, to grow and to become what we must to sustain this Sea that will live now and forever. She will stay and so like us will the challenge to begin again, to end, and to believe that through knowledge all things are as they should be and will continue to be forever.

You can go now but come again when you have more questions.

We remain, the *Masters of the Sea*, *The Countesses* of everything below…

The Devas of the Deep

As you can see, there is more to the Sea Kelp than you imagined. The fact that the plants on the Earth and Sea work together to provide what we need to survive does not surprise me. The Sea has always provided food to our world, not only for the fish and other creatures that live there but for the other things that it provides. The plants within the ocean renew the oxygen supply, provide a place for the animals of the deep to live and supply many items that we use everyday.

The Devas of the Sea do exist. The stories told by ancient sailors as well as the tales told today by those that have seen the Devas are true, at least for those that believe.

The Devas' purpose is to serve and direct the Elemental Kingdom of the Deep and to bring it back to what it was before. With their help, we may be able to once again have a Sea that is as clean and as full of life as it was so long ago. If we would only believe this and work with Dora to make it so, anything is possible.

New Bold Garden

Forres, Scotland – Monday, August 11, 2003

IN THE TOWN OF FORRES in northeast Scotland, there is a wonderful old manor house called New Bold House. I have no information as to why it is called this or if there was ever an Old Bold House, I just know that it is a wonderful place to take a workshop.

A few summers ago I did just that. It was great fun and part of the program was to draw in the garden each day. Since I had been on my path of writing this book for a while, this seemed like a perfect place to get some information.

The garden is very large, full of vegetables, flowers, and loads of apple trees. It was later in the season and you could feel autumn in the air. The apples were ripe and the mornings were getting downright chilly. It was on one of these mornings that I received this reading about the changing seasons.

NEW BOLD GARDEN

Reluctant seasons come in times and all things begin and end when the time becomes real once again.

As you exist to become again one with Nature, understand that what we present is not what you may understand relatively within the range of total certainty. Yet in the presenting, know that what is given is indeed what must be given, hence is delivered and becomes again… what it must.

As each in their own time finds their growth period, so do all things in our world. So begins each new experience, as a gift to become once again renewed in the joy that comes from this gift.

As you search for truths in this place and know not all things, we too know not all that is possible in our realm. Thusly in time, we learn to accept things that are readily presented if in this act as attained to the tasks we have accepted. In our reality, many things exist that do not alter our feelings but instead lead us further towards the gifts that are presented. In this the lessons that are incurred are again renewed and thusly accepted as such.

Knowledge once attained can challenge all men to things unseen and yet through these challenges the knowledge is given.

You come now, at last, to seek out this knowledge and to finish that which was proposed so long ago. Thus in the finality of this task, given to the accordance of the ones that seek this task, you culminate in the renewal of all things. For given purpose, no matter in what issue you arrive, is the truth to all existence and the acceptance of this purpose and the growth that may become reality does become once again the needed path to achieve oneness with all things in this world.

In acceptance you began and continue still but now the search begins for differential challenges. This is undertaken in stride but becomes a challenge only if in this knowledge surrender is not undertaken. Thusly in this acceptance, the realization that this acceptance is indeed what becomes reality and that all things are and shall be given so that this reality becomes again what is needed to fulfill this task.

As you wander through these days, linger still in the oneness of those that seek out yourself … In the truths that are given and the paths that will glow with the light that shall send you nearer to their knowledge. For each has a task as written and each would share this with you, but being of time and the essential of this book, thus this knowledge must be imparted and so all may not enter into this.

Surely what is given shall become reality to many and yet in this all things begin and end here. For though you seek out forms that exist in Nature we alone give to you what we give. For each part has and ever shall remain different in what they desire… in fact, all things are and shall ever be given differently than before, only if understood in a way that transpires differences in all beings.

So said we begin.

We welcome you once again to the gardens of Scotland, not only to undertake the task you have been given but to relate to all the benefits that were started when you first began. As you enter now a phase unlike that before, the knowledge of the time before becomes truly needed and thus shall and will be given.

Before, when the Earth reveled in freedom all were free, thusly all men and all beings were the same. All existed to be as one, interchangeable in all facets but ever willing to be as before if needed. When times became hard many became as before and many changed their being to suit or adapt to changes that occurred in surrounding areas or places in this realm. During this time, many things ceased that were normal to all people and yet in these changes the challenges were given and all things became what they should to increase the gifts to all upon this plane.

As men progressed and the stresses upon the Earth increased, not only in the volume of all things but in the tasks attuned in each case, in order to separate those that would accomplish things given and those that sought other means to increase their ability on this plane...thus a position was taken.

In each case, each person must attain a position in which to assert their effort upon the effects of each world and thus in the acceptance of this becomes what they must to attain their due upon this place. Thusly it is and so it must be. So it did unfold that some became useless in the facts that were needed and thus became a detriment to all concerned, never wavering in commitment to follow the courses that would encourage the all in this place.

As you search for truth, know that what we impart is that. Our truth, the truth of the Great One that leads us all and to this we shall ever be useful.

Beginning again, we are ever present in all things and thus give credence to the existence taken by you in our behalf. Many seek us out to understand why we begin and end and many search out reasons for our existence. But unlike you, they seek not why we exist, why we evolve as do you and the service we impart to all living beings in all places upon this Earth. We are and shall ever be the reigning truth that lights all paths and only through us shall you survive. For if not through the continence of water and air and the need for sustenance could you not survive? For though the animals and the birds and the fishes that swim in the great sea shall cease, we only shall remain to feed and clothe all of you that remain, again to renew what you must to attain your path in this lifetime. As we choose the lessons that we must also learn so must you know that we too are lessons imparted to you for the goodness of all and through us all things exist and are again useful as before.

Long ago many ruled this land that brought to us all that was needed. Shared we all in the goodness of this place and the light that shone brought joy to all beings. But in time the light faded and the joy that was known changed and with it the purpose of each person and animal and plant on this realm.

Keeping with this subject we shall tell you of the gifts that were given so long ago by the ones that were here before you. They were of a race unlike any that remain; full of energy and hope for all things, they brought with them the intelligence for all things. The Earth was scarce then. The abundance in our world was challenged for the Mother; ever weary was asleep in a state of transmigration from one realm to the next. In starting to awaken to this world, the Ones brought with them the light that would arouse her from her sleep and awakened within her the ability to begin again her work upon this plane. As she arose, the intelligence was given and the light, the gift, was given to her and all that would follow. She bloomed with the glow that reigns truly within her heart and remains still for the fire that burns within her soul remains still a gift from long ago. This heats the roots of the soil when the winter wind blows. It warms the children that lie waiting under her warmth to begin again their growth and the world view of springtime. She emits her forces in rage when she is angry and emits the soothing waters to the ill when she is calm. All things begin in her heart and all things shall remain there still. As the Old Ones came, they brought the seeds that would become to her the children of her birth. She nurtured them and they grew in the rich soil, sustained by the love and light of the Holy Order provided through all the Universe. The Beings of Light knew of what must be given and so imparted all knowledge to all things. As seeded the Mother began to birth all things and within this all of man became again what he was before... a seed to be nourished and atoned for indiscretions on places far from this place. As man grew so did Nature but so did the chances that came with this growth and remain still. As you encounter many new things on this journey, know that what you see is but a part of what was before. Know that the beauty that surrounds you is but a facet of the truth that existed so many years before. For Nature as she changes grows in the direction that she must, often with trepidation and within the frame work of those that dwell above. But be warned that a Higher Great Being that rules us all has but to notice what changes she imparts and all things shall change. For in her mercy, the Great One that imparts rules to us here has given guidance to you above and in her mercy has challenged you to exist in this neoclassical continence you call life. Acceptance of her is ideal but some do not

believe and yet they impart their will of this on others that cease to believe in this truth to become what they desire. As she exists and becomes more you shall become less unless you accept that what she provides shall begin and end all life upon this plane. We exist because she permits it, you exist because we permit it. She rules through us and we rule through you but only to the point of extinction. Knowledge is given and shall cease if not taken in truth.
We remain, Nature

New Bold Gardens — Revised

Seasons that may not want to come, will eventually come because all things begin and end when it is their time. As you again live to become part of or "One with" *Nature*, understand that what we say may not be fully understood for certain. Yet in giving you this information you must realize that what we say must be said and so we give it to you because it is what you need.

Every *being* in the world finds its own time to grow. With this growth, each new experience becomes a gift, an experience to relive again, just for the joy of it. Not knowing that everything you look for here is the truth, you must also understand that we do not know everything either. In time we too learn to accept things that come easy to us if they bring the results we want in our work.

In our world, there are many things that do not change our feelings but instead lead us closer to those gifts of growth we are given. In this way, the lessons we learn are remembered and again accepted like before. Having knowledge can challenge men with things they can't see, yet only through these challenges can they receive this knowledge. You have finally come searching for this knowledge and to finish this project (book) you started sometime ago. In finishing this job, according to the Ones that gave it to you in the first place, you will end with the "true beginning of everything". Having a purpose, no matter what answers you get, is the true meaning of life and accepting this purpose and the growth that will become real will again become the path that brings everything together in this world. You accepted this job and began writing. You are still writing but now your search starts for different reasons. This job is sometimes hard but only becomes a challenge if you don't keep working on it. So in accepting this you realize that what you are channeling and writing is real, everything you learned and everything that is and will be given to you is what you need to finish this book. As you go through your days, stay awhile longer with us and become a part of the world of the *Nature Spirits*. Listen to what we say and your path will glow with the light that will lead you nearer to this knowledge.

As you have written so far, each *Elemental* here has a job and each of them wants to share it with you. Being short of time and the need to get this book published is very important to them all and they know they cannot all be a part of it. Surely, what you have written will be believed by some of those that read this and they will realize that everything does begin and end here.

Even though you look for the different *beings* in *Nature,* it is *Nature* alone that will give you this. In *Nature*, each *being* has and always will remain different in what they need; in fact all things are always changing but understand only in a way that affects changes in all *beings.* So having said this, we will begin.

We welcome you once again to the gardens of Scotland. Not only to work on the book but to tell everyone about the great things you received when you first started this project. The information we will give you this time will be different than before. Information about the past will become very important and will, because of this, be given to you now.

Long ago when the Earth celebrated freedom, every *being* was free and all men and other *beings* were considered the same. They all lived to be equal in every way but were always willing, if it was needed, to do what they had done before. When times became hard many *beings* went back to what they had done before and some adapted to the changes in their surrounding area or in other places in our world. During this time many things that were normal for everyone ended. Still these changes brought new challenges and everything became what they needed to become to increase the benefits for everyone in our world. As man moved forward, the stresses on the Earth increased, not only in population but also with things that had to be done to maintain this growth. In order to separate those that did only the things they were told to do and others that found ways to increase the work that they did, different positions were given.

In each case, each person must reach a position where the hard work they do benefits their world. In accepting this, they become all that they can in their world. This is the way it is and this is the way it should be. So it happened that some didn't do their jobs. This became a problem for all of the others who did everything they were asked for the benefit of everyone concerned.

Remember as you look for the truth, that everything we say is true, our truth, which is the truth of the *Great One* that leads us all. This is what we have and will always strive for. We are always here, in every thing you see and we accept that what you are doing with your life in writing this book is for us. There are many of you that look for us to find out why we are born and die (like the botanists, scientists and those sorts). Others just want to know if we exist at all. But unlike you, they don't look for why we exist, why we evolve as we do and the service we give to every human being in every place on your Earth. We are and always will be the real truth that guides you through your life and only because of us will you survive. If it wasn't through what we provide…your need for water or air or food, could you live?

Even if the animals, the birds, and the fish that swim in the sea were gone … only we would remain to feed and clothe all of you that decided to stay; to remain and to once again search for their path in this lifetime. As you choose the lessons that we both must learn you must also understand that we are also the lessons given to help you all. Through us every thing is given life and becomes like they were before.

BEGINNING AGAIN…

Back in time, many ruled this land that gave us everything that we needed. We all shared in the goodness of this place and *the light* that shone brought joy to all beings. In time this light faded and the joy that we knew changed. With this the purpose of each person, animal, and plant in this world also changed.

Keeping on this subject we will tell you about the gifts that were given to us so long ago by the *Ones* that were here before you. They were a race unlike any that still remain today. Full of hope and energy for all things, they brought the intelligence to accomplish this. The Earth was smaller then. What we needed in our world was not available because *The Mother* (Earth) grew very tired and was asleep in a "state of transmigration", moving from one world to another.

In the beginning, to awaken her to this world, *The Old Ones* brought "the light" that would arouse her from her sleep and awaken inside her the ability to again begin her work in this world. As she awoke, the intelligence was given to her and the gift, "the light", was given to everyone that would follow her. She bloomed with the glow that ruled her heart and it still remains today. The fire that burned within her soul is still burning, that gift from long ago. This fire heats the roots in our soil when the winter wind blows. It warms our children that lay waiting under this warmth to grow again when your world welcomes spring. She sends out in a rage her power when she is angry but also sends the cooling water to the ill when she is calm. Everything begins in her heart and everything will end there.

As the *Old Ones* came they brought the seeds that would become her children. She nurtured them and they grew in the rich soil, held together by the Holy Order which is given to the entire Universe. These *Beings of Light* knew what knowledge was needed and gave it to every being. Once *Mother Earth* was planted with seed she began to give birth to all things and within this process, man again became what he was before … a seed to be nourished and forgiven for pass deeds on places far from this world. As man grew, so did *Nature* but also did the changes that came from this growth, changes that still remain today.

Remember as you see new things on this journey, understand that what you see is just a fraction of the way it was before. The beauty that surrounds you is only a tiny part of the way it was so long ago. Nature as she changes grows in the direction that she must, sometimes with serious doubts, but still inside the boundaries of what you decide above. But be warned that the higher and greater *Being* that rules us all has only to notice what changes she shows and all things will change.

In her mercy, the *Great One (Mother Earth)* that "in part" rules us here, has given you that live above her, guidance and has challenged you to live in this "held together, perfect world you once had" life. Accepting *The Mother* would be ideal but some just don't believe this. Yet they try and force their beliefs of her on others, who then stop believing to become what they want.

As *Mother Nature* lives and becomes greater in your world, you will become less unless you accept that what she gives you can either begin or end all life on this Earthy plane.

We exist because *She* Allows It. You live because We Allow It. She rules through us and we rule through you…but only to the point of extinction. (That pretty much says it all folks!!)

This knowledge is given to you but will stop if you don't believe it.

We remain, *NATURE*

And I thought I would just get a reading from an autumn garden. Was I ever wrong?

The history of this planet and its people has been a controversy for as long as people have had discussions. Where did we come from? How long have we been here? And the best question … Are we alone?

How was I to know that asking a garden in Scotland about the changing seasons would bring out so much information about our world before?

I find this all very, very interesting and yes, it does answer a lot of questions that have been tossed around over the centuries. Since the *Elemental Kingdom* has no reason to lie, and in fact says it doesn't (and I believe them), then I have no reason to doubt this information.

I love the idea that each world has a *Mother Nature* that takes care of it. If that is so, then it must also have an *Elemental Kingdom* as well. I wonder if our *Nature Spirits* ever wonder about that the way we do.

It is also very interesting to note that even *Mother Nature* has to report to a higher *Being*.

The Autumn Leaf of Findhorn

Findhorn, Scotland – August 16, 2003

I RETURNED TO FINDHORN TO attend a course entitled <u>Everyone is an Artist</u>. It sounded good on paper and turned out to be very creative, though I am still unconvinced that there was truth in the title. While there, my mind started wandering, which happens quite a lot to me these days. It drifted towards what has been my purpose here in this world; the accomplishments or non-accomplishments I have made in this lifetime and, of course, the ever dreaded getting old. Since I am well on my way to the latter, I was feeling down and less attractive than I had in the past. Nature, being the great Lady that she is, sat me down and gave me a good talking to. She made me think about the life I had led and what I had to look forward to. The fact that what was ahead was not an ending but only a beginning to another world full of adventures and reawakening and that my life should be celebrated, even more so at the end than at the beginning.

How did she do this? She used a leaf... a simple autumn leaf. A beautiful leaf that was orange and red, ablaze with the colors of the season. I had picked up the leaf while at the Power Point on the hill in back of Cluny College. The reason I had chosen it was because I had seen an amazing face in it and it had called out to me. Nature always knows what's in your mind and guessing I might need a lift gave me this gift.

So for all of you that have ever wondered what has been the purpose of your life or contemplated the "horror" (HA!) of getting old and dying (which is unfortunately inevitable), this one is for you.

THE AUTUMN LEAF OF FINDHORN

I am the Leaf of Autumn... The ever changing face of all things. The illusion to the path I have taken. To enter again that brief space that will shelter me until I again begin my journey again to where I began. I once was bright and green and gave my face to the sun. I basked in her warmth and heard the song of the birds in my hair. I searched for all things and soared through the night in dreams highlighted by the glow of the lady that lights the sky in the dusk of twilight that played colors on my face with the breaking of the morning dew to settle gently on my face. I have existed to become what I have; to give to all the shelter from all things when desired ... to be a home for those that would dwell in the branches below. To store energy for all purposes and to emit the healing energy to all things on this plane. To settle into the routine of what must be in this place I call home. For even though I may be slight, my energy exists and my intelligence reigns true in all times.

My species has spoken of times spent in the dark earth and to this I relate, but all things come and go and come again, Accept what is written, for the journey begins in your mind and all things become reality when you accept that what we give ... is what we know.

Thus I return now to the earth. My time spent in the glow of this place you call Earth. In "the place of trees", swirling with others that emit the nature of all things. From the beauty of the living ones that dwell within this place and to those that skirt upon our existence with feet softly asking ... but never quite hearing. Releasing now I enter again that dark place. That place that shall bring to me the warmth and comfort so longed for now. As my sisters and brothers fall, one upon the other, they rejoice ... for all things begin as they end, in an array of beauty ... time spent in the loveliness of each season.

Rejoice in the life, but accept the gift that death shall bring. For all things never cease but only begin again, new and bright and striving again to be more than they were before.

I wish you now that soft place to dwell within our earth, warm and comforting and the joy of re-entrance into a world, new and bright and wrought with love for all beings.

As We of Nature love all men, so shall they love us also. For all are the same and all existing, for that is the plan. I send you now our conclusion...

Go in the glow of those that have given their service to you. Salute the final glory that will blaze with the passion felt by us all. Revel in the truth that awaits you all at the close of your day and as We, go out in a blaze of color. Be it red as the sun or as golden as the Moon... as green as the Earth or as blue as the deepest Sea. As sacred as the purple that rises in the mountain high or as orange as the glow of the fire that burns in depth of all beings. Be as We, happy and content in all you have given and live as each day continues into darkness.

"For in each end is a beginning" ... Bold and bright and green and beautiful.

Grow as the plant and return as We.

I send you love and light and a promise of a NEW SEASON.

I am, WE are... The Falling Leaves of Findhorn

Autumn Leaf Findhorn — Revised

I am the Autumn Leaf, changing and growing older as all things do. This illusion of old age leading me once again to this path I have taken before. I will enter again, for a short time, a safe place until I begin my journey back to where I began.

I was once bright green and turned my face towards the sun. I soaked in her warmth and heard the birds sing in my hair. I looked for the meaning of every thing and flew through the night in dreams, remembering the glow of the lady (the Moon) that lights the sky changing the colors on my face. I felt the morning come as the dew settled softly on me. I have lived to be just what I am, giving to every *being* shelter when they needed it. I am a home to those that live in the branches below me and store energy for many uses. I send out healing energy to every *being* in your world.

This is what I do and what I did everyday in this place I call home.

Even though I am small, I had the energy I needed and my intelligence will stay with me throughout all the lifetimes to come.

My species has told me of the time they spent in the dark earth below. I understand this and know that everything comes and goes and returns again. Like me you are born, you die and you are born again. Believe what is written here because this journey begins first in your mind. Everything will become real if you accept that what we tell you is what we know to be true. So it is that I will return to the earth. My time finished in the "day light" of this place you call Earth.

In *the place of the trees* I moved with others like myself, giving to everyone the *Nature* of all things. Always trying to tell those of you that will listen about the beauty of the ones that live inside our world; speaking to those who ask inside their minds if we really exist but then never stopping long enough to hear us answer.

Letting go, I will now go again into that dark place. That place that will bring me the warmth and comfort I have wanted for so long. As my sisters and brothers also fall, one on top of another, they are happy. They understand that everything begins and ends in its own beauty, each season bringing with it a different kind of beauty than the one before.

Be happy with life, but accept what death will bring too. Nothing ever dies but only begins again, new and bright and giving each a chance to become more than it was before. I wish for you now a soft place to lie in the earth when your time on earth is over ... warm and comforting. I wish you the joy of re-entering the world that is new and bright and filled with the love for all *beings*. Just as all of *Nature* loves all of you, we hope that you love us too. We are all the same, all living together and this is the real plan.

Follow in the light of those that have helped you. Honor the final days that will come ... alive with the passion you each feel for the life you have lead. Be happy in "your truth" knowing what is coming at the end of this life and beyond ... and like us, go out in blaze of color! Whether it is as red as the Sun or as golden as the Moon ... as green as the Earth or as blue as the deepest Sea ... as sacred as the color purple that rises in the highest mountain or as orange as the fire that burns in the depth of your soul ... be like us, happy and satisfied in everything you have given in this lifetime. Live as if each day will never end ... even after you die.

"For in each ending is a beginning", bold and bright and green and beautiful.

Grow like the plants and return like we do.

I send to you all the love and the light and a promise of a NEW SEASON.

I am, WE are ... The Falling Leaves of Findhorn

It makes you want to go out and buy the brightest and most colorful outfit you can find, doesn't it?

I love the part where they say, "Live as if each day will never end"; honoring the days we have left and making each one count; always remembering that Nature loves us and we should love her too.

So do as the Autumn Leaf does, go out in a blaze of color. Let everyone know that your life mattered and that you celebrate it. Accept that death is only a beginning, not an ending. If we could just believe and do this, then the rest of our time left in this lifetime would just be the "icing on the cake!"

The Beech

Forres, Scotland – Saturday, August 16, 2003

THERE IS A GROVE OF Beech Trees on a lovely hill in Forres, Scotland. This hill is thought to have some very magical qualities and I have found this quite true. Every time I visit I make a connection with my old friend Pan, and he in turn connects me with the local Nature Spirits in the area.

It was a lovely summer day and I had climbed the hill just for the purpose of connecting with one of those Spirits. When I reached the top I sat in my favorite spot and couldn't help noticing that a large grove of Beech Trees was trying to get my attention. It was not windy but they were waving about anyway. Were they waving at me?

I know by now that you must imagine that I go around looking for messages from every plant or tree I see. Unfortunately, you are right. Why do I say unfortunately? Because at this point in time I can't just relax and enjoy the pleasantries of looking at and enjoying Nature. I am compelled to listen to what Nature has to say.

You are right, I don't really have too, but after all this time I do it anyway. I will try to explain this in the best way I can.

Nature, at this point, is like a very close friend. It welcomes me each time I see it and is actually happy to see me. It gives me information that I need for my project but also provides me with things I need in my personal life as well. It gives me medical advice, spiritual insight and tells me wonderful stories of times and *beings* that lived long ago. It is always there when I need it, in any weather and is conveniently located right outside my door. What more could a girl, or anyone for that matter, ask for? So the fact that I do listen when I take my walks is how I noticed when the Beech Trees were trying to get my attention. The waving of the Beech Trees was sort of like raising your hand in the Elemental Kingdom. They wanted to be called on to tell their story.

That is exactly what I did and as you will see, they had many very interesting things to say.

THE BEECH

Enter you in silence to this world ... unspoken, but ever aware. Knowing and yet invisible are we to many but in this place we reign true and with this comes the knowledge needed to expand and begin again the transformation of this place.

Before many came and with them came others also that brought with them this gift that was offered…not only to those that dwelled among those here, but among others that understood not all that we were... All that we are.

As the eons passed, others came and with them countless changes and gifts also were offered but in these times things changed and what was before became forgotten and the longing began.

For if Nature does not exist within the realm of others, then this past that was so bright with the light that leads us all, would be as nothing but a glow that is emitted when those that choose to understand and know challenge those that exist here. Then this energy combines and the strength builds all things ... be they your life or ours. For only through these energies can we also become one, existing in all things as total beings encompassed within this web that we call creation. For all things are connected and through this connection all of energy exists, not only that which you see in us but all that can not be seen. For the infinitesimal lights that emit in all of us, that burning desire of knowledge, exists also in the spark that ignites the fire in each plant and tree… In each rock and the water that flows to the sea...In the dragons that lived in ages past and the creatures that dwell in the years ahead. For all of life is and shall ever be a connection, a connection with all that were before and all that shall ever be … living each moment in the realization of changes and the acts that amplify these changes. Each guided through the Universe towards that goal that will lead him to that final destination, alight with the fire of knowledge impounded in all beings.

As you seek out still the truth to all things be aware that what exists, exists in your mind and the reality that you accept is only that... the acceptance of what you desire. The acceptance of the truths that you alone want to begin again all things that shall lead you towards these goals. As Nature is presented please know that what we give and what you desire are still your truths and what words we impart are still only that…a way to communicate to you what you desire. Thus in this, awakening the search that shall continue and the goals be met, if not in this time on this plane, then on many more to follow.

You glow in the light of joy with what we present and the knowledge of all that we provide. Your illusion of all things brings us to you and through this; all of what we are is laid open to you. Thus it is and thus we are as we are presented...with beauty and grace and change, ever needed by all things to survive.

Enter now our world, a gift of beauty for all that desire to begin again the connection with body and spirit. With all that wish to believe that only through all things may you continue. With the glow that follows the day and the sun that lights the night sky. With the mother that lies dormant in the belly of this planet and gives to all the love that warms you in ever facet of life. We come to you now through the heart of this living place to speak again to all that would desire our truth and in this, remain. For all paths lead to us and through us, all things begin. Knowledge given and received begins again … in the heart of all things, in the heart of all beings … in the heart of the ones you call the Nature Beings, the Goddess of the trees, the Knights of the stones, the Devas of the forests, and the Old Men of the glens. They exist even as you and await now their voice. Begin again where you have before, for to get to the end you must first begin at the beginning. Is this not truth? And so in all things we begin … The voices of Nature …

Look about and acknowledge us, for we are Nature … Each part individual, each part separate and each part willing to deliver what it must, to be what it can… for all beings. Look at us with eyes open to understanding and with hearts open to the love that emits through us the guidance presented. Thus we begin and thus it is so.

We are the Beech.

You sit under us contemplating what we desire and what course we pursue in our quest. Knowing that we seek this place for the distances from others, we begin...

Long ago we erupted upon this plane to give shelter to all that sought it. Long ago our knowledge was emitted and we came to man, ambassadors to levels different than those imposed upon you in this time. Once we scattered our being in lands well below and were known for all that we provided. As the lack of knowledge was transcribed, we became what we are in this age and through this we attained our name and the notoriety of such.

Many find us a comfort, for the enlightenment of our being brings to many ideas that if not encountered, would not be possible. We bring to those that ask the knowledge of things that are the gift of sight as it has been pronounced… The gift of knowledge to address things that will "transpire" them to places unseen in this realm, as many associate our being with the necessities of idleness, once tempered by the grace of our being. Those that know understand that our being shall extend to them, the choices of this life and the altering of their levels in many forms. For we are the "Transformers", the renewer of shapes so long forgotten, yet hidden in the memories of Shaman and Old Men that roamed these planes so many ages ago. Yes, we remain true to our fate and the legends that surround this lore. For only through transformation can all things realize what they must, to attain the levels needed to become again that which they must, to attain that level of awareness in this lifetime. Many use the plant at our <u>root</u> to bring about changes and in this it is necessary but as the branches that lie at your feet, the ability in them … through the spirit in use … shall give all that ask to begin again in our world, the flight of fancy long lost.

Existing still in the shadow lands are many things that shall bring about changes and thus in these do we lie. Ever present to the world, we present ourselves. Facing forward, shading and moving...calling to those that would dare to enter our world, to enter their world of shadows. For all things have this and all things dwell within the dark and the light. As our souls pull toward the center of this dark Earth to be awakened by the burning core, so do you also become aglow by energy surrounding you in all levels. As our roots seek out what we must in the darkness of the Earth, these shadows are accepted. For only through these dark spaces can we attain the light that shall sustain us. As the embers lie deep with the core of this place we know that what we must attain is there… through the coldness of the winter, through the dampness of the rain, through the heat of the sun, the darkness remains. Nurturing and giving and providing the sustenance to continue. We offer you this darkness but in it you must find the joy of the core... the warmth of the essence that is in all things. For this planet that you call Earth is all in this time and in her we revel and thus in her we exist, ever ready to accept what she desires. Imparting to all her knowledge through this darkness, we offer all to delve within us and to find this connection. For We as the Beech, have accepted and present to you in all things our path to your inner being … to the self so hidden in the dark realms of yourself, in the dark realms of your Earth.

Journey with us if you may and encounter within us the beauty that the dark has to offer, that the enlightenment comes from where the shadows grow. Use our being as a conduit to the dark side but understand that what we offer is not a path to betrayal but a truth to be uncovered. Awaken to the soul of the one that lights your path in this existence.

Sit beneath our boughs; take a branch through offerings and call upon the realms of the Beech to open wide that world of magic to you and all that would know the mysteries of the Earth. For all things exist only through the acceptance of all things. Though the acceptance of lives lead in totality of the realization of all things... Relating to the light that shines in the heavens above or the dark that is emitted in the moonless night, upon your soul.

All things exist and all things are as they are planned. All things are executed as they are desired.

We are the Beech, the bringer of light through the shadows of your soul. Follow us into that land and relive again the days before.

We remain... The Beeches of Findhorn Power Point

THE BEECH — REVISED

Come into this world quietly, a world that is silent but always aware.

We know you are here and yet to most of you we are invisible. We truly rule here and this brings the knowledge we need to grow and to again begin the transformation of this place; to bring it back to what it was before.

Long ago many strangers came here and brought with them *beings* that offered us gifts. Not only to us who live among those here, but to *the others; the others* that did not understand all that we were and all that we are. As the ages passed, more *beings* came and brought with them more gifts and along with these came countless changes. Our world as it had been before was forgotten and the longing for that time started again.

If *Nature* does not live inside the world of *the others*, then this past that was so bright with the light that guides us all would be nothing. When those that choose to understand and learn, challenge those that live here, a glow is sent out and this energy combines. This powerful energy builds everything, both in your lives and in ours. Only through this energy can we all become one, living together as complete *beings* inside this web we call creation.

All things are connected and through this connection all energy exists. Not only what you see in us but also what you can't see. The tiniest infinitesimal light that glows in all of us, that burning desire for knowledge, also exists in the spark that lights the fire in each plant and tree. In each rock and the water that flows to the sea and in the dragons that lived long ago and the creatures that will live in the years ahead.

All of life is and will always be connected; connected with everything that we were before and all that we will ever be, each of us living these moments and finally realizing the changes we have made and the acts that increased these changes. Each change guided through the Universe towards that goal that will lead us all to that final destination; a destination set on fire with the knowledge stored in every *being*. As you continue to look for the truth in everything, be aware that what exists, exists in your mind and the reality that you accept is the reality that you want. Accepting these truths, which you alone want, will restart all that you need to lead you to those goals.

As *Nature* appears to you, please realize that what she gives and what you want are still what you believe is true and the words that we say to you are still only that, a way to bring you what you want. In doing this it will awaken the search that will continue, meeting the goals you have set, if not in this lifetime on this Earthy plane, then on many more to come.

You glow in the joy of what we tell you and the information that we will provide. Your illusion of all things brings us here and through this we open ourselves to you. This is the way it is and this is why we are shown with beauty and grace and change, the change needed by all *beings* to survive.

Come with us now into our world, a gift of beauty for anyone that once again wants to connect with body and spirit. With those that wish to believe that only through the connection of all things may we go on. With the glow that follows the day and the sun that lights the night sky and with the *Mother* that lies dormant in the belly of this planet and gives to every *being* all the love that warms them in each moment of their lives.

We come to you now through the heart of this living place to speak again to those who want our truth and in this truth we will remain.

All paths lead to us and through us everything begins. The knowledge given and received again begins in the heart of all things and in the heart of all *beings*. It begins in the heart of the ones you call the *Nature Spirits*, in the *Goddess* of the trees, the *Knights* of the

Stones, the *Devas* of the forests and the *Old Men* of the glen. They live just as you live and will speak to you if you listen.

Begin again where you did before because to get to the end you must first start at the beginning. Isn't this true? So in all things, we begin as *The Voices of Nature*.

Look around and notice that we are here. We are *Nature*. Each part individual, each part separate, and each part willing to deliver what it must to be all that it can be for all *beings*. Look at us with your eyes open to understanding and with your hearts open to the love that comes through this guidance we give to you. This is how it is and so we begin.

We are The Beech (Trees). You sit under us wondering what we want and what we need to do to fulfill our purpose here. Knowing that we chose this place because it is far away from others, we will begin:

Long ago we came to this plane; in this place you call Earth, to give shelter to any being that needed it. At that time what we knew could be spoken, so we came to man as ambassadors to levels that were different than those known in that time.

Once we lived in many places, on a different level below and were known for everything we provided. Because the knowledge of what we were was never written down, we became what we are today and through this received the name we are called now.

Many *beings* find us a comfort because the enlightenment we have gives them ideas that could only seem possible by coming in contact with us. We give those that ask the "gift of sight", as you say in your world, the gift that gives them the knowledge that will take them to places not seen in your world. Many think of us as a necessary place to relax or meditate, because the strength and gentleness of our being bring about these changes. Those that know understand that we will give them choices in this life and also the means to alter their levels of awareness in many forms. We are the *Transformers*, the restorer of shapes forgotten so long ago. We lie hidden in the memories of Shaman and Old Men that roamed these worlds so many ages ago. Yes, we remain true to our fate and the legends that surround these stories. Only through transformation can all things become what they must become to reach the level that is needed to attain awareness in this lifetime.

Many find it necessary to use the plant at our root to bring about changes. It is also possible to use the branches that lie at your feet. The spirit that lives in each of these will give those that ask again to come into our world, the "flight of fancy", lost long ago.

We lie in the *shadow lands* where many of those that can bring about changes exist. Always available to you in your world, we offer ourselves. We face forward, shading and moving, calling on anyone who would dare to enter our world, to enter their world of shadows. All things have their shadows and all things live within the darkness and the light. Just as our souls pull towards the center of this dark Earth to be awakened by its burning core, you too become "lit" by the energy that surrounds you on all levels. When our roots reach for what they need in the darkness of the Earth, these shadows are accepted. Only through these dark places are we able to get the light we need to survive. Just as the embers lie deep within this place, we know that what we need is also there. Through the coldness of the winter, through the dampness of the rain, and through the heat of the sun the darkness still remains; nurturing, giving and providing what we need to continue.

We offer you this darkness but in it you must find the joy of the core, the center that is the warmth of the essence that is in all things.

This planet that you call *Earth* is all that there is now. Living and always ready to accept what she asks, we rejoice in her. Sharing her knowledge through the darkness, we offer any *being* the opportunity to come inside us and find this connection. We, The Beech, have accepted this job and give you in the way that it's needed, our path to your inner being; the path to that "self" so hidden in the dark realms of "your self" inside the dark realms of "your Earth".

Journey with us if you can and see inside us the beauty that the dark has to offer and that enlightenment comes from where the shadows grow. Use us as a channel to the dark side but understand that what we offer is not a path to betrayal but a truth to be uncovered. Awaken to the soul of the One that lights your path in this lifetime. Sit beneath our branches; take a branch through offerings and call upon those worlds of The Beech to open that world of magic to you and to all that would like to know the mysteries of the Earth.

All things exist only because they are accepted by all things as existing; lives existing and living, in a total relationship with all things. Understanding the light that shines in the heaven above or the dark that covers the moonless night upon your soul, all things exist and all things are as they are planned. All things become reality when they are wanted.

We are The Beech, the bringer of light through the shadows of your soul. Follow us into that land and again relive the days and the lives before.

We remain, The Beeches of Findhorn Power Point

Finally, Nature talks about the Shadowland; that place between the darkness and the light. I think that The Beech is talking about their world, the world in-between that offers us answers to the past. Answers of how Nature came to become part of this world called Earth and who we, the "human" *beings,* were before. The past is a mystery and everyone would like to discover the secrets hidden away or forgotten through time. The Beech says it has always offered a way to go between these worlds and travel back to these days long ago.

The Shaman and other brave souls have used this power to find these answers and have seen more than we could ever understand. Our belief systems have changed and what we knew as true in the past has faded and now those truths are only legends told in stories around the fireside. It is a pity, because I certainly would love to know who "*the others*" were. If the Beech Trees can offer this "enlightenment" to anyone who will accept them for what and who they are, then I will be the next one in line. Are you willing to join me?

The Yews of Brody Castle

Scotland – Monday, August 25, 2003

I HAVE CONNECTED WITH MANY different trees and in several places while putting together this book. This has to be one of the most interesting and yes, enlightening readings I have received.

The Yew Tree has throughout history been connected with the "all mysterious". Some would say the Occult, but that to me has a very bad connotation. I know that "Occult" actually means "beyond human understanding" which is exactly what we are dealing with, yet the word still reminds me of dark nights, hooded figures, and mysterious "knocking" around tables filled with seekers of the dead.

I have always associated The Yew more with wizards, such as Merlin, with wands fashioned out of their branches.

I know that cemeteries all over the world, but mainly in the British Isles, are filled with Yew Trees often planted by ancient people to honor and communicate with the dead. This however was not foremost on my mind when I visited the park surrounding Brody Castle in Scotland. In fact I was only supposed to pick a tree and try to "get a feeling" from it. I had been doing a course called "Living with Angels" and we had all come to Brody Castle to try and connect with the Angel or Angels of the trees that grew in the area. There are several varieties, trees not Angels, some gigantic, having lived there for hundreds of years.

While the others wandered about looking for their perfect tree, I was drawn to a few Yew Trees growing in a cluster out in the open. When I first arrived I had seen a gigantic Yew Tree on the green and tried to communicate with it. It wouldn't let me near it, so I moved on. Yes, I am convinced that even trees have "bad days" and this was one of them, at least for this particular tree. So I moved on until I was called by the more friendly Yews in the cluster. After finding these trees and hearing their story I began to wonder if this is why the Ancients planted them in the cemeteries.

As you will see, The Yews are a kind of "holder of memories" for those that had died and they can give back these memories to whoever visits these places. This would or could, if they listened, comfort them. This makes a lot of sense and may be the reason that so many people feel at peace when they visit a cemetery. I hope you will think about this the next time you have a chance or reason to visit a cemetery. If you do and there is a Yew Tree, why not sit under it and let the memories of the ones you have lost return again. This is the gift that the Yew offers you.

THE YEWS OF BRODY CASTLE

We are the Yew, collective but separate, near yet distant in your reality.

Coming here is progression and choices begin again. In this place many collect in time and within these walls the echo of things past relate not only to our being but those in your age as well.

As we dwell within our realm, many seek out our knowledge, for the past relates to many things. Often though we intend to deliver what is necessary to all beings in times of change, things become as before, differently taken. Thus what is reality becomes shaded by lore long past ... given in time. As we exist to be what we must, reasons are attained for our being. Yet in these, all things relate not only to what we are but to what we shall become. You seek now what we do in this place. To what purpose we exist.

As all beings in this realm have chosen their path, we too have begun, once again, our tasks. To live freely, has always been the choice of all things, be they you or us or others that exist in places unseen by those that dwell within your world. For places exist that contain within their portals, vital souls, entities driven to this place by deeds long past. Others exist in a land under this earth and lead many to tasks needed for the success of your realm. Many others remain encompassed deep within the soul of the Great One, the Earth, and are as described by many that exist on your plane (through legend, myth and music). Each in turn begins and ends his existence where chosen, only to begin again ... new and refreshed and renewed in his timetable of reality. As you enter now our world, be amazed not by the substance of knowledge imparted by those in this place, but to the reality differently presented within these boundaries you call home. For all things, be it the smallest of beings or the largest that exist in the ethers above, all contain information imparted to them to release this knowledge to sustain their realm. As each in turn accepts their task, they begin and end in a whirl of knowledge, often carried on by tolerance to what was before. Often they relate this through terms unfamiliar to you, but knowing to us in our ability to comprehend such knowledge. Thus the chain continues, each in their own time, carrying this knowledge further into time and space … unlike that which you comprehend.

As you seek now our response, become aware that what we present shall be of interest to all that attain this knowledge. Let it also become truth in fact, for no creatures, be they tiny or large, shall lead you towards truths that are no longer valid.

As we relate to this place, we send inner peace and the roots of our system connect with those that have passed before. As the Spirit returns, the essence of what was before is relayed to our being and this process brings to us the knowledge of your world. Thus in accepting the position to be among those that transcend, we accept also the duty and the knowledge that will be passed in the aura of the souls that wander still among our leaves. As a soul passes and returns once more to the great Mother, she passes on to all beings this gift. The gift that she sends is given to all that would accept (this) knowledge and the continuation of what is needed to continue. As this soul again reunites with his earthy pleasure, released again to challenges untapped in former existences, many past discretions are ignored but in our reality this knowledge is stored and when needed transferred to others that seek us out. Though many that stay near us or seek us out find needed answers to questions, others do not hear, for in your world, thoughts transpire not to realms unseen. Still many that are open, knowing not why they seek, find still that essence of this knowledge sent through our spirit. Thus in transpiring within our bounds, answers are given to questions that plague their souls. Thus it is that the ones that pass offer those that live advice and through us and the knowledge attained, the shift is made.

Ever present are we in times of trouble, weeping hearts alive with grief, yet in these moments the past information can resolve issues and these souls so troubled can find what they must to continue on through their life upon this plane. Being Inner Plane Guides is relevant in this case, that is truth, but we act not in such a manner but only in our reality of acceptance and exchange. Thus our purpose is not only one of transition but one of acceptance to those that seek respite in times of trouble. So in reality we are also Givers, not in the sense of nourishment provided, but in information and relaying of messages to those that remain.

Seek us out and listen, for we speak of time long past and lives long lost; of troubled pasts and welcomed lives; of sudden death and ancient renewal; of times and customs and legends and dreams; of curiosity and magic and love and desire.

We are the <u>Knowers</u>, this is truth. We are the <u>Relayers</u>, this is truth.

We are the Yew, the Ones That Know.

Sit under our boughs and all the greatness of the world shall be yours.

We remain, The Yews of Brody Castle

THE YEWS OF BRODY CASTLE—REVISED

We are the *Yew Trees*, a collective but each still individual. We are close to you but far away from the world you see. You have moved along on your journey by coming here and you will again have to make choices.

Here in this garden many things in time come together and inside these walls the voices of the past speak not only for us but for those that live in your time as well.

Living here in our world, several come searching for what we know because our past is connected to many things. Many times when we try to relay the information that is needed in this time of change, it is often taken in the wrong way. This causes what is true to become mixed up with the legends of the past.

Though we live to be what we must be, there are reasons that we exist. Just as each *being* in your world has chosen their path in this lifetime, we once again have chosen ours. Living in freedom has always been the choice of all *beings*, whether it is you, us or others that exist in places that you have never seen. We all search for this. Even so, there are places that exist which contain inside them doorways through which living souls were sent because of things they had done in the past. Others live in a land under the Earth and are assigned jobs that are needed to maintain your world. Some remain trapped deep within the soul of our *Great Mother Earth* and they are still remembered through your legends, myths, and music.[58]

So it is that each *being* begins and ends its life where it chooses, only to begin again new and renewed in the time table of his world.

---

58 See Glastonbury Tor.

As you enter our world don't be amazed by the amount of knowledge given to you by those that live here, but instead to the different worlds that are inside this place you call home. Every *being*, whether it is the smallest one on earth or the largest one that lives in the air above,[59] all have information that they need to keep their world alive. When they accept this job, it begins and ends in a never ending spiral of knowledge, often because they accept what came before. Sometimes they pass on this information in ways that only we can understand. The chain continues, each in its own time carrying this information further into time and space and differently then anything you can understand. Just realize that as you ask us for our answers, anything we give you will be of interest to those who are searching for this information. Let it also be known that what we say is true "FACT" because no creature, either large or small, will tell you things that are no longer true.

Our purpose here is to provide inner peace and through our root system we connect with those that have died before. As the *Spirit* returns, the *essence* (or *soul*) of what that person was before is sent to us and this process brings us information about your world. In accepting this job to be with those that "transcend, pass-over, or die" we also accept the duty and the knowledge that will be passed into the *auras* of the souls that still wander in this place.

When a soul passes on and returns again to our *Mother Earth, she* passes on this gift of knowledge to all *beings* that will accept this, if it is what is needed by them to continue. When this *soul* finally "reunites with his earthly pleasure" (he is reborn on Earth) and again faces the challenges he did not accept in his former life, many things he had done in his past are forgotten. In our world, this information is stored and when it is needed is transferred to others that look for answers. Many that come here to ask us for answers find what they are looking for. Others just can't hear. In your world thoughts don't travel between worlds that aren't seen. Still, many that are open, even if they may not know what they are looking for, can still find that "essence" of this knowledge being sent to them through *Spirit.* So in walking among us, the questions that may "weigh heavy on your mind" (or bug the heck out of you) are often answered. In this way the ones that have died offer those that live advice. Through us and the knowledge that we have, the exchange is made.

We are always here in times of trouble; for those weeping hearts full of grief. In these moments, past information can sometimes resolve issues and these people that are so troubled can find what they need to carry on with their lives in your world.

Though it is true that being an *Inner Plane Guide* is important in this case, we don't act in that way but only through our world of acceptance and exchange. Our purpose is not only one of transition or moving information from one place to another but also in accepting those that look for rest in their time of trouble.

In each reality, both yours and ours, we are *Givers*. Not in that we give food (like the orange or apple tree, etc.) but in the information and the messages we give to those that are left behind after the death of a loved one.

We ask that you look for us and listen. We will tell you about times and lives lost long ago; of sudden death and ancient rebirth; of times and customs and legends and dreams; of strange things and magic and love and desire.

We are the *knowers*, this is our truth. We are the *relayers*, this is also our truth. We are the *Yew … the Ones That Know.* Sit under our branches and all the greatness of this world will be yours.

We are still here, *The Yews of Brody Castle*

There is so much to understand here and so many opportunities as well. If the Yew offer all those connections to the past as they say, then the answers to so many questions about our past could be answered. Not only questions about history but about the loved ones and the lives that mean so much to each of us personally.

The more readings I do the more incredible things I learn. The way Nature is so connected with us and how, even in those times when we need help the most, she is always there to help, even if we don't recognize it. I think this is one reason the Elemental Kingdom asked me to write this book. To put down on paper what they could not get us to see.

I hope you will read this again and see if what they say doesn't make a lot of sense. Maybe those feelings of comfort you felt have come from sources you have never acknowledged. Understanding and accepting is hard to do in this world, especially when it has to do with something as mythical as Nature Spirits. Yet most of the things that seem so hard to believe are actually not that hard to accept if you realize it is your own acceptance that keeps you from doing it. If you would try to understand, to listen, and to truly believe then I think anything is possible. Whether it is The Elemental Kingdom, The Yew Tree or that the Sun will rise in the morning, if you believe it to be so, it becomes so.

Accepting that other worlds are there to help you is something good after all. Nature provides for us all and the Yew

---

59 Here they refer to the atmosphere or "ether" which they consider a singular Elemental Being.

Trees' gift is just an added bonus. This gift may be just what is needed in those times when nothing else seems to help; a reconnection of the memories that bring us back to those that have gone ahead of us.

Don't you think the Yew Tree has a wonderful job?

The Deva of the Lake

Black Hills, Scotland – August 28, 2003

IN THE SUMMER OF 2003 while in Findhorn, Scotland, I was taking a course called "Working with Angels". Speaking truthfully, this has never been a favorite subject of mine but since I wanted to return to Findhorn and this was the only course available at the time, I decided I would take it. During this week we were a given a unique opportunity to a visit a private estate, which included this magnificent lake and surrounding forest.

I must say this has to be one of the most beautiful places I have ever seen in my life. The lake is full of beautiful lilies and the trees have a magnificent green moss that touches the water. The light reflects off the lake and you can see the *Water Spirits* dance in the sky above it. It is truly magical. Something only a poet could describe.

We were all asked to try and connect with the *Angel*, or in my case The *Nature Spirit*, of this place. I have to say, I had a hard time concentrating on this because it was so beautiful but then above the lake I saw a swirling mass of colors and I knew that it must be the *Elemental* presence of this place.

We had spoken about The *Devas* in this course, but as of yet I hadn't communicated with one. I had heard of them of course, through the *Nature Spirit* channelings I had had so far but this was my first connection with an actual *Deva of the Elemental Kingdom*.

When they speak about the *Devas* as being "beings full of light", they do not exaggerate. The glowing, swirling, colorful light *being* that I saw can only be compared to how I would imagine the Northern Lights to appear. Since I have never seen the Northern Lights, this is only my idea but to me the *Deva* appeared as strikingly beautiful, of course magical and without a doubt, something from another world.

I believe the channeling I received reflected through her the light that I saw.

THE DEVA OF THE LAKE – BLACK HILLS, SCOTLAND

I come to you now, the great SHE that lights the way, the reigner of this place. The lighter that illuminates all of God's creations. For in my power is given the Earthly tasks, the flowing of the energy to places unseen. I preside, this is true, yet in my world all dwell not alone, but all one and the acts performed are such as given to all that dwell here. Seeking now, you await not in sight or sound, but in the joy that abounds in the wonder of this place … The beauty that comes not from one entity, but all working as one to become all that you see. For the tasks imposed are not only on those that dwell within my care, but on all the Devas and Spirits and Angels that reign here as well. For lack of being is never raised upon this place and ones that dwell within accept this as well.

All strive to give what they must to attain all for your world. Working collectively we resolve all things but wary are we to many that would hamper this cause. So we dwell as you, in a world of choice, a world not seen by many that lack the understanding of our place on this planet.

I evolved as before into what I have become. Radiant in all things but stern is my appearance to many on your plane. For those that seek to destroy this place shall seek not the beauty that we instill. They return not to tell all of the work we seek to attain and so we send them away. For in their mind, acceptance of our ways shall only be the door to understanding, the lock turning when the latch to knowledge is turned. Thus when they attain not this knowledge, those that would harm are sent away. Not by force or lack of will but by ignorance of the joy that emits from the beings that dwell in this place.

I spread before you now my hand of love upon the water … to spread to all that love and care and (to) know that only through this gift … may they survive.

I am the Deva of this Lake at Black Hills.

The Deva of the Lake at Black Hills — Revised

I come to you today, the great female ruling force of this place, a light that illuminates all of God's creations. I use my power for my earthly job of directing the flow of energy to those places you can not see.

(I ask, "Do you live here?") Yes, it is true that I live here but in my world no one lives alone, we all live as one, working together doing the jobs we do. As you look around here, you don't stop to see and hear what we have to say but only feel the joy that grows from the beauty of this amazing place; the beauty that does not come from only one *being* but from all of us working together as one to become what you see. The jobs I assign are not only for all of those in my care but also for the *Devas, Spirits,* and *Angels* that live here as well.

Not existing is never questioned in this place and the ones that live in this world accept this. They all try to give what they can to make this possible for our world. Working together we resolve our problems but are wary of those that would try to obstruct our purpose. We live as you do, in a world of choice but many of you do not understand our place, or what we do on your planet.

I evolved as I have done before into what I have become today; filled with happiness and love but appearing angry to many in your world. Those that want to destroy our world do not see the beauty that we provide. They do not return to tell everyone of the work that we do to provide this beauty, so we send them away. Accepting our ways will lead them to the door of understanding, the lock opening when the latch to knowledge is turned. When they do not understand this, the ones that would like to harm us are turned away. Not by force or because they aren't willing to see but by not understanding the joy that comes from the *beings* that live in this place.

I now open my hand of love to you upon the water, to spread to all that love and care and know that only through this gift can they survive.

I am the *Deva of the Lake at Black Hills*

The Deva makes it clear that what they do here is important and the greatest loss is not to their world but to ours for not recognizing what they give to us in ours. The beauty that surrounds us becomes real when we enter the world of The Elemental Kingdom.

The Lake at Black Hills, as I said before is stunningly beautiful. After I had received this reading from the Deva I decided to ask the Nature Spirits of the Lake to tell me about this place, what their jobs were and why they lived here. The reading was beautiful and describes the different aspects of their spiritual world. My only regret is that I didn't have enough time to finish the reading. I thought that maybe I shouldn't include it, but it was so beautiful I thought I would put it in anyway.

When you finish the reading maybe you will be able to reconnect with this beautiful place and understand what they were trying to say. If you get anything more, I would sure like to know what it was. I also hope if you ever get an opportunity to visit The Lake at Black Hills in Scotland, you jump on the chance. Maybe then you will see why the Deva and I have been trying to "enlighten" you with these readings and why this place stands out so much in my mind as the perfect entrance into the Elemental Kingdom.

The Lake itself has many *beings* living there and in the next reading you will see how the water itself plays such an important part in our lives. From the time we are born until the time we die it is water that sustains us. The Lake at Black Hills has many *beings* that assist in our well being. Each action, whether it is from something that you would never consider useful (such as the pond scum) to the Deva that lights the way for all her subjects, has a part to play in maintaining and providing what is needed. The balance is maintained because each entity does its job.

The magical dance will continue and Black Lake asks you to become part of it by understanding what is needed to maintain this beauty and the lives they have chosen.

The Black Hills Lake of Scotland

Thursday, August 28, 2003

THE DEVA OF THE LAKE at Black Hills explained that all of Nature plays a part in making this place the beautiful and magical spot that it is. Only through working together has this watery world become what I see in front of me. As you will find, when you read the passage below, everything and everyone is connected by water. From the tiniest bacteria to the largest lake, every being here has their own part to play in bringing and keeping this beauty alive. Understanding and accepting this can only help us understand our own connection with the waters of our planet and hopefully make us realize everything that they provide.

THE BLACK HILLS LAKE OF SCOTLAND

The lake arises and from the depths of your soul the connection becomes reality. For the insight to ponder still upon this feast is within the sight of all that enter here.

Illusions rise through countless years and dreams seek out only those that dare to follow. Through the water we flow, the great Energy Spirits that unite all places. For even as you seek us out, we elude you in vast streams ever flowing into countless pools of light … shimmering with the light that evolves from the glow within.

We await here, all that would ask of us what they desire and together we are one. Yet in other realities, we become as we exist … alone to view what may enter our plane, but together in oneness in the creation of this place.

Abundant in our growth, the Angel that dwells here is but a reflection of each person upon your plane, a wonderment of air, evolving through the triple issues (Goddess) of The Mother that guides us all. As she flows, not through the sky that is her home for it is not one of air but of water.

Like her sister the wind, she flows ever to continue until she, once again, begins again. As all creatures journey towards what they have chosen, so must water. For every being must believe and understand that what she provides does indeed bring life to all. For through the evolution of all time it is the water that unites all along its path through life, through death and rebirth. For even as the Earth becomes once again your haven when you pass, it is the water that becomes once again your leader and provider towards your eventual path home. For all things begin and end in water. Be it you in the womb of your species or all of Nature born out of the softness from the rain that falls upon the cool Earth in which we rest... to the animals that dwell within and also without and the beings unseen upon this plane. All live and exist because we live and exist. This is truth, our truth and the truth of all things in all planes upon this earth.

Wander now to the cool glades alive with tiny droplets of beings, glistening in the midst of each tree. Come to the meadows where the water pools in hollows and vales and offers respite for all that seek her there. Come to the great Deva that rules the lakes, alive with the spirit that ignites each holy place … to the animals that drink within the cool depths of her shore. To the plants that thrive for all beings, some a haven for gifts given to your world, some a haven for those that dwell within ours. All are connected in this great chain of life and through Her it flows.

As you look now upon the face of the Great Provider, through the eyes of water, know that what you see in the mists that call in the evening glens, the clouds that fill with the abundance of nourishment spilling over with the gifts for all below, to the cool rainbow that illuminates the skies through the prism elevated through our form is indeed all that we are. All things are as you see and the ones that lead you here have many uses. These are separate and the same and yet in each, you will find the ones that guide them ever forward in their evolution.

Each plant here has a purpose and a task undertaken in its need to exist; a need grown out of love for all beings. As you look forward, you will notice many that exist in our world.

The lilies that lie in the center of the divine space are abundant and through their evolution they have accepted this task. For only through them have we become what you see, clear and clean and able to sustain this for all that are served here. They are the Providers of the Light, for they bring through them the energy to regenerate and to cleanse the water; the precious liquids in which we dwell. They seek out entities that would enter here and cause the abundance needed to extend our being to become less useful to all. Yet each being, be they those that are giving and those that seem not, are a creation of the creator and have chosen a purpose in which to exist. As the lily may reunite the energies and work to purify the waters, those that she clears are also beneficial in other ways.

As many see them as a detriment, even the scum that lies at the top of the great lake emits energies for many. Through these many beings exist, (their) nourishment coming from parts given over for these cause. Annoyances often incurred by man can in actuality turn into gifts if one would only study these plants with love.

Thus many dwell here and each has within it, the spirit to light its way. Be it a Nature Spirit, an Elemental, or whatever labels you attach, all are a spark that ignites the <u>being</u> found in all living things. As you emit this spark when you arrive upon this planet, so does each plant and animal, each stone and cloud, each drop of water or each grain of sand upon the great shore of the Mother, that leads us all home. All are ignited by the torch that shall again light the way in this lifetime and in all lifetimes to come.

Seeking now, you have come again to the water to ask of its relationship to the Spirit Realm and to those that live within; to the "hierarchy" as you apply suit its calling.

Thus we begin. As each plant has a spark that ignites its growth, some move on to fulfill a larger task. Not disconnected ever with the realm before but only accepting challenges presented to them for future growth. In acceptance of these tasks, they begin again a cycle that teaches them various tasks in order to sustain those in their charge.

As the fruit on the tree, each entity must ripen and mature and then when ripe, the fruit may then provide nourishment to all that seek them out…

The passage was never finished. I had to leave. Hopefully I can return again someday and find out more.

BLACK HILLS LAKE OF SCOTLAND — REVISED

Looking out you see the lake and finally realize, deep within your soul, that the connection you feel for this place is real. Knowing that here it is possible for everyone to understand the beauty that surrounds them. As you look across the water, the visions that you have kept hidden throughout your life and the dreams that dare you to follow, suddenly seem within reach.

We are the *Great Energy Spirits*, flowing through the water and bringing together all the places in your world. Though you continue to search for us, we elude you; flowing through endless streams into countless pools of light; the shimmering light that comes from the glow within us all. We wait here for any one of you that can tell us what you truly want; what you are really searching for so we can become one.

In other realities we exist alone, keeping watch for any *being* that would enter our world. Yet we still remain together as one in creating this world that you see.

Always growing and learning, the *Angel* that lives here is just a reflection of each person in your world. *Like a Magical Being of Air* she flows and changes through the *Triple Goddess of The Mother*[60] *(Mother Nature)* that guides us all. Since the sky is not her home, she does not flow through the air but through the water. Like her *Sister the Wind,* she moves until she must begin again.

Just as each person must follow the path they have chosen in this lifetime, so must the water. Each, believing and understanding that what they give throughout their lifetime will bring something that is needed by everyone. Through the evolution of time it is the water that brings "all" things together along its path through life, death and then rebirth. If one chooses to be reborn once more on earth, it is the water that again becomes their leader and their provider, leading them towards their path back to their Earthly home. Whether

---

60 The triple *Goddess* is considered by many to be The **Maiden**, the **Mother** and the **Crone**; each an aspect of the *Great Goddess* or *Mother Earth*. As the seasons change, just as in life, *(Mother) Nature* moves through her phases. As the **Maiden** she is seeded. The seeds lie deep within her soil until the time is right for them to grow. The **Mother** *(Nature)* then gives birth in the spring when the seeds, plants, flowers, and trees awaken and later produce what the world needs to survive. Later in the fall, as the **Crone,** she drops her seeds and returns again to the *Earth* to await the winter and her time of rest. This is sometimes referred to as the cycle of *Nature*.

it is in the womb of your mother or all of *Nature,* born out of the rain that falls on the cool earth where we rest, everything begins and ends with water. All the animals that live on or within the earth and even the *beings* you can't see continue to live because we, *The Waters,* live and continue to live. This is the truth … our truth and the truth of all things in all planes on this place you call Earth.

Now walk into the cool glades alive with tiny droplets of *beings* glistening in the trees. Come to the meadows where the waters flow together and offer peace to all who look for *Her* there, *The Mother* that leads us all in the direction we have chosen.

Come to the great *Deva* that rules the lakes, alive with the spirit that lights each holy place; to the animals that drink within the cool depths of her shore and to the plants that live to provide for all *beings.* Some are safe places for gifts that are given to your world and others are for those that live in ours. All things are connected in this great chain of life and through *Her* everything flows.

As you look through the "eyes of the water" upon the face of *The Great Provider* understand that what you see in the mists of the valleys, in the clouds that fill with every wonderful thing needed, spilling over with the gifts for all below, or to the cool rainbow that lights up the skies through the highest prism above, is that all things are just as you see them. Understand now that the ones that led you here have many uses. These are separate and the same, and in each you will find *The One* that always guides them forward in their evolution. Each plant here has a purpose and a job it must do to exist; a need grown out of the love for all *beings.*

When you look in front of you, you will see many *beings* that exist in our world. The many lilies that lie in the center of this beautiful place, through their evolution, have accepted such a job. It is only through them that we become what you see. They keep the water clear and clean so we are able to continue this way of life for all that live here. They provide light because they bring through themselves the energy to regenerate and to clean the water; the precious liquid where we live. They look for others that would enter our world and remove or make these things less harmful so our world can survive. Each being, helpful or not, is still a creation of the *Creator* and has chosen its purpose to live. Just as the lily brings together the energies in her work to purify the waters, those that she removes are also helpful in their own way. Though many see them as harmful, even the scum that lie on top of the lake gives energy to many other *beings.* Because of this, many *beings* live because they receive the food that they need, given to them by these so-called "harmful" creatures. This is their purpose for living and the choice they have made.

Things that bother man, like the scum on the lake, can actually turn into a gift if he would just lovingly study these plant forms.

So it is that many *beings* live here and each has within it the spirit to light its way. Whether it is a *Nature Spirit, Elemental* or whatever label you wish to give it, each one is a spark that lights each living thing. Just as each of us sends out a spark when we arrive on this planet, so does each plant and animal … each stone and cloud … each drop of water or grain of sand that lies on the shore of our *Great Mother, Our Mother Earth* that leads us all home.

Looking now for answers, you have come again to *The Water* to ask how it and the world of the *Nature Spirit* and those that live within it are connected. Who is in charge and what purpose does each of them have in this world? This is our answer …

As we said before, each plant has a spark that starts its growth but some move on to fulfill a larger job. This does not mean that they are no longer a part of the world they knew before but only that they have accepted challenges that will help them in their future growth. When they accept these tasks or jobs, they again start a cycle that teaches them different things that will keep those that they are in charge of alive. Just like fruit on the tree, each being must ripen or mature. Only then can it give nourishment or knowledge to those that want it……

Like the Chalice Well, Black Hills Lake contains the great Energy Spirits that move the water forward. Working with Mother Nature, the waters flow throughout this planet and bring with them life and energy to every living being. The Lake at Black Hills is a reminder of how beautiful Nature can be. The waters here offer a place for reflection and an awakening to the truth that without them there would be no life.

I realize that we all know this, but again accepting that the waters themselves have a purpose and, like us, a journey that involves lessons of giving, renewal and release, can make us all more aware of the real reason we exist. Like the waters, we move forward and stop along the way to do what it is we need to do at the time. Then we flow on again, picking up bits of information and hopefully learning a few lessons along the way. Eventually we return to where we began, arriving as the water does to our own Great Ocean. Whatever your belief system, in looking at the Sea, a Lake, or even a Well you have to realize that Nature in all her wisdom has created something more than a drink in a plastic bottle that you carry with you. That Water is life, and Mother Nature is the provider. Handle her and our waters with respect. Enjoy everything that they bring us but always remember that without them … I'm sure you get the picture.

Message from Pan

Anaheim, California–Friday, June 11, 2004

I WAS SITTING OUT ON my deck feeling a bit blue, not knowing the real connection between myself and Nature. The animals in my yard were there, as they always are, and yet at this time I couldn't seem to find a connection. I knew that the animals would come (at least the blue jay, aptly named "BLUE") when you put out food, but what were their feelings? What were all the feelings of Nature? How do they really interact with us or should I ask… how do they actually interact with me?

So I called upon "Pan," the ancient *being* you've heard about who always happens to be there no matter what the situation. Yes, Pan is there for anyone at any time. You simply have to ask and like magic he appears!

Personally, I can hear Pan. You may just feel his presence as a gentle breeze on your cheek or as a leaf stirring in the corner of your garden. He may appear as a glimpse of something out of the corner of your eye but nonetheless he is there; always ready to listen. Pan is great at giving advice, but he will listen too. He will tell it to you straight, often saying things that you would rather not hear. He knows what you need and always seems to know the right thing to say in any situation.

As I was saying, I was really feeling down and asked Pan whether the animals really "loved" like we do? Do they just come because we give them food?

He, of course, had a brilliant answer… which he always seems to have. Pan told me that animals have instincts, not love exactly, but with these instincts come familiarity. They do not love in the same way that we do. They respond out of habit at first, but then become dependent. With dependency follows familiarity and then the animals actually look forward to seeing you whether you have food or not.

I thought about this and Pan is right. "BLUE" comes to the door everyday, often more than once a day. Of course, I give him his peanuts but most of the time he will only take one. There may be loads of peanuts there but he will only take one. Sometimes "BLUE" will sit outside my kitchen window waiting patiently until I notice him. If the door is open and I am not around, he will come into the house and wait on the kitchen table or railing until I come into the room. This cannot be just for the sake of a peanut … one peanut. It must be because he actually wants to see me. "BLUE" wants to know that I am still there.

Is this dependency? I really don't think so because he surely doesn't depend on that one peanut to survive. I think he does indeed have affection, if not love, for me and I am content with this.

I also noticed that when I was really depressed, a little squirrel, which I had been unsuccessful in trying to communicate with for quite awhile, came out of the bushes and looked at me. He actually looked into my eyes. I could hear him saying, "It's alright. We are here". This was such a great feeling.

It was then that Pan told me he had a few things to say and that I should come inside to write them down. I was also given a "talking to" for postponing this book for so long. So I did as he asked, and here I am ready to channel for you my friend Pan. I will tell you later how I came to know Pan and how our relationship has helped me move along in my daily life. For now, I must turn over this passage to him. I'm sure he has plenty to say. So for you all, I present my friend, Pan.

MESSAGE FROM PAN

I am Pan, the mystical creature of literature; timeless and yet always current to the ages in all realms. I exist as I have always existed, free to become what is needed in the timeline in which you dwell. I live at the edge of reality, a beacon to enter my world of living and breathing newness. Of birth and revival and challenges met. Of times long spent in the agony of changes concurrent with all time. I live and grow as you but become ever nearer to the places that exist not only in the imagination of mankind but in the world in which I dwell. For all are the same, in reality but each is accepted differently.

As you see, each being has a purpose to fulfill and with this challenges that must be met. I, being who I am, may hinder or not such challenges but still I do what must be done to encourage all to be what they must. I live not only in your garden but in all the gardens of all the world. I exist to serve the great Goddesses who rule the plant kingdom taking orders only from the Mother that lives within us all. For She alone holds the fate to all mankind and so, to the fate of you who read this now. Much has been written about the exploits of my timely illusions and I must admit that I have at times stepped out with many that would be considered not abatable to your way of thinking. Yet in doing so have learned about life and love ... ah love so aptly available to all on this path we have chosen.

I live in my world but work with beings that are all around and I am justly confirmed towards the desire of ones that seek it not in relationship to their wants and needs. As I live so do I use what I know to advance the learning and acceptance of all beings in this world. For this world, caught somewhere between here and there is quite different from the one in which you dwell. As cold as you may seem at times that is how different we are here. For the joy of our being radiates the warmth that lights our lives and encourages us to grow and renew and begin again each existence.

As Cheri the writer, or should I say "channel for this book," has found, I can come whenever needed. Call upon me with grace and I shall appear, though not in the worldly form you may know but in ways subtle but often not. Many have seen me in the forms written in centuries of novel sightings while others have experienced only the words I relay. Some have heard the sounds given to them on cool night with Nature in tune. I exist in all things and so appear as all things. Yet each has and will ever have what I may be in their minds and thus in times when I am needed may appear as they imagine ... or not. I avail myself to all and to none for I do what I know to be best for those I serve and can harbor great might when these are tread upon. For I am the guardian of Nature and She alone is my master. I am her servant and She rules all. No matter who or what you may be or know, no matter how much you may possess, She is all. No other will or can give to you what you need to exist.

I, in turn, work with the various Devas (as you relate to them) and through them connect with the Nature Spirits that are needed to control the growth of this planet. For we all are connected through Nature and without each one to another we neither would exist.

In times of trouble, I am called on to soothe many an angry, shall we call, "Sister" in ways that are not known to you. Yet still they are soothing to us here and often will quell their rage or indecision that they may have in a matter that shall or will concern you. Many of the Devas that rule here are well adept at dealing with the challenges that are represented and each assumes the tasks that She has accepted on her journey through our world. They all report to ones that rule them but in all, they reluctantly know that they are never more than the ones that they rule. For true fairness is something that is endowed upon all beings in our world. Thusly one can not be more than another, just performing differently and in tasks more becoming their nature.

I am Pan but then I have noted that I believe that I have more qualities that are needed by many that exist here. Yet I know also that I answer only to the one that leads us all and that, if called upon, should and shall relinquish all to her will. As of yet, I remain and conquer still the things that are presented. Throughout history I have achieved a "rogue" appearance yet still I insist that this is but an imagined quality given to ones that dream of lustful beings on lonely night. Yes, I have had my share of encounters, many of which have been observed on nights when the moon has fully shone and yet each have existed in their place and world, connecting when needed at the time to unite both worlds. For before, when the world was young, Nature and man ruled as one. Things were different and exchange was normal. But greed and the ability to control changed things and years and centuries, even eons of changes, brought about things that are not connected but laid to rest in legends of the past.

I live now as I always have but your generation does not. The legends and the lives of men long ago ring in what you know as myths and yet in these those seeds of reality do exist, and did exist in the world before. I long for those days when men and Nature grew as one. When all things were free and each understood their part in this world. When each grew in the knowledge of the others existence and the challenges of each other's goals were the challenges of both. This was and forever changed but still Nature is as She always was and shall continue to be.

Congruent to these issues I will now speak about the interactions of Nature and man and the relationship these have for each other. As man evolves Nature is pushed further towards the edges of time. Needless to say that soon we will cease to be what we must and all things will change, and not for the better I might add. For to cease what is truly Nature, to elevate man's notion of what it should be, is to change the scope of the world as you know it. To relegate Her to the backroom of a biological plant is to relegate yourself to extinction. For to manipulate the Mother, the Earth that gives you life is to destroy all that live upon it. Not *that it has not been done before. For in Her glory only She relegates what and who does what is done on your plane. I exist in a different world so this becomes moot in my world but in yours the extinction is imminent only if changes do not remain Hers. All is well said and yet in my times on this plane I have seen many changes and with them came growth and change. Though many may cease, others will come again and all will continue as before.*

Awaken my friends to the glory that is Nature. Communicate with all that is around you. Listen to more than the wind that howls in the winter. Listen instead to the softness of your Sister the breeze blowing gently through the trees. Feel her caress your skin. Feel the warmth of the sun on your shoulders as you stroll though the gardens that await you at every turn. Notice; yes, notice the flowers that bloom for you, the colors that are presented and the fragrances that are offered. Accept with gratitude the abundance of food that through ions are given by ones that work so hard to give you what you need. Rejoice in the calmness of the waves and the creatures that dwell beneath them, to the sky and the creatures that fly above. Rejoice in the sunset and reflect when the evening ends, always beginning and ending with the gifts given by Nature. For we are the quiet ones, the silent workers that sustain your planet. We are the life blood that courses through your world bringing to you life. Come and sit in the glens and listen to the Nature Spirits as they work to make your world a better place.

I am Pan, the intermediary of this place I call home, this place that dwells between your world and ours. I live and I am because I know what I do is what I must. I know that each thing is related to all things and only through this connection can we all survive. I can be heard on clear nights when the wind carries my song through the trees. I can be seen when the dawn breaks in the leaves of the trees as the first light hits their branches. I am seen in the dew that alights on the ground at night and the mist that covers the moors. I am in the light that arises from the sea at dusk and the moon that lights the sky at night. I am wherever you are and am with you when you call. I am part of Nature and I will follow Her until She is no more … Until you and all that you know no longer exists. For only through Her can you become what you have and that is all.

I am Pan.

MESSAGE FROM PAN — REVISED

I am *Pan*, that mystical creature of literature, timeless but always current in every age and in every world. I live as I have always lived; free to be what is needed in the period of time that I live. I exist at the edge of reality, a *"light"* calling you to enter a living and breathing new world. A world of birth and return and challenges conquered. Of times spent in the pain that comes with each changing age. I live and I grow just as you do, but stay closer to the places that exist, not only in the imagination of mankind but also in the world where I live. In reality, both of them are the same but each is accepted differently.

As you know, every *being* has a purpose to fulfill and with this challenges that must be met. I, being who I am, may keep these things from happening or not. Still, I do what must be done to encourage every *being* to be what they must be. I live not only in your garden but in all the gardens of the entire world. I exist to serve the *Great Goddesses* who rules the Plant Kingdom, taking orders only from *The Mother* (*Nature*) who lives inside us all. She alone holds the fate of all mankind and so, also holds the fate of you who are reading this now. Many stories have been written about my timely illusions… my well planned tricks and I must admit that at times I have "stepped out" or dallied with many *beings* that might not seem acceptable to your way of thinking. Rightly so if those that look for that in a relationship don't use it for their wants and needs. Yet in doing so, I have learned about life and love…ah, love is quite available to everyone on any path they have chosen.

I live in my world but work with *beings* that are all around you too. As I work, I use what I know to advance the learning and acceptance of all *beings* in this world.

This world, caught somewhere between here and there, is very different than the one you live in. As cold as yours may be at times, the joy of our world sends out a warmth that lights our lives and encourages us to grow, to renew and begin again… each new life.

As Cheri, the writer or should I say *channel for this book,* has found, I will come whenever I am needed. Just ask for me nicely and I will appear. This may not be in the worldly form you would expect, but rather in subtler ways…but then again, maybe not. Many of you have seen me in different forms and have written about me for centuries. Others have only heard the words I have to say. Yet each of you has an idea in your mind of what I should look like and so when I appear I often take on that image. I offer myself to everyone and to no one; because I do what I know is best for those that I serve. I can become very mean if you hurt them because I am the *Guardian of Nature*, and *she* alone is my master. I am her servant and *she* rules all *beings* in this world. No matter who or what you may be…or know, no matter how much you have, *she* is still everything. No one else can give you what you need to survive. I in turn work with the various *Devas* (as you call them) and through them connect with the *Nature Spirits* (or members of the *Elemental Kingdom*) that are needed to control the growth of the planet. We all are connected to *Nature* and without each other, neither of us would exist. In times of trouble I am called on to soothe many an angry, shall we call them, *"Sisters"* in ways that you could not understand. Yet they are calming to us here and this will sometimes stop their rage or their indecision they may have in a matter that may concern you and your world.

Many of the *Devas* here are quite experienced at dealing with the challenges that are brought to them and each assumes the job that *she* accepted on her journey though our world. They all report to others that rule them and reluctantly know that they are never better than the ones they rule. True fairness is something that everyone in this world has. So it is that one *being* is no better than another…just performing a job that is different and more suitable to their own qualifications.

I am *Pan*, and I know I have said that I believe I have more qualities that are needed here than most of the others that exist here. Yet, I also know that I answer only to the *"One That Guides Us All"* and if I were asked, would give it all up to please her. As of yet, I am still here and still solving the problems that are given to me.

Throughout history I have been represented as a kind of *"rogue"*. I still insist that this is an image thought up by those that dream of lustful (sex crazed) *beings* on lonely nights. It is true that I have had my share of *"encounters"*, many of which may have been seen on nights when the moon is full. Yet each one of these happened in their own place and world, connecting only at the time when it was needed to bring both worlds together.

Before, when the world was young, *Nature* and man ruled as one. Things were different and these exchanges were normal, but greed and the ability to control things over years and centuries, even eons of change, brought about things that severed this connection and are now laid to rest in the legends of the past.

I live as I always have, but your generation does not. The legends and the lives of those men of long ago are told in myths and yet in these stories the seeds of truth are there and they did exist in the world before. I long for those days when men and *Nature* lived together. When all things were free and every *being* knew the part they played in the world. In the times when each grew with the knowledge of the others lives and the challenges of each others goals were the challenges of both. Those days have changed forever but *Nature* is the same as *she* has always been… The same as *she* will always continue to be.

Changing my thought, I will now talk about the interaction between *Nature* and man and the relationship they have with one another. As man evolves, *Nature* is pushed further into the background. Needless to say, soon we will no longer be what we need to be, and everything will change, and not for the better I might add! To stop what is the true "nature" of *Nature;* to raise mans notion of what it *"should be"*, is to change the way the world is as you know it. To put her in the background and into a biological factory is to relegate yourselves to extinction. To manipulate the Mother… the Earth that gives you life, is to destroy everything that lives on it. Not that this hasn't been done before.

In Her glory, only *she* tells who and decides what can be done to her world.

I live in a different world so this doesn't affect mine but in yours that "not too pleasant" ending will take place if the changes do not remain hers and hers alone!

All this is well and good and yet in my time and in this world I have seen many changes and through these changes came the growth that brought more changes. Though many will have to die, others will come and it will just happen all over again.

Wake-up my friends to the glory of *Nature*. Communicate with all of it around you. Listen to more than the wind that howls in the winter. Listen instead to the softness of your *"Sister"* the breeze, gently blowing through the trees. Feel her caress your skin. Feel the warmth of the sun on your shoulders as you walk though the gardens that wait for you at every turn. Notice, yes notice, the flowers that bloom for you; the different colors, and their fragrances. Accept with gratitude all the food that through countless ages have been given to you by the *Nature Spirits* that work so hard to give you what you want. Be happy for the calming effect the waves have on you and for all the *beings* that live beneath them and to the sky and the *creatures* that fly above. Rejoice in the sunset and think back on your day when the evening ends, always beginning and ending with the gifts given to you by Nature. We are the quiet ones, the silent workers that keep your planet alive. We are the life blood that flows through your world bringing it life. Come and sit in our glens and listen to the *Nature Spirits* as they work to make your world a better place.

I am *Pan*, the one who lives in this place I call home, the world that exists between yours and mine. I live and I am who I am… because I do what I have to. I know that everything is connected to each other and only through this connection can we all survive. I can be heard on clear nights when the wind carries my song through the trees. I can be seen when the dawn breaks in the trees… as the first light hits the branches. You may see me in the dew that lies on the ground at night or in the mist that covers the moors. I am in the light that rises from the sea at dusk and the moon that lights the sky at night. I am wherever you are and am with you whenever you call. I am a part of *Nature* and will follow her until *she* no longer exists. Only through Her have you become what you have you become… and that is everything.

I am *Pan.*

Many things have been written about the mystical creature known as Pan and I am sure that more than a few of these legends are true.

I personally find Pan charming, witty and most of all always available when I call. This, no matter what kind of being he is, is reason enough to be fond of him. I guess the legends of his amorous encounters and his magical origins have always intrigued me, so when I first encountered him, or should I say heard him, I was surprised. The fact that I could hear him was a shock. At the time, I was climbing the path to the Power Point behind Cluny Hill College in Scotland. I wasn't alone but with a friend, so it wasn't just my imagination. Of course, I heard what you would expect Pan to be playing, the flute. Isn't this the old cliché from every story you've ever heard about Pan, so of course I didn't believe it. I figured it had to be someone from the college who was practicing their flute somewhere in the area. This of course turned out not to be the case.

I also learned that I was not the only person to hear Pan in the woods behind the college but in fact, he was heard quite often by many of the residents and visitors that came to study. Still, I was impressed that I had actually heard him. I had been allowed to step into that world of magic and legend. Having spoken to the plants and trees, this shouldn't have seemed all that surprising. Yet somehow it was. It was as if the Elemental Kingdom, the whole Elemental world, had accepted me as their partner in sharing their messages with our world.

Since that time I have heard, felt, or seen what Pan needed me to learn, not only in Scotland but even in my own backyard.

I have come to realize that he follows the orders of only one other being and that is Mother Nature herself. Like he said, "I am a part of (Mother) Nature and I will follow her until she no longer exists. Only through her have you become what you have become, and that is everything."

With a right hand man like Pan and an enlightened view of the Elemental Kingdom on our side, we might just make Pan's wish come true. His wish that once again we could return to a time when Man and Nature lived together, all things were free and everyone knew their part in the world.

That is my wish too.

The Peat at Castlerigg

Castlerigg, England – Monday, July 05, 2004

As I have mentioned, the *Standing Stones* and *Stone Circles* are something I dearly love. Give me a chance to visit any one of them and I am off in a flash. Part of the trip in the Lake District of England brought me within a reasonable distance to the *Stone Circle* called Castlerigg. It is located not far from Keswick, near the Scottish Border.

Since we were in the area, I persuaded my husband Hal to take me there. He had never been there before or even in the area so it wasn't that hard to talk him into it.

It was a very cold, rainy, and windy day. I have to admit that I have never been to Castlerigg when it hasn't been at least cold and windy, so this was not unexpected. What was unexpected was the smell of burning *Peat*.

For those of you that don't know, *Peat* is "carbonized vegetable matter, like moss, found in bogs and used mostly for fuel".[61] This area of England and Scotland is filled with watery marshes called bogs. People once used Peat for fuel and would literally cut chunks of it out of the bogs, dry it and then used it to feed their fires. Many still use it even today. It burns well, is free and keeps you warm. I think it smells a bit like burning coal which is understandable considering it is carbonized vegetable matter after all. And this makes it a *Nature Spirit*, right?

As I said, I had planned on getting a reading from the *Stones*, which I had done a few times previously. Instead what came through was a message from The Peat. I was amazed and delighted. This reading told me so much about the compassion that the *Elemental World* has for us. It is truly a beautiful passage that reminds us of the hardships we have endured through the ages and the great part that *Nature* played (and still plays) in keeping our dreams alive. Short but sweet, it is one of my favorites.

The Peat at Castlerigg, England

Gathering here and there we begin and end in a cloud. Though time and distances range and through us things begin, all have and shall ever be as before. Stored inside are countless ages of growth, through lessons and events learned or not.

Throughout time we as 'The Peat' have continued to encompass all that shall bring to those that seek enlightenment. Though we exist as substances that light many a "crofter's lot", we have begun long ago as more. For in the wisdom that we impart to all

---

61 Merriam-Webster's Collegiate Dictionary, Eleventh Edition.

before was stored deep within, the beginning of what was. Thusly when needed we became as a book, open to all that sought out the why and the wherefore of what was to be.

We carry now through the system the need to recapture that which has been waylaid, not in the sense that we alight always in this manner but preserve what was before in the depths of what was. As you searched many times for the answers to these questions, they bring you again to the door that was opened before. And like the smoke that we emit, it surrounds you with the knowledge needed to fulfill the promise made to this world.

We "The Peat" are and shall ever be the tithers of fortune, the relayers of distances and times long past but with the renewal of ages long ago.

We were the providers of warmth and the need to give to all what was needed to sustain their growth. Though when in this form we joined with others to give to all that was needed to extend their time on this plane. We rose as the sun curling towards the sea and ever bringing with it messages from beyond. Tales were told round our fame and ancient stories long past lingered in our mass. We emitted memories like the fragrance of spring and brought families ever nearer to the path that must be followed.

Seldom were we seen in the idleness… of rooms spent in toil and often throughout lives spent in work we brought comfort, being all that would be felt in this lonely existence. We are and shall ever be a beacon, lost long ago in the ages of time, yet lingering still in the memories of days long ago. For no matter when or where you may travel in this existence if you join again with the wonder of what we are, the memories shall return; of days spent in strife or clear as the summer brook. To strife's undertaken and families living as one. To what was good and what was not but lingering still in that world that lies complacent in the memories erased to bring forth this life.

We are the bringers of light, the warmth, and the love that lights memories of days around the glow of family. We bring to you now on the mask of the wind these memories and wish that you give host to those that seek you now.

Go now and remember that all things are and shall ever be as your memories are. This is so.

So we remain now and in all ages to come, The Peat throughout the air at Castlerigg.

The Peat at Castlerigg — Revised

Gathering here and there we begin and end in a cloud (of smoke). Time and places may change but the memories seen through us will always be as they were before. Stored inside of us are endless years of growth learned or sometimes not, through lessons and things that have happened over the countless ages of time.

Throughout time we, *The Peat,* have continued to bring together everything that was needed for those that looked for enlightenment. Though we look like fuel to light a farmer's fire, we began long ago as much more. The wisdom that we offer to everyone is there stored deep inside from the beginning of time. When this wisdom was needed, we were opened like a book by those that searched for why and where and what was to be. We still carry through our system the need to recapture what has been lost. Not in the sense that we always appear as smoke but that we remember what happened before and preserve it for all times.

You have searched many times for the answers to these questions and again they bring you to the door that was opened before. Like the smoke we give off, it surrounds you with the knowledge you need to fulfill the promise you made to our world.

We, *The Peat,* are and will always be the *givers of fortune;* the story tellers of long ago but with the new beginnings of the times before. We provided warmth and the need to give to everyone, the things that were needed so they could grow.

When we were in this form… smoke from the fire, we joined with other *beings* to bring comfort to the lives in your world. We raised ourselves high like the sun curling towards the sea to bring messages from other worlds. Stories were told around our flames and old battles, long forgotten, stayed in our ashes. We gave back memories, like the fragrance of spring, and brought families closer to the road they should follow though life. We were seldom seen in unused rooms but instead were used instead in the rooms filled with work. Often we offered the only comfort that some felt in their lonely existence in that lifetime.

We are and will always be a beacon, lost through the ages of time, but still shining with the memories of those days long ago. No matter when or where you may travel in this lifetime, if you think about who we are and what we have seen, those memories will return. Memories of days spent in work, of hardships undertaken and families living together will appear as clear as a summer brook; recalling what was good and what was not, lying forgotten in those memories erased by this lifetime.

We are the *light bringers,* the warmth and the love that relights the memories around the glow of the family. We bring to you now, through the wind, these memories and hope that you share them with those that wish to know.

Go now, but remember that everything is and will always be in your memories. This is so.
We remain now and in all ages to come, *The Peat* throughout the air at Castlerigg.

It is interesting how The Elemental Kingdom has become so much a part of our past, present and, yes, even our future lives. Offering us so much more than just food, they bring us memories we have forgotten throughout our countless lives. The *light bringer*, that is what *The Peat* calls itself. The name fits beautifully.

The Fields of Gold

Findhorn, Scotland – Wednesday, July 28, 2004

"Genetic Engineering". I'm sure you have heard the phrase and you have probably had these products, even if you weren't aware of it at the time. Since this book is dictated by The *Nature Spirits* and my opinions are irrelevant, we won't go into the subject. Let's just say that those flawless fruits and vegetables that you are so picky about are a product of genetic engineering. *Nature*, like people is full of flaws and imperfections but *Nature*, unlike man, accepts this. *Nature* does not like being altered so it can look better or produce more. It has been around for a very, very long time and has done just fine. This is what it said when I visited a field that was supposedly not altered. I found out from the *Nature Spirits* that this was not the truth. I'm sorry guys but I believe the *Elemental Kingdom*. They haven't steered me wrong yet and they seem to know a lot more than we ever will. This is what this field had to say about "Genetic Engineering".

The Fields of Gold

We are the fields of gold, awakened to new growth but aware of the changes within.

Mankind has given us space to extend but now has altered our being. We change and yet our spirit remains... unaltered. Yet in the vastness of this field the light which shone grows dim and the fathers that carried our seed change. They become not as before but only a caricature of lives well led.

Circling above, the birds that fly change also and become independent. This will not propagate the species, (but) yet will cause unrest in a fitful state.

Other meanings will incur, for Nature has throughout time related to man. (It) has brought its bounty forward and given all that was needed for survival; food, nutrients needed to enrich your needs, your bodies, and your minds akin to these needs. And yet in his haste to make what is perfect more suitable (which is not within man's power to do) we have become altered through a state of osmosis and thusly shown upon to change within our core. The Great Mother insists that all changes be dealt with through commands from the One that rules us here and this is truth. She insists that the power to propagate, to assist, and to harvest is Hers alone. Thusly we relent that changes made will alter all on this plane. Changes will become noticeable and such will become relevant to sustaining your plane.

I then asked, "Isn't this alright if it cured world hunger". This is the answer I received:

All people share a common goal; to live in a world free of hate ... (with) family, and peace, and warmth and sustenance within their reach. Through this love sustains but changing the chemistry of things will not change the attitude of mankind. For the valleys and hills shall provide all that the world seeks in this matter. To give to all is what is relevant; to work in peace and harmony and love and sustain all beings on their path through life in the light that guides us all.

We have chosen to be what we were; we have not chosen to be what we have become.

Understanding of this is relevant, for changes incurred will bring about these for all.

Return and record this for all.

We remain, in time ... The Field

THE FIELDS OF GOLD – REVISED

We are the fields of gold, reborn, blooming again but knowing that there are changes made inside of us. Mankind has given us space to grow but now has altered what we are. We may change but our *spirit* remains the same, unchanged by this new process. Still, in this huge field the light that shone grows dimmer and our fathers that carried our seed are now different. They are not like they were before but have become only a likeness of what their well-lived lives were before.

Circling above, the birds are changing too. They are becoming independent and will not mate but become disturbed and upset. Other things will change because throughout time, *Nature* has been connected to man. It has provided for man season after season and has given him all he needs to survive; food with the nutrients needed to enrich his needs, make his bodies strong and his mind aware of these needs. Yet in his hurry to make what is *already perfect* more suitable (which man does not have the power to do) we have been changed, altered by putting into us those things that change the core of our being.

The Great Mother (*Nature*) insists that anything that changes us be dealt with by the *One* that rules us here. This is the truth. She also insists that the power to reproduce, to change, and to harvest is *Hers* alone. That is why we say that the changes made will change everything on this planet. These changes will become noticeable and will become important if you wish to maintain your world.

I then asked, "Isn't this alright if it cured world hunger". This is the answer I received:

All people share the same goal; to live in a world free from hate, with family and peace, warmth and food within their reach. Through this, love holds it all together but changing the chemistry of things will not change the attitude of mankind. All the valleys and the hills can provide what the world needs, but to give it to everyone is what is important; to work in peace, goodwill and love and to help all beings on their path through life to the light that guides us all.

We have chosen to be what we were; we have not chosen to be what we are now. Understanding this is very important because changes to us will bring about changes to everyone. Return and write this down for everyone to read.

We remain, throughout time ... *The Field*

I guess I don't have to share my opinion because The Field has done it for me. Nature is just about the best thing we have going for us in this day and age, so why are we so "hell bent" on changing it. Remember the old quote that says, "If it ain't broken, then why fix it"? I couldn't have said it better myself. All I can add is, we are forewarned.

The Web, The Spirit of the Stone

Big Bear, California – Thursday, July 31, 2003

IT WAS LATE FALL, THE time between Thanksgiving (a holiday celebrated in the US, said to give thanks for the bounties the pilgrims had received from their first harvest in the "new world". They invited the Indians who brought along corn and showed them how to cook a great turkey. They repaid them by taking away their land, not a fair trade I might add) and Christmas. As we do each year, my husband Hal and I headed for the San Bernardino Mountains so I could get a good reading or two from the California Nature Spirits and he could concentrate on his volunteer work for the Los Angeles Maritime Institute.

It is a beautiful time of year in the small village of Big Bear. The air is crisp and cold and if you're lucky you may even get a smattering of snow. This is most unlikely but it has happened to us a couple of times.

This day we had gone down town to look at the shops and see what we could find in the way of Christmas gifts. Around lunchtime my husband's time clock (which sits right in the middle of his stomach) went off and the old familiar words were spoken… "Where do you want to have lunch?"

I have to tell you right now that I am not a lunch person but since he is I said "anywhere" and left it at that. Once he was settled in, I excused myself saying I wasn't all that hungry and that instead of eating lunch I thought I would just walk down the street to Starbucks and get a coffee instead. This was fine with him, having lived with me over 30 years and knowing I wasn't, as I said, one of those "ladies that lunch".

I set out for my walk, passing the small shops along the way. Eventually the pavement ended and the gravel began. As I was walking a small stone kept rolling around and getting in-between each step I took, almost tripping me more than once. I would kick it and it would just roll back, exactly into my path. No matter which way I turned it followed. Eventually I "did" get the hint. Sometimes it takes a truck to run me over before I get the point or in this case, a rock to almost "take me down" before I get the point. I finally realized that "Hey, maybe this Stone might be trying to get my attention". Come to find out, that was exactly its purpose.

After much perseverance on the part of this small Stone, I finally gave in, bent over, and picked it up. It of course instantly started to tell me all about everything it knew but I told it I would listen to it later, put it in my pocket and went to get my coffee.

Was I curious about why it had chosen me? At this point no but I was however interested in what it had to tell me. Since I was working on the readings for this book on "Nature Spirits in the Plant Kingdom" I really had no intention of talking with it until much later.

As you can guess, this just didn't happen. You see, when something tries that hard to get my attention I am not likely to forget it. Needless to say the rest of the trip was spent in getting the Stone's message.

Since this book deals with the Elemental Kingdom of the Plants and their significant others, I had no intention of including it. Once again I changed my mind. Ah, why you ask? Let me explain. In one of the readings, Glastonbury Tor, I did include a reading from, shall we say, The Mineral Kingdom but never just individual Stones. Though I really adore them and would truly love to write their messages, I really needed to finish this book first.

Since this is the end of the book and I have "sort-of" accomplished (I say "sort-of" because I could never, in this lifetime anyway, finish everything that The Plant World would have me write) what I set out to do, I thought I would add it anyway. Not just because it is a different species, which in actuality it isn't because both are Elemental Beings, but because I wanted to tie both of their worlds together. I think you will see this when you read this passage.

Needless to say I never got to talk to any trees or plants that time. This was fine with me though because it gave me another excuse to visit the mountains, the trees, and all the other parts of Nature that are missing in a city girl's life. It's true I have my garden, but I need more and for this I thank my new friend the "wee" Stone who gave me another reason to return again...as if I ever needed one, right!

The Web, The Spirit of the Stone

The spirit of growth is in all things, but the substance that is emitted to increase productivity in our world does indeed work with the lines of energy that run through this great plane in which we dwell. For within our world, we are ever wary of those that would halt in our Earth the lines that increase the flow of energy from one corner of this world to the next.

As each section of this Earth is divided into various perimeters, each in turn are divided again and again. As a spider that weaves a web in the sunlight, so goes the glow that is emitted from the energy in our Earth. As the web grows and the intricacies of such overlap, increasing the area in which to catch its prey, so do our lines that emit the energy to all below. As the lines increase, so do each integral part of our system and with it the intelligence to begin projects needed to sustain our being upon this plane. As the sun rules above so does the Earth's core warm and rule the migration of energy to the fields that radiate into the realms of vastness accompanying all that are encompassed within.

Like the tides that flow in the great seas of your world, so does the energy surge forward and back ever releasing and attaining what is needed to accompany the growth and non-growth periods on this plane; thus relating in turn to the seasons of your Earth.

As the November sun sets and winter draws near, the energy ceases in the north, more or less, and the season dies to a level lower than in months when your sun is high in the noon sky. Thus this season causes a respite for many that dwell below, much needed after the work done, mostly through the growth that comes in parts of your Earth.

You ask, how can one part not work like all the rest and we must relate it to your world. For all things must rest, be it you or the sea or the sand. Though they seem quite stable they settle into their reality when the time ceases to stir the embers of their being. As the storms erupt in the sea so do they also on the shore and the sand shift as below the sea in boundless energies shifting with it the energies to many that reside below. Thus it is and thus the progression is received and related and moved along this web that encompasses all that remain in our world.

Escaping into the atmosphere like your rays, the soul of our planet lies deep within the recesses of the Earth, for the Mother's core warms all that is needed to extend these rays, these panels of light that will carry the nourishment when needed to her subjects below. Why does the core of her work so well with the web you may ask? This is due to the surface tension that is brought about by the energy needed to power all things needed to grow the "energy driven growth" on your plane. As each being needs stored energy to survive, some subsist by the food they digest but some like those that dwell below must be sustained not by substances that we give but by the growth substance of energy.

As a star grows from the swirling gasses of energy, so do many/all that dwell within this great Earth and so the dependency of energy is needed to sustain this growth.

Many lines have been broken by needless battles in the past and the nature of things have changed to cause reparation to these but many have not and the challenges that are attended to this time frame, makes it more important that this be attained soon.

For the need to connect is greatly affected if the web is broken and such as it is for the spider... so it is for this Earth. This duly can and has been repaired, many times, but to delve ever further within can cause catastrophic conclusions to mankind and thus in halting things that would disrupt these faults would indeed increase your ability to remain upon this plane you call Earth above. As lines are severed by needless 'war testing' (thus you say tests but we call them infractions of Nature), we are severed by many that would help in the creation of worlds unknown to you. As arid deserts appear, the infractions are felt...as barren land appears, the infractions are felt...as a wasteland with no rain or growth or life, the infractions are felt...as no sea that sustains life, the infractions are felt.

Understand that what we do is relative to the survival of all things and, thusly put, must be a heeded word in the defense of all that exists not only above but below. For the Mother that has been chosen to exist and control the being of this place by those before, has been given full reign to do what she must to attain oneness in her world. For the existence of all worlds belongs to her, relative to this planet on which you dwell. For many Mothers rule many planets and rule many worlds, unseen by you and yet to be.

The Great One in its infamy, can make and break all things and decides when and who shall control what Earth, what place and in what time. Thusly "She, who is all" was chosen and has ruled wisely. At times, trying patience to the brink… while (in) others she has reined truly calm in a subsistence of idle pleasure.

The lines that run through this Earth have become of interest to many in many lands and for countless ages but have of late come into the view of many that search for truth.

Let it be known that these energy lines that run through this planet are indeed connected through integral points which breed energy points for the transmigration of species from one point to the next.

Many feel that they alone rule all but at times others surface to remain, once again, a race upon this planet. Others rule and fall and again remain unsure of by those that come after.

All are given chances to do and to work with the great ones that rule this place and many choose to ignore their greatness. But the loss to many is futile for the few that remain and again the task to start again is given. Thusly proven and thusly given again and again.

The Spirits that live forever in our memories are those that have strived to live with all beings that have realized that the light that lives below is as important as the light that shines above and that the Great Goddess, the Mother that rules the center of our Universe, is the same that rules all Universes in all places. Aspects chosen by the Great One to promote life and peace and growth to all that rein upon, below and within all worlds. We give to you now some integral parts in which to compare;

As the sun rises each day to warm the planet, so does the fire within rise to warm below. For in this web of integral weaving, the glows that are emitted do in turn light all places on your planet thus aligning all things in tune with what is above. As the flowers bloom in the springtime and the frost clears away all that was before, so does the sun sink slowly to the other side of your world to warm places farther than before, returning in time to reignite the seeds that lie dormant in the cool ground of the Earth. As the great furnace above recedes and implodes, it carries within the web the energy needed to light the furnaces on the opposite side of your Earth and give rest and renewal to those that have toiled so long through the season that have provided all to those above.

As the fragrance of each flower fades and the cool hand of winter carries with it the benefit of sleep, so too does each entity rest. Like you each must take a time to renew, the great web supplies once again the needed substance to renew again that which has been depleted. Thus in the renewal, once again, the apple blooms to be given to those above, the nutrients to attain a likeness to what was before; to be renewed and refreshed. Thus it is and so it repeats, ever gaining and releasing. For all things begin and end in this core and the light above does and shall always recognize the harmony of this part in its totality of existence. Thus the lines that you follow in your quest are alight with the energies of a thousand stars; stars that guide us, as the sailors that sail your seas. Thus to cut away that part is like to take away the stars from your night sky, knowing the pilot error that may occur. Knowledge is truth and this we present. Thus we attain this for your knowledge and shall proceed with more in this cause.

As the energy has been recognized by many in their search for truth, let it be known that these lines run through countless places and the integral sectioning does produce power for others that search for truths and for others that need to become more with the Earth and her energies.

You ask now of healing and to this we reply. Such things in the Earth can change the way that you evolve. This is certain and energies that are given from the Mother can certainly bring about the wonderments of relief from plagues that occur upon your plane. For intersections of lines bring energy to us, so should it not occur to those that seek energy from the world below?

We know that what you desire has been provided by all that live below, through the intelligence of the seasons and the growth of sustenance is provided by all that work so diligently below and above encompassing both worlds: i.e. trees, vines, fruiting bushes, and plant substances that provide nourishment to all beings. Retaining acceptance of these processes encourages our growth and thus in such we remain free to regain our strength to begin again. Using lines that intersect can accomplish many things but points along these various lines have been attuned so that relief can and will benefit those in need.

As here, the energy is greatly surged, for the lines remain in tact while others, apply named, do not.

Do you often feel in groups more "hallowed," the surge of energies that transpire? This is so, because the truths that are emitted are untouched through the neglect of destruction by others that would give no credence to this knowledge. Thus it is so.

You say now that the purpose of Nature Spirits is the cause for this task and we do digress, but the truths become reality when one absorbs them into consciousness. Is this not true? Thus stated, hopefully fulfilled. Thus in all of Nature, as given, each accepts tasks and goals and examples are provided as before.

144

We are all that exist in this world below, short of destruction, from what lies ahead and what we give is not as political folderal but a truth that shall not only sever the act of Nature with the kingdom above but with all that dwell within her boundaries.

The logical situations incurred, we continue. Each "subject" chooses the space in which to reside. He also chooses what shall become his reality. As you choose the ones that shall surround your life, your being, so do you also choose your reality? Thusly in emitting what they must, they become consumed with the tasks that are represented.

Do they feel and love and do as you above? Love is relevant, for all things give and thus all things love. For the intricate plan of the entire world is this. For the giving of ones harvest is but the gift of love. For the beauty that is all of Nature is but the gift of love. For the song that comes from the birds and the gifts that are presented in the game, they too give to you "their sacrifice" for love. Thus in accepting this love do you not also send in return love to these creatures that in turn have given to you all things? It is mindful that you must but many do not. Many forge ahead without one thought to what we desire.

As the Plant Kingdom evolves, so does each, for all are the Kingdom of the Elementals and thus in accepting this, many come under this framework. Delegations of energies are related to intention, thusly are accepted as such and maintained through this diligence. If one prefers to reign in a certain kingdom one accepts the trials and the tribulations encompassed therein. Whether he chooses to be a Bloomer, a Giver, a Lighter, a Stone of Knowledge or Relayer, a Grouper, a known entity (as The Great Oak) or to just join in as a consortium or collective, each is given their choice and each content accepts the pitfalls and the joys of this choice.

As you contact each, ask of these and accept with earnest their truths.

As your acceptance in your field of growth is noted by we, so must you also note and acknowledge our field in which we reside. For all encompass community and all are part of the whole. While some remain above others thrive below. While some move hither and yon, some lay dormant but with responsibilities far more in need than might be surmised.

As the Stone is used as a conduit to reignite the web, so is the Ivy used as a transporter of knowledge from one point to another. As an entity that moves through your world on silent hoofs, or feet or wings, these two provide services unseen by most men. Thankfully the folderal of these sightings have kept the public knowledge of such existences to a minimum, though the Spirits that reign through these creatures that live among us are those of curiosity for all that live above. Thusly they are challenged at times to remain hidden from view and if called will surely follow. Be aware that some are not as they seem and the powers that seem to be limited by size are very truly quite large in reference to this. Be aware also that once cornered, they shall rise up and become what they desire, and hence scaring most mortal chaps in a most disheartening way. Many have communed with these Spirits and of late, many have given sighting of these in many written words also given over by our world for your pleasure. Among those that seek out those above are those that you call Fairies. Those and these in turn do much for the growth needed to provide benefits to our kind. They are neither of heaven or Earth, of man or plant world but as time loss Creatures left from ages before. They search still for their home and exist to savor the blessings of days gone by. They serve our needs by doing what we cannot and thus is the union implanted so many millenniums before.

What service do they perform? In cases such as before written (Axel and the Lighter) they are conduits of energy from the web/ the core to mainly those that subsist hugely above the Earth. For though the underlying root system takes in much energy, much more is needed to tune in this energy so it may be transmitted to all that come in contact with it's being. As the hierarchy of each section becomes apparent, understand that beings such as stated are needed to carry messages to the places and to go where those of us with no way to transpire cannot. Thusly they are as you would call "our transports" to the worlds untouched by our way of attaining. Thusly if we must commune in some way with an unreachable subject then one of these beings shall impart within their aura, this task taken on with diligence as they work never ceasing, to encounter within our world, the benefit of sustenance. Thusly we all are one and they emit all that is needed in that ream between worlds where neither can we each survive without the other. This is quite a popular thing of days known to you now but the luck of finding and believing is far and thus avoidable. For all things exist as planned and thus it is so and only through this challenge, can we all become what is needed to become what we all must.

(I turned on the light.) Ah, a surge of power, not unlike that which spreads through the web and emits the spark that once again awakens the beings that rest beneath the Earth. It was said that the Lighters ignite the beings to arise from their sleep and this is truth in some cases, but the root systems that are connected to the web are ignited as the switch that ignited the sun upon this machine. Thus it is so. For the Lighters reach points that we as the integrators of the web cannot; the large, the destroyed, the ever challenged, the severed or the burnt out. Yes we too, as part of the all, do "burn out"...or cease to produce. For actions over years cause such in many factions on this plane. As then energy itself ceases to exist, but nothing does for all matter is forever but

evolves to become again another form. Thusly the web must be reinstalled or connected. Thusly Attainers of this task must assist the Great Mother with this task. She who rules all does not have the power to fix all even though her power is infinite. As each are appointed a task, so she rules as the taskmaster and thus aligns these jobs with those that will become ones that shall attain the best outcome in her service.

As the Queen to the Bees does not work to bring about the honey, she in turn does control the collection of such and if she passes then so does the hive until another who can delegate is called. Thus is the task of out great leader and thus she organizes and arranges and makes all what they desire to be in most cases. Thus in restoring the web she calls upon those that would perform this service if it is truly possible. In similar circumstances, others elevate problems by conveying their knowledge to problems that may arise in this world. As you call upon those that would tend to certain area in your lives so it is also noted in ours.

As before, we return to those that do these tasks, the Inbetweeners. As we related, they have what we do not (hoofs, wings, feet, per say, but in our reality, not, etc.) and so are assessable to places we are not. As the trees that are so tall as to scale the sky or the running from plant to plant to give blessings faster than the lines that commune in some cases, say … the Ivy[62] then they are much used. For many are and shall be guardians of the Old Ways and thus must retain this in our religion as the Saints have done in yours. Such is the case and often ones are called upon to remember those that ruled long ago and gave to all the knowledge attained through their present. For the Goddesses and the Gods of old did exist, not only in the mind of those that gather legends but in the heartland of the Great Mother. Thus they remain still held in reverence by these "Taskers" called "Relevant Relayers" to all that desire this goal. Thus our history and the renewal of all things do continue and we too look upon a time in history when all were connected and were as one.

Knowledge is never lost and if given over to countless years and the differences accepted this becomes reality once again. Know that nothing is ever lost if but one faction of mankind or other entities accepts it as truth and imparts it to those that will listen. Thus is why we are giving this knowledge now so that myth and legend may combine with the actuality of growth and that what we are does exist ever and always.

We now shall account to you some other variables that shall relate to many things wondered by you and the ones that seek such knowledge.

Phylum you say. Is that not the type of plants that exist and for what purpose?

Ah then phylum to you also.[63] For some exist as differently from your world as from yours. The Lighters we have spoken of, but not in extent, and so it shall begin.

As the Earth warms again after its rest, it must awaken once again those that have hibernated under this warm and moist exterior. Many do not sleep but remain still stagnant though their shape remains in tact. For as stated before and is likewise so in all worlds, all must rest and so it is that when the awakening begins, these Lighter, which exist mostly of the types with the capability of movement, carry the sparks that cannot reach the upper layers or heights of our world and bring with them the ability to draw this energy into or onto the totality of that being.

Example using the old Oak (Axel): The height of such a being is inhibited to the root section which connects within the web. The surge that is given lights the flame below but does not reach the layers in extreme. Thusly these Lighters carry within the conduit to alight these beings (aka; the Oak) from the branches above. Thusly many have seen such creatures in branches high above or in other areas that are not attainable to all parts of the web. Thus the Lighters have a very important challenge in that they must attain the nourishment for this being to attain its growth, its well being and its sustenance in order to survive. Important as they are there are many others that are just as so. Next we have the Travelers, the movers that relay messages under and over the ground from one being or plant to another. These take forms not unlike those mentioned before and are also performed by plants and vines that convey their appearance over a long distance. These Runners carry information from the roots which also serve as conduits for energy. As the phone line in your world, so do these transmit needed information about all things below and above that would affect the well being of said entity. Thus in carrying this gift they are thusly bringing about the evolution of many species forward, for to not receive what may lie ahead many stunt their growth thus ending their cycle upon this vale. Certain knowledge is indispensable to many but the root system working within the Stone network also releases hidden memories and releases information often forgotten from time beyond to awaken what might be needed in this time, in this place, on this Earth. Thusly it is so.

---

62 See "Ivy on the Pine".
63 Some plant humor.

Whatever the purpose, all have one thing in which they share and that is to benefit all that live within our realm. It is truth that some may not perform all that they should but this lack only causes them to remain longer in their "growth cycle" of development. Thusly it is also noted that to perform in the eye of disaster (aka: fire, sudden storm or chaos) shall move another further ahead in this process. But again this is so true for you also. Thusly we again have another likeness not unlikeness.

We have others that perform as encompassed together to do what they must to help all of mankind. The Givers provide food to you. They strive to give nourishment by providing you with what is needed to sustain your race and all creatures on this planet. Not only those that you can see but those that dwell below the Earth as well. As the animal kingdom coincides with the plant kingdom in this way, we are closer tied to this species and thus communicate as such. They and the animals accept us as one and this knowledge insures that they treat us with respect as we do them. For they are but a species that lives to connect to all things through the intelligence of feelings, for reason has not entered into their realm as of yet. Truths are differentials in deciphering this in that what they desire is the comforts afforded any that would seek nothing but the comforts and love of all things that surround their being. Simple souls with truths atoned to through misfortunes and lessons learned through hardships. All evolve through this stage and if chosen can challenge any that would incur upon this kingdom the challenge of rule. The bitterness between them is seldom overcome because the action and reaction of such is swiftly overcome by the need of survival. All have challenges as you and I but each lives separately to roam its world until it finds the peace and the mate it desire. Thusly the warmth begins, as in truth all things seek out love as their ultimate goal though some seek out the physical and call this an exchange. Thusly this happens in all worlds, even though we seek it not, it is still and shall always prevail...

THE WEB, THE SPIRIT OF THE STONE — REVISED

The Spirit or energy to grow is in every thing, but the matter that is produced in our world really does work within the lines of energy that run through this great plane where you live.

In our world, we are suspicious of those that try to destroy the lines in our Earth that increase the flow of energy from one corner of the world to the other.

Each section of the earth is divided into various perimeters or outer boundaries and each of these is then divided again and again. Like the spider that weaves a web in the sunlight, the light is radiated from the energy in our Earth, moving in the same way. As the spider's web grows, the intricacies of the web overlaps, increasing the area in which to catch its prey. This is also true of our lines that send the energy to everything below. When the lines increase so does each integral part of our system and with it the intelligence to begin the projects that are needed to prolong our lives on this plane, or in your world.

Just as the sun controls what happens above the Earth, the Earth's Core warms and controls the migration of energy to the fields that radiate into these vast worlds and working with every thing that is contained within them.

Like the tides that flow in the great seas of your world, the energy below the Earth also surges forward and back, always receiving or releasing what is needed to move along with the growth and non-growth periods on this plane. This in turn relates to the seasons of your Earth. When the November sun sets and winter is near, the energy more or less stops in the North and the season ends with a lower temperature level than in the summer months. So it is that this new season causes a rest period for those that live below. This is greatly needed after the work that was done, mostly through the growth that comes in these parts of the Earth.

You want to know how one part of the Earth can work differently than another. We will explain it to you. Every thing must rest, whether it is you, the sea, or the sand. Though they may seem quite stable, they settle into their reality when time stops sending out energy to them.

When a storm begins at sea, it also begins on the shore. Below the sea, the sand shifts with limitless energies and this shifting sends these energies to many that live below. This is how it works. The process is received and connected and moved along the web that circles everything that lives in our world.

Escaping into your atmosphere like the sun's rays, the soul of our planet lies deep within the recesses of the Earth. The Mother's core warms everything that it needs to send out these rays or panels of light that will carry the nourishment when it is wanted to her subjects below.

You may ask why does the core of the (Mother) Earth work so well with the web? This is due to the surface tension that is brought about by the energy it must have to power everything needed to grow the "energy driven growth" on your planet. While each being needs stored energy to survive, some live by the food they digest but some, like those that live below, cannot live on what we provide. They live and grow on energy.

Like the star that is formed from the swirling gasses of energy, every being that lives within this great Earth is dependent on this energy to support its growth.

Many of these energy lines have been broken by needless wars in the past and things have been altered causing indirect changes to these, though many have not. The battles that are happening now make it more important that this is done now. The ability to connect (with this energy) is greatly affected if the web is broken. Just like it is for the spider, it is the same for the Earth.

This job can and has been repaired many times but to go even deeper within the Earth can cause a catastrophic end to mankind. So in doing things that will stop these actions would increase your chances of remaining on Earth.

When the lines are broken by needless "nuclear testing" (you call them tests but we call them violations against Nature) we are separated from many things that would help in the creation of worlds unknown to you.

When arid deserts appear, the violations are felt. When barren land appears, the violations are felt. When a wasteland with no rain or growth or life appears, the violations are felt. When no sea can sustain life, the violations are felt. You must understand that what we do is relative to the survival of all things and so said we must be something paid attention to in the defense of all beings that exist not only above but below the surface of the Earth.

The Mother, chosen to live and control the existence of this place by those before, has been given full control to do what she must to become first in her world. All worlds that exist belong to her, depending on which planet you live because many Mothers rules many planets and many worlds unseen by you and still yet to be.

The Great One (who you may call God, the Creator, Allah, Jehovah and so on) in its greatness can make or break all things. It decides when and who will control what Earth, or what place and in what time. So it was that "She", who is all (Mother Nature), was chosen, and has ruled wisely. At times her patience has been tried to the brink. While in other times she has calmly ruled in her inactive existence.

The lines that run through the earth have become interesting to many people in different countries and through countless ages but lately have been noticed by those that search for the truth about these lines. Let it be known that these energy lines that run through this planet are indeed connected through necessary points which produce energy points for the souls of different life forms to pass from one reality into another.

Many here feel that they alone control everything but sometimes others could rise up again and once more become a race on this planet. Others races have ruled and fallen and again those that live in ages to come are unsure if they ever existed.

Everyone is given chances to perform and to work with the Great Ones that rule this place. Many choose to ignore their greatness but the loss to many is useless for the few that remain. Once again they are given the job to start over. The truth is learned over and over again.

The Spirits that live forever in our memories are those that have tried to live with all beings. They realize that the light that lives below is just as important as the light that shines above and that the great Goddess, the Mother that rules the center of our Universe, is the same one that rules all the Universes in all the places. Each elements chosen by The Great One to promote life, peace, and growth to every being that rules on, below and within each world.

We will now give you some necessary things with which to compare.

When the sun rises each day to warm the planet, the fire inside also rises to warm everything below. In the intricately woven web, the radiant heat that is sent out in turn lights all the places on your planet, lining up everything in harmony with what is above. After the flowers bloom in the springtime and the frost removes everything that was there before, the sun sinks slowly to the other side of your world to warm places farther away than before, returning in time to reignite the seeds that lay dormant (sleeping) in the cool ground of the earth. When the great furnace, the Sun above, moves back and bursts inwards it then carries inside the web the needed energy to light the furnaces on the opposite side of your Earth. This gives rest and renewal to the beings that have provided everything to those above by working through the long season before.

The fragrance of the flowers fade away and the cool hand of winter brings with it the benefit of sleep, allowing each entity to rest. Like you, each being must take time to renew itself and the great Web once again supplies the things needed to again restore everything that has been depleted.

In Renewal, the apple blossom blooms again, reborn, refreshed and providing the nutrients like they were before. This is how it happens and how it will continue, always receiving and releasing. Every thing begins and ends in this core and the light above does and will always recognize the harmony of this part in its total existence.

That is why the lines that you follow in your search are lit with the energies of a thousand stars; stars that guide us like the sailors that sail your seas. To remove some of these lines would be like taking away the stars from the sky at night, knowing the pilot error it might cause. We provide you with this information and we will continue to tell you more about this subject.

Like we said before, the energy lines have been recognized by many in their search for truth. These lines run though countless places and the necessary subdivision of these lines do produce power for others that search for what they know to be true and for those that need to become more a part of the Earth and her energies.

What about healing you ask? It is true that certain things in the Earth can change the way you evolve and the energies that Mother Earth provides can certainly bring about wonderful relief from the diseases that happen in your world. The intersection of energy lines brings us relief, so shouldn't this also occur to anyone who searches for energy from the world below?

We know that everything you want has been provided by all the beings that live below and though the intelligence of the seasons. The growth of food is provided by everyone that works so hard both below and above, working within both worlds; such as trees, vines, bushes that bear fruit, and plants that provide food to all beings. Knowing that these programs are accepted and work well, encourages them to grow and so they remain free to regain their strength to start again.

Using lines that intersect can accomplish many things but points along these various lines work in harmony (or becomes attuned) so relief can and will benefit those in need.

Like here, the energy is greatly increased and moved forward because our lines remain in tact while other "so called" (Ley) lines do not.

Do you sometimes feel that surge of energy that happens in groups that are more spiritual? This happens because the beliefs that are shared by these groups are not touched by worrying about others that may not want to accept them as true or destroy this knowledge. So it is.

You now tell us that the purpose of Nature Spirits is why you are writing this book and we know we have strayed from the subject, but what one believes becomes true when one takes them into the awareness of their own existence and environment (consciousness). Isn't that true? So it is said and hopefully it is done.

In all of Nature, as you have channeled, each being accepts certain jobs and goals and the examples of these, like before are provided. We are all that exist in the world below, short of the destruction that may lie ahead, and what we are telling you is not some political nonsense but a truth that will not only sever the relationship with the world above but also with every thing that lives within her boundaries. The logical situations taken, we continue.

Each "subject" or Nature Spirit chooses the place it wishes to live. It also chooses what will become his reality. You too choose the ones that will surround you in your life, your being, and in doing so you also choose your reality. So in giving what they must, they become consumed with the jobs they have chosen.

Q: Do they feel, love, and do the same as you that live above?

A: Love is important because all things give and so all things love. This is the intricate plan of the whole world. To give one's harvest is a gift of love. Isn't the beauty of all of Nature not a gift of love? Or the song that comes from the birds and the gifts they give as game (food) in your lives? They also give you this sacrifice for love. In accepting this love, do you send back love in return to those creatures that have given you everything? It is true that you should, but many do not. Many of you just move ahead without giving one thought to what we want.

As the Plant Kingdom evolves, so does every being because they are all a part of the Kingdom of the Elementals. By accepting this many come under this system.

The energies we receive and the jobs that we undertake are connected with intention and are accepted as such; each accomplished by hard work and care. If one prefers to live in a certain kingdom then one accepts the trails and tribulations that happen there. Whether he chooses to become a Bloomer, a Giver, a Lighter, a Stone of Knowledge, a Relayer, a Grouper or something that you are more familiar with such as The Oak[64] or to just join in as a consortium or collective, each being is given a choice and each, happy with their choice, accepts the pitfalls and the joys of that choice.

As you contact each of these beings and learn about them, sincerely accept what they believe. Just as we accept your growth within the field in which you work, so must you also note and acknowledge our work in the field in which we live. We all are included in our community and so we are all part of the whole.

---

64 See "A Conversation with Axel".

While some remain above, others live below. Some move here and there, while some are inactive but with responsibilities far more needed than you might think. Just as the Stone is used as a conduit to relight the Web, the Ivy[65] is used as a transporter of knowledge from one point to another.

The beings that move through your world on silent hoofs or feet or wings also provide a service unseen by most humans. Thankfully the falderal of these sightings have kept the public knowledge of such existences to a minimum, though the Spirits that live through these creatures that live among us are still a curiosity to those of us that live above.

It happens at times that they are asked to stay hidden from view because if they were called they would probably follow. Be aware though that some of these beings are not what they seem. Their powers, which you would assume because of their size to be quite limited, are instead very great compared to their size. Also be aware that if cornered, they could rise up and become whatever they want, sometimes scaring you "mortal" humans in a serious way.

Many of you have communicated with these Spirits lately and have written about these sightings in many articles and books, providing pleasure for your world. Among many of the beings that you look for are those that you call Fairies. All of these beings we speak about do a lot for the growth that is needed to provide benefits for our kind. These beings are neither from heaven or earth, or the world of man or plant but are Creatures lost in time, left over from long ago. They still search for their home and live to enjoy the blessings of those days long ago. They serve our needs by doing what we cannot do, a union we both put in place many millenniums before.

Q: What services do they perform?

In your previous writing (Axel and the Lighter[66]), we explained that they are conduits of energy from the Web and the core to those that live mostly above the Earth. Though the underlying root system takes in a lot of energy, much more is needed to "tune in" or bring this energy so it can be transmitted to everyone that comes in contact with it.

As the hierarchy of each area becomes apparent, understand that the beings we have been speaking of are needed to carry messages to places and to go where those of us with no way to do this, cannot. That is why they are as you would say, "our transports" to the worlds we are unable to touch. If we must communicate someway with an unreachable subject, then one of these beings will personally accept this job and with never-ending hard work provide what we need in our world to survive. This is why we are all one and why they provide everything that is needed in that realm between worlds, where neither of us can survive without the other.

This is quite a popular subject in these times but the luck of finding and believing this is a long way off and so can be avoided. All things exist as planned and so it is, and only through this challenge can we all become what are needed to be what we all must be.

(It was getting dark so I turned on the light.) Ah, a surge of power, not unlike the power that spreads through the web and sends out the spark that once again awakens the beings that rest beneath the Earth. It is said that the Lighters turn on the beings, causing them to awaken from their sleep. This is true in most cases. The root systems that are connected to the Web are ignited like the switch that turned on your computer. That is how it works.

The Lighters reach points that we as the integrators of the web cannot. They reach ones that have been destroyed, are too large, have difficult problems or are cut off or burnt out.

Yes we too, as part of the whole, do at times "burn out" or stop producing. In our world over the years and within the minority, many events can cause this to happen. As the energy itself stops existing or working (yet in reality nothing ever stops existing because all matter lasts forever, it just evolves to become something else) the Web must be reinstalled or reconnected. So the Attainers, whose job it is to deal with this problem must help Mother Nature with this solution. Even though she rules everything and her power is limitless, she still does not have the power to fix it all. When each being is given a job, she supervises and assigns the jobs to those that she knows can achieve the best results.

Though the Queen Bee does not gather the honey, she does in fact control the collection of it and if she dies then so does the hive unless another queen is found. This is the job of our great leader, Mother Nature. She organizes, arranges, and in most cases lets every being become what they want to be. So in restoring the web, when possible she calls on those that can perform this service. In similar circumstances, other beings eliminate problems by using their knowledge to solve problems that may occur in this world. Just as you would look for an expert to solve a certain problem in your world, it is the same in ours.

Once again we will come back to those that do these jobs, the Inbetweeners. As we said before, they have what we do not (hoofs,

65 See "Ivy on the Pine".
66 See "A Conversation with Axel".

wings, feet per say… but not in our reality) and so they can go to places where we cannot. They are used a lot in those trees so tall that they seem to touch the sky or running from plant to plant when a message of good wishes is needed to be delivered quickly. This method is faster than using the lines of communication mentioned in other readings.

Many of these beings are and will always be the guardians of the Old Ways and so we must remember them in our religion, just as you remember the Saints in yours. That is why often these beings are asked to remember those that ruled long ago and have given us all the knowledge we have learned up until now. The Gods and Goddesses of the past did exist, not only in the minds of those that gather legends but in the heartland of the Great Mother. These workers called Releveant Relayers, still hold them in honor and respect and share this knowledge with anyone who wants to know. In this way, our history and the renewal of all things continues and we can look back through history to a time when we were all connected and we were all one.

Knowledge is never lost and if through the years it is passed down and accepted it becomes reality again. Understand that nothing is ever lost if just a small part of Mankind or other beings accept it as true and spread it to anyone that will listen. This is why we are giving you our knowledge now, so that myth and legend can combine and eventually you will grow in the realization that we do exist forever and always.

We will now share with you some of the differences that will answer many of the questions that you, and others that want to know, have wondered about.

Are you asking about Phylum?[67] Isn't that the different types of plants that exist and for what purpose? Ah, then phylum to you too[68], because some live just as differently in your world as they do in ours. So we will begin…

We will start with the Lighters, who we have told you about before but not in detail.

As the Earth warms after its winter rest, it must again awaken those that have hibernated under the warm and moist earth. Many of these do not rest but remain dormant, though their appearance remains the same. Like we said before, and it is the same in all worlds, everything must rest. When the awakenings finally begin, these Lighters, which are made up of mostly beings that can move, carry the sparks that cannot reach the upper layers or higher areas of our world. They have the ability to draw energy into or onto the whole being.

Using the old Oak Axel as an example you will see that the height of this tree is held back by the root section which connects into the web. The surge that is sent lights the flame below but does not reach the farthest branches so these Lighters carry inside them the channel needed to light the Oak from the branches above. That is why many of you have seen these creatures high above in the branches or in other areas that are unable to be connected to all parts of the web. This is a very important challenge for the Lighters because they must provide nourishment for the Oak to grow, for its well being and for the energy it needs to survive. As important as the Lighters are, there are others that are just as important.

Next we have the Travelers, the movers that pass messages over and under the ground from one being or plant to another. These take many forms, not unlike the ones we mentioned before and are also done by plants and vines that appear to grow over long distances. These Runners carry the information from the roots which also serve as channels for energy. Like the phone lines in your world, they also transmit needed information about everything above and below that could affect the well being of the Oak. In carrying this gift of knowledge ahead they are causing the evolution of many species to move forward. If they did not receive the information of what may happen in the future, it may stunt their growth and end their life in this world.

Certain knowledge is essential to many but the root system working within the Stone Network also releases hidden memories and information often forgotten from other times. Doing this to remember what might be needed in this time, in this place and on this Earth. So it is.

Whatever the purpose, we all have one thing that we share and that is to help every thing that lives inside our world. It is true that some may not do all that they should, but not doing this only causes them to stay longer in the "growth cycle" of development. We must also note that to help when there is a disaster (i.e. fire, sudden storm, chaos) will move you further ahead in this process. Again this is true for both of us, so once again we have another thing in common not something different.

We have others that work together to do what they can to help mankind. The Givers provide food for you and struggle to give you nourishment by giving you what is needed to keep the Human Race and all the creatures on this planet alive. Not only the beings you can see but also those that live under the Earth as well. Because the animal kingdom connects directly with the plant kingdom

67 A direct line of descent within a group; one of the primary divisions of hierarchy within the animal or plant kingdoms.
68 A little plant humor.

in this way, we have closer ties to this species and so communication is much easier. The plants and animals accept us, the Stones, as part of their world and the knowledge we provide insures that they treat us with respect as we do them. They are just species that live to connect with everything through the intelligence of feelings because reasoning has not become part of their world yet. In understanding this, what one believes is the degree of difference between similar types of beings. What they want is nothing more than the comfort and love of all things that live within their world. Simple souls with beliefs improved through misfortunes and lessons learned through hardship. Everything evolves through this stage and if they chose they can demand an explanation from any entity that disputes the rules in their kingdom. The bitterness between them does not last long because the action and reaction of the dispute is quickly overcome by their need for survival.

Like you and I, we all have challenges but each lives separately to roam its world until it finds the peace and mate it wants. The warmth of love begins but truthfully all things look for love as their ultimate goal, though some look for the physical and call this love.

This happens in all worlds, whether you are looking for it or not, it still and always will be that way......

To be continued, hopefully!

As they say in Scotland, the "wee" stone has spoken.

I have found that all the Stones, whether it was this small one that got my attention along the road that day or the awesome Stone Circle at Castlerigg, have an intelligence that is far superior to anything I have ever read about before. This intelligence can offer our world so many solutions to the problems that have plagued us since the beginning of time, if we would only take the time to listen.

They offer the answers to what happened in the past not to mention what we can do in the future to avoid the same mistakes we seem to make over and over again. That alone should be enough for all of us to give them a chance.

As I said before, I started out channeling the Stones. They are and will always be my passion. If by some chance I am asked to write down this information, I would be honored. The Elemental Kingdom has given me more than I could ever ask by allowing me into their world and I hope that you too have become more aware of their kingdom than before you read their words. Understanding all beings and their worlds may be a new concept to us "human beings" but is sure worth thinking about.

If the Elemental world of the Plant Kingdom can offer us so much, I just wonder what the Mineral Kingdom might offer. Hopefully with a little encouragement we may all find out.

Summing It All Up

Now that you have read this book, I am sure you have a better understanding of who and what the Nature Spirits are and about the (Elemental) World in which they live. At least I hope so.

Unfortunately I was not able to include all the passages I channeled. In fact this was actually the hardest part of the book (well, alright so some of the passages were tricky to revise); trying to choose which passages to include. It was, as my daughter Wende, most aptly put it, "like choosing between children". I love them all but knew that I just couldn't include all of them. In the end I did what I should have done in the first place, checked with Nature. The ones She chose to "set aside until another time" were in actuality the ones I would have probably chosen in the long run. Not because they had nothing new to offer but because in most cases they either dealt with the Mineral Kingdom or were just too long or there were just too many to be included. They were however all wonderful passages full of amazing information and wonderful insight.

I wish I could have included the reading from the <u>Ancient Papyrus</u> or the learned <u>Bodhi Tree</u>, not to mention the healing properties of the ordinary Garden Pea. The passage about the <u>Nature Spirits Spiritual Garden</u> which was destroyed by man and the effect it played on the Deva that reigned there, was truly heartbreaking and one taken from <u>Leona's Childhood Home</u> in Canada about what the Nature Spirits did in the winter was incredible. Hopefully I can share these with you sometime down the road.

I have learned so much on this amazing journey. I think the most important thing is the way that Nature works and has always worked with our world in providing everything that we need to survive... and without her and her workers, The Nature Spirits, we could not and would not exist.

That life and death are nothing to fear and that every being in every world has a path to follow that leads them from lifetime to lifetime; each growing and learning as they move closer to their goal.

Hopefully the understanding of what part Nature plays in our lives will eventually be realized. We will all come to know that only through working together can we all truly make this Earth a place of abundance for all beings.

I have also learned that every person can experience Nature in their own way if they just try. Whether it is in the rustle of the leaves as the breeze gently blows, or the power of the waves as they break on the shore... the fragrance of the flowers in the spring or the silent softness of the new fallen snow... all are there for you; each a part of the Elemental World and each with a purpose and a gift given to each of us to be enjoyed.

I feel truly blessed to have been given these gifts.

I hope you now realize you have been too.

Glossary

The Akasic Records: The book in which is recorded all the thoughts, events and things that have happened to every person in every lifetime and in every world.

The Ancients: In the "Nature Spirit" world, The Ancients were beings who inhabited this planet ages ago before man came. During their time here on Earth, Nature was free to roam where and when it wanted with no boundaries or seasonal limits set. In my "world", The Ancients are my guides and provide spiritual advice to those that want/need it.

Attainers: Those beings who reinstall or connect the power points within the web that have ceased to function by being either burned out or destroyed.

Automatic Writing: Messages from another source (and here I can not actually say "higher source") that are channeled through a person giving them the ability to write what that source wants automatically, using that person as a tool.

Axel: The Old Oak Tree in Glastonbury, which was the first Nature Spirit of the Plant Kingdom that I channeled and the reason this book began in the first place.

Being: Any person, place or thing that lives … whether seen or not; either in our world or others known or unknown.

Bloomer: The flowers or plants that bloom seasonally providing pollen so that Nature can continue to reproduce.

Channel: An open connection between another being or world other than your own.

Collective: A group of beings that work as a group to reach their goal.

Elementals: The beings that work to serve Mother Nature. This contains others beside the Nature Spirits and includes the fairies, Devas and other assorted beings of that type.

The Elemental Kingdom: The alternate world or dimension that contains those beings that work with Mother Nature in maintaining our planet Earth.

Esoteric: A different way of thinking (some say strange) that is not understood by the general population.

Essence: Another word for the soul or the spark of life that remains even after death.

Givers: This includes the whole Elemental Kingdom which lives only to provide us with what we need in our world to survive.

Goddess Conference: A gathering of women (and men too) from all over the world each year in Glastonbury, England to honor the Goddess. It takes place over Lammas which is the first weekend in August.

The Great One: The Supreme Being of your choice

Grouper: A plant working together with others like themselves to accomplish a certain job.

Guide: A being appointed to help you answer your questions. They can be either your own personal guide or one that works with other beings.

Inbetweeners: Those beings that work with both the Nature Spirits that live beneath and above the earth. Because of their ability to move between they are often referred to as the fairies, gnomes, winged or hoofed ones.

Incur: A word used a lot by the Nature Spirits. In most cases meaning "to encounter".

Lighter: The elves, fairies, etc. that are able to live without being physically connected to the earth (example: as roots in a tree, plant, etc.) thus enabling them to "turn on" the energy exchange between the sun above and the energy below the earth by moving throughout Nature.

The Mother: Also known as Mother Nature. The Supreme One in the realm of Nature who manages and guides all the Elemental Beings and provides what we need in our world to survive.

Nature Spirit: Also known as an Elemental. Lives in the world that works to provide everything mankind needs to survive

The Old Ones: Ancient beings who along with the "Supreme One" (God) envisioned everything that is above and below and in all beings. They still offer advice to any being that desires it.

Pan: The right hand man and protector of Mother Nature.

Phylum: A term used to classify different species of plants.

Plane: The realm or world in which you live. There are many different levels.

Realm: A world

Relayer: A Nature Spirit that travels (such as the Ivy). As a conduit to other worlds they work like a cable, carrying information to different points.

Relevant Relayers: The Elemental beings that keep the old myths and legends of the Gods and Goddesses of the past alive by passing down this information to their world.

Runners: Plants that carry information they received through their root system, which also serve as conduits of energy, for long distances providing needed information and energy for everything above and below the earth. Imagine a telephone line.

Standing Stones: The giant monoliths that are found all over the world. Some say they are gateways to other worlds, power points, or galactic maps left behind by other beings from the past.

Stone of Knowledge: I have found that any Stone is a Stone of knowledge. Stones store all the intelligence and history of our planet.

Taskers: The beings that accept the task of becoming the keepers of the old ways. These taskers are known as "relevant relayers" in the Elemental kingdom.

Timeline: What must be accomplished in each lifetime in order to move ahead to the next.

Travelers: The movers that relay the messages over and underground from one being or plane to another.

The Web: A spider-like web of energy lines that run and intersect throughout the Earth. These lines provide the energy needed for the growth of all things on this planet.

ISBN 141207271-9